Ernest Hemingway's *The Sun Also Rises*

A CASEBOOK

CASEBOOKS IN CRITICISM

General Editor, William L. Andrews

ERNEST HEMINGWAY'S

The Sun Also Rises

◆ ◆ ◆

A CASEBOOK

Edited by
Linda Wagner-Martin

OXFORD
UNIVERSITY PRESS

2002

OXFORD

UNIVERSITY PRESS

Oxford   New York
Athens   Auckland   Bangkok   Bogotá   Buenos Aires   Cape Town
Chennai   Dar es Salaam   Delhi   Florence   Hong Kong   Istanbul   Karachi
Kolkata   Kuala Lumpur   Madrid   Melbourne   Mexico City   Mumbai   Nairobi
Paris   São Paulo   Shanghai   Singapore   Taipei   Tokyo   Toronto   Warsaw

and associated companies in
Berlin   Ibadan

Library of Congress Cataloging-in-Publication Data
Ernest Hemingway's The sun also rises : a casebook /
edited by Linda Wagner-Martin.
p. cm. — (Casebooks in criticism)
Includes bibliographical references.
ISBN 0-19-514573-9; ISBN 0-19-514574-7 (pbk.)
1. Hemingway, Ernest, 1899–1961.   Sun also rises.   I. Wagner-Martin, Linda.   II. Series.
PS3515.E37 S9234 2002
813'.52—dc21   2001036041

1 3 5 7 9 8 6 4 2

Printed in the United States of America
on acid-free paper

Credits

George Cheatham, "'Sign the Wire with Love': The Morality of Surplus in *The Sun Also Rises*" in *Hemingway Review* 11, no. 2 (Spring 1992), 25–30 (University of Idaho Press, 1992). Reprinted with permission.

Matts Djos, "Alcoholism in Ernest Hemingway's *The Sun Also Rises:* A Wine and Roses Perspective on the Lost Generation" in *Hemingway Review* 14, no. 2 (Spring 1995), 64–78 (University of Idaho Press, 1995). Reprinted with permission.

Scott Donaldson, "Hemingway's Morality of Compensation" in *American Literature* 43, no. 3 (November 1971), 399–420 (Duke University Press, 1971). Reprinted with permission.

Ira Elliott, "Performance Art: Jake Barnes and 'Masculine' Signification in *The Sun Also Rises*" in *American Literature* 67, no. 1 (March 1995), 77–94 (Duke University Press, 1995). Reprinted with permission.

James Hinkle, "What's Funny in *The Sun Also Rises*" in *Hemingway Review* 4, no. 2 (Spring 1985), 31–41 (University of Idaho Press, 1985). Reprinted with permission.

Keneth Kinnamon, "Hemingway, the *Corrida,* and Spain" in *Texas Studies in Literature and Language* 1 (Spring 1959), 44–54. Reprinted with the author's permission.

Wendy Martin, "Brett Ashley as New Woman in *The Sun Also Rises*" in

New Essays on Hemingway's The Sun Also Rises, edited by Linda Wagner-Martin (New York: Cambridge University Press, 1987). Reprinted with permission.

Debra A. Moddelmog, "Contradictory Bodies in *The Sun Also Rises*" in *Reading Desire: In Pursuit of Ernest Hemingway,* 92–100 (Ithaca: Cornell University Press, 1999). Used by permission of the publisher.

George Plimpton, "An Interview with Ernest Hemingway" in *Paris Review* 18 (Spring 1958) 60–89 (*Paris Review,* 1958). Reprinted by the permission of Russell & Volkening as agents for *Paris Review.*

Mark Spilka, "The Death of Love in *The Sun Also Rises*" in *Twelve Original Essays on Great Novels,* edited by Charles Shapiro (Detroit, Mich.: Wayne State University Press, 1958). Reprinted with permission.

Daniel S. Traber, "Whiteness and the Rejected Other in *The Sun Also Rises*" in *Studies in American Fiction* 28, no. 2 (Autumn 2000), 235–253 (Northeastern University Press, 2000). Reprinted with permission.

Contents

Ernest Hemingway's *The Sun Also Rises*

A CASEBOOK

Introduction

LINDA WAGNER-MARTIN

◆   ◆   ◆

ERNEST HEMINGWAY'S 1926 *The Sun Also Rises* provided readers a startling example of the newly modern novel. People accustomed to fiction by Charles Dickens or Jane Austen, books in which a leisurely narrative told a recognizable story about well-described characters, found Hemingway's cryptic introduction of characters—people whose actions did not often seem to be purposeful—puzzling. And for a novel said to be about people who had survived the debilitating trauma of the First World War, *The Sun Also Rises* contained almost nothing about that cataclysmic event. Strangely, Jake Barnes's wound, the most apparent evidence of the war's damages, seems to have made him a strong and almost wise protagonist.

The Sun Also Rises was not the novel readers expected it to be. Its style was so unusual as to be just plain troublesome. How did one interpret the quick shifts from one scene to another; from the initial focus on Robert Cohn, boxing champion of his undergraduate years at Princeton University, to that on Pedro Romero, the admirable young Spanish torero? Where were the assumed lead characters of Jake Barnes, Brett Ashley, and Bill Gorton? If this were an American novel, as it was advertised to be, why did none of its action take place in the United States? And if it were a truly moral book, as its author Ernest Hemingway insisted, why did its plotline consist of a great many sexual liaisons embedded in an even greater number of eating and drinking scenes? Considering that life in the United States had been operating under the laws of Prohibition since 1920, Hemingway's emphasis not only on the fact that his characters spent much of their time drinking but also on deciding whether or not a person was a good drunk or a bad one appeared to be teasingly irreverent.

Hemingway was lucky. Instead of being damned for its irreverence, not to mention its irrelevance to the Prohibition culture of the United States, his first novel was comparatively well-received. The reception of *The Sun Also Rises* was determined by the highly favorable response influential critics had given his slim earlier books. In 1923, his *Three Stories and Ten Poems*, several of which had already appeared in Harriet Monroe's premier magazine *Poetry*, had been published in Paris. In 1924, *in our time*, a pamphlet of one-page prose poems, appeared from Three Mountains Press, the conduit for Ezra Pound's book series. Reviewing *in our time* and *Three Stories and Ten Poems*, Edmund Wilson commented for *The Dial* in 1924 that Hemingway's prose was "of the first distinction":

> He must be counted as the only American writer but one—Mr. Sherwood Anderson—who has felt the genius of Gertrude Stein's *Three Lives* and has been evidently influenced by it. Indeed, Miss Stein, Mr. Anderson, and Mr. Hemingway may now be said to form a school by themselves. The characteristic of this school is a naivete of language often passing into the colloquialism of the character dealt with which serves actually to convey profound emotions and complex states of mind. It is a distinctively American development in prose.[1]

The young writer's fame was not only conferred by critics: African American writer Claude McKay recalled that "Ernest Hemingway was the most talked about of young American writers when I arrived in Paris. . . . *In Our Time*, that thin rare book of miniature short stories, was published, and it was the literary event among the young expatriates."[2]

In 1925, while a good bit of the international literary world was reading F. Scott Fitzgerald's novel *The Great Gatsby*, Hemingway's short stories were published in *In Our Time*, the longer version of his 1924 collection, a version that kept the short prose pieces about bullfighting and the war as small interchapters between the fourteen short stories which Hemingway had managed to write by that time. Again, U.S. critics noticed. Paul Rosenfeld wrote in *The Nation* that "Hemingway's short stories belong with cubist painting, *Le Sacre du printemps*, and other recent work bringing a feeling of positive forces through primitive modern idiom. The use of the direct, crude, rudimentary forms of the simple and primitive classes and their situations, of the stuffs, textures, and rhythms of the mechanical and industrial worlds, has enabled this new American storyteller, as it enabled the group to which he comes a fresh recruit, to achieve peculiarly sharp, decided, grimly affirmative expressions; and with these acute depictions and half-impersonal beats to satisfy a spirit running through the age."[3]

Above all things, Hemingway wanted to be seen as new. His mentor, Ezra Pound, wore the storied scarf with "Make it new" inscribed upon it through the streets of Paris; his other prominent mentor, Gertrude Stein, was even more visibly an icon of modernism—in both her persona and her art collection. As all younger artists had learned, being connected with the innovation of modernism was a bonus in the publicity-crazed 1920s: an era that used the 1913 Armory Show and Sigmund Freud's psychoanalytic theories as touchstones for the new was eager for writing that could be compared with a Duchamp painting. But what writers of all time had learned was that it takes only a few rave reviews in the right places to make a book into a best-seller. While Edmund Wilson did not like *The Sun Also Rises* as much as he had Hemingway's earlier fiction, his *Dial* comments paved the way for the novel to find an admiring reception.

Titled *Fiesta* in its British edition, *The Sun Also Rises* captured readers' imaginations. In it Hemingway had written about exotic settings and equally exotic pastimes. Few American readers had been to Spain: indeed, were it not for the fact that Gertrude Stein and her companion, Alice B. Toklas, had themselves earlier found the Pamplona festival, with its superior bullfights, Hemingway and his friends would never have made their pilgrimage. As he had with scenes and vignettes about World War I, Hemingway described the Spanish culture—its churches, restaurants, tables in the sunny squares, fishing streams, bus rides, hotels, and bullfights—with detailed authenticity. He still knew what made good journalism, and he was not above creating some of journalism's vivid effects in the genre of serious fiction. Hemingway wanted to publish a book that people would admire as well as talk about; he defined himself as a serious writer, not someone who wrote for the movies or for titillation. He did not mind if his books were not best-sellers. What he wanted was standing, respect, and the accolades of his friends, people who were themselves serious about their art.

The overwhelming first impression of Hemingway's 1926 novel, then, was that it was different. No one else had written about these topics and these settings. Only the Spanish knew Spain in this way. Even as F. Scott Fitzgerald helped him break into big-time commercial publishing in the

United States, by acting as a liaison to Max Perkins, Fitzgerald's influential editor at Charles Scribner's in New York, Hemingway knew that his writing would outshine the kind of cultural panorama that Fitzgerald usually built his novels around. Readers devoured Fitzgerald's *This Side of Paradise, The Beautiful and Damned,* and (to a lesser extent) *The Great Gatsby,* but they did so because his writing was romantically poignant, almost formulaic: did the right man win the girl? did college students really live like this on their elite campuses? Had Hemingway written about the same topics—the by-now familiar "jazz age" characters and situations, his work would have been marketed as a copy of Fitzgerald's. Hemingway learned from his friendships with not only Fitzgerald, but also Sherwood Anderson, Ford Madox Ford, Gertrude Stein, Ezra Pound, Glenway Wescott, Harold Loeb, John Dos Passos, and others that the only American writing that would make its mark would be writing that was innovative. His anger when his early short stories were compared with the work of either Anderson or Stein was his attempt to blot out—or at least disguise—their influence; he wanted to be a master, not an apprentice.[4]

Critically, of course, he was learning fast from everything he read, and from everyone in the art world as well as the literary. There are certain similarities between Fitzgerald's 1925 *The Great Gatsby* and Hemingway's 1926 *The Sun Also Rises:* the use of oblique characterization so that some characters remained shadowy; the creation of a beautiful and sexual woman protagonist (Fitzgerald's Daisy Fay exaggerated into Hemingway's Lady Brett Ashley); an observer-narrator who kept some of his blessed naivete (the Nick Carraway of *Gatsby* who became a more involved, and less naive, Jake Barnes in *Sun*); and reliance on description that gave the reader the atmosphere, and the geography, of place, as well as of class. While the East and West Egg residents were themselves conscious of the difference between real money and new money, and the Long Island setting gave Fitzgerald a way to achieve the glamour of the 1920s culture of success, Hemingway achieved the same kind of glamour by having his characters travel in Europe: taking in the *Fiesta,* with the exchange rate as it was in the mid-1920s, was possible for even less romanticized, middle-class people, for even people (like Jake Barnes) who had to work. But Hemingway could see what sold. He knew readers were intrigued by the mysteries of class and affluence, and he positioned *The Sun Also Rises* to appeal to the voyeurism that readers felt when they could share the excitement of the lives of the wealthy. Hemingway's novel, however, did not chronicle those lives. Except for Count Mippipopolous, no one in *The Sun Also Rises* could easily pay a bar bill. What Hemingway achieved in his novel was the aura of the exotic, and he achieved that effect largely through placing *The Sun Also Rises* in France and in Spain.

Because Fitzgerald was impressed with Hemingway's early work, and was himself an impressionable kind of man, Hemingway chose to remain friends with him even after he had broken off his early relationships with both Anderson and Stein. Fitzgerald's championing of Hemingway's skills was invaluable.[5] And it was Fitzgerald's Princeton friend, Edmund Wilson, who had given Hemingway his first rave review.

Fitzgerald, too, became the reader who provided for Hemingway the striking structure for his visibly modernist novel. Because they were friends and because Fitzgerald had secured the Scribner's contract for Hemingway, Hemingway asked him to read the manuscript of *Sun*, even though he had already submitted it to Max Perkins. Fitzgerald's response has become, rightly, famous. For Fitzgerald told Hemingway to omit the first chapter and a half of the draft version, the heavily romanticized biography of Brett Ashley (this change is the reason the book begins with Robert Cohn); more important, Fitzgerald asked him to change the tone, to get rid of what he called "condescending casualness." He went on to emphasize that "there are about 24 sneers, superiorities, and nose-thumbings-at-nothing that mar the whole narrative."[6] Since much of the narrative is in the voice of Jake Barnes, Fitzgerald's comments about tone also were comments about Hemingway's protagonist.[7] He continued in that vein to ask that Hemingway say less about himself—that is, the author figure, who was clearly egocentric and proud of it—and to let the book's action play itself out among its characters. The noninterference of the modernist author was thereby achieved. In *Gatsby*, Fitzgerald had achieved that effect by letting Nick Carraway tell the story; in *Sun*, nobody told the story. Hemingway's book was a step ahead: it *was* the modernist novel.

So Hemingway did cut and revise. Although it was difficult for him to accept criticism of any kind, he appreciated Fitzgerald's candor: he wanted his novel to succeed. In monetary debt to Fitzgerald and perhaps to John Dos Passos and Gertrude Stein, Hemingway was also tired of the fact that he and his family—his wife Hadley Richardson and their infant son, John Hadley Nicanor, to both of whom the novel was dedicated—lived almost entirely on Hadley's trust fund. It was time for Hemingway's fiction to pay off.

Critic Leonard Leff, in fact, sees Hemingway's novel, and his efforts to place it with a top U.S. publisher, as a calculated step in a careful campaign to make the author into a celebrity. The popularity of movies as well as of glossy fashion and arts magazines coincided with the rise of advertising.

Leff contends that Hemingway, even at this early stage of his career, "was acutely aware of audience" and had supplied Scribner's with "retouched studio portraits" of himself in unusual settings—on ski slopes, as well as in Spain—for the book's publicity.[8] (One of his reasons for leaving Liveright, his first publisher, was that he considered their advertising ineffectual.[9]) Leff also assesses the content of *The Sun Also Rises* to be aimed at the 1920s' somewhat melodramatic emphasis on "sensationalism," because the book's characters were "fashionably indecent" yet its style was never difficult—remaining totally distinct from James Joyce's modernist style.[10]

This recent and somewhat cynical view of why Hemingway chose to write the novel he did is at variance with much earlier criticism of *The Sun Also Rises,* which has always taken the frustrated love between Jake Barnes and Brett Ashley as the center, the deftly placed vortex, of the narrrative. As Robert W. Lewis, Jr., wrote in his 1965 study, readers have been unified through "the common theme of suffering for love. . . . Brett and Jake are really sick with love. And thus the essential comedy of the whole story—of any romantic love story—in which the lovers claim a special role and ask for a special sympathy."[11] No matter what else happens in the book, "the love never dies."[12]

Love was, in many respects, still the answer to the increasingly technologized society of the twentieth century. People feared the impersonality of the binary, of the numbers-based lives shared by even the most stalwart humanists by mid-century. It was useful to find in the books we cherished the replication of people's deepest-held values. So Hemingway's *The Sun Also Rises* became a novel about love, rather than about love's debasement.

For the influential Lionel Trilling, Hemingway became the proponent of piety, if not of religion. As he explained, "In Hemingway's stories a strongly charged piety toward the ideals and attachments of boyhood and the lusts of maturity is in conflict not only with the imagination of death but also with that imagination as it is peculiarly modified by the dark negation of the modern world."[13] Richard P. Adams agrees, finding in *The Sun Also Rises* (with which he compares T. S. Eliot's *The Waste Land*) a searching but positive representation of humanity in the chilling throes of the war to end all wars. He reads the travels to foreign lands and the immersion in other cultures as rites of interrogation, emphasizing that San Fermin is a religious festival as well as a bullfighting one (or, rather, that the bullfight is part of that festival) and that the book is filled with churches, with the monastery of Roncevalles, and with discussions about prayer's effectiveness—or lack of it. Adams concludes, "in *The Sun Also Rises* Christian and pagan religious feelings work together in perfect harmony."[14]

For Frederic Svoboda, the untwisting of the strands of place and theme in *The Sun Also Rises* leads the reader to the same comfort Hemingway finds in nature and the many dimensions of the natural, and therefore unspoiled, world. As he states it, "another aspect of nature's importance may derive from the way in which the connection to nature also raises the stakes in Hemingway's writing. The ironies of nature are always there: the earth reliably turning, however else the lives of the characters of *The Sun Also Rises* may descend to chaos."[15]

Michael S. Reynolds sets the novel in the context of 1925, the year it was written, and claims that its much-vaunted modernity was largely the function of Hemingway's style. As Reynolds sees the book, which he reads as a novel of World War I, "The war merely put a period on the end of a sentence that had been twenty years in the writing. The stable values of 1900 had eroded beneath the feet of this generation: Home, family, church, and country no longer gave the moral support that Hemingway's generation grew up with. The old values—honor, duty, love—no longer rang as true as they had in the age of Teddy Roosevelt. For Hemingway and for the country, the loss was not permanent, but in 1926 it seemed that it was. If his characters seemed degenerate, if their values appeared shallow, so did the world appear, at home and abroad, in those postwar years. To read Hemingway's indictment of his age as a paean to the 'lost generation' is to miss his point badly."[16] Working as extensively as he was in not only the John F. Kennedy Library Archive of Hemingway materials, but also in all collections pertinent to what would be his masterful five-volume biography of Hemingway, Reynolds had the proof of his statement ready to be published in the second volume of his biography. What he had found in the manuscripts of *The Sun Also Rises* was Hemingway's specific statement about the "lost generation" epigraph. Reynolds quotes the unpublished note, referring to all the damage already done to the generation that fought—or at least lived through—the Great War: "There will be more entanglements, there will be more complications, there will be successes and failures. . . . My generation in France for example in two years sought salvation in first the Catholic Church, second DaDaism, third the movies, fourth Royalism, fifth the Catholic Church again. There may be another and better war. But none of it will matter particularly to this generation because to them the things that are given to people to happen have already happened."[17]

The life of any piece of literature depends in part on the culture of its readers—both the culture contemporary with its publication and initial response, and intermediate responses, and the culture of the present readers' lives. The aim of this collection is to bring together criticism from a range of years, giving today's readers a way to create a montage, a palimpsest of ideas that may help to give *The Sun Also Rises* a life relevant to the twenty-first century. Hemingway's novel has been historicized over and over, and a few of the essays that were influential in that mode of criticism do appear here. But the real reason for this casebook is to help the reader find the permanence of the literature, its luminous value rather than its past value. As a last part of this composite, a letter from Ernest Hemingway to his older sister Marcelline helps to set the crucial importance of the war—and his frighteningly serious wounding—in memory. On November 18, 1918, months after his being wounded and taken to various hospitals for various surgeries, Hemingway wrote from Milan, Italy, to Marcelline in Oak Park, Illinois:

> Child, I'm going to stay over here till my girl [the nurse with whom he was in love] goes home and then I'll go up north and get rested before I have to go to work in the fall. The doc says that I'm all shot to pieces, figuratively as well as literally you see. My internal arrangements were all battered up and he says I won't be any good for a year. So I want to kill as much time as I can over here. If I was at home I'd either have to work or live at the folks. And, I can't work. I'm too shot up and my nerves are all jagged. . . . You won't know me. I'm about 100 years older and I'm not bashful. I'm all medalled up and shot up.[18]

By the time Hemingway created Jake Barnes and placed him amid his less serious companions in *The Sun Also Rises,* he had learned that the best way to heal injuries—and soothe nerves—was to hide, or disguise, them. But that they existed, at least for the author and his surrogate character Jake, gave the novel its weighty purposefulness. Laconic and steady as he was, for the most part, Jake knew what existing meant. And he also knew that it was not always pretty.

READING THE PLIMPTON interview with Hemingway, published in 1958 in the *Paris Review,* reminds one how keenly interested the literate world was in the American modernist writers. William Faulkner had won the Nobel Prize for Literature in 1949; Hemingway received it in 1954. John Steinbeck was to win it in 1962, and Sinclair Lewis had been the first American novelist to be so honored in 1930. The prominence of these startlingly innovative writers, whose works had already been translated into countless languages, was an early sign of what would continue through the rest of the twentieth century: the absolute dominance of U.S. writers on the international scene.

The fallout of the dominance remains with us today. The novels of these Nobel winners—and their friends F. Scott Fitzgerald, Gertrude Stein, John Dos Passos, Glenway Wescott, Katherine Anne Porter, Djuna Barnes, and others—remain essential to any consideration of writing in the past century. It is for that reason that classes at the secondary school level, as well as in universities and community colleges, are frequently built around novels by, particularly, Faulkner and Hemingway. The work of the former illustrates the forceful comprehensiveness of the modernist reach: a text wide-ranging and allusive, a fiction that not only creates a world full of characters but creates the world itself. The work of Ernest Hemingway, in purposefully designed contrast, aims for the effect of non-art. "The Racing Form" referred to in the epigraph to the *Paris Review* interview is Hemingway's joke, his personal stripped-down answer to what he sees as the over-intellectualization of a human being's life in the chaotic modern world. But there is so much serious commentary from Hemingway in this interview that it is almost an essay written/spoken by the author himself.

Mark Spilka's essay about the death of love in *The Sun Also Rises* was also published in 1958 and has been reprinted often. Carefully assessing human relations from a heterosexual perspective, the norm in 1958, Spilka finds in the book only damaged characters, "cripples" as he names them. The novel, then, becomes a metaphor for the damage of war in the culture entire, and Brett Ashley—who was often harshly criticized for her numerous sexual encounters—comes off no worse than the male characters of the book. Evenhanded in terms of gender, Spilka's essay focuses on Pedro Romero as the true—and only—hero of the book.

Thirty years later, Wendy Martin contextualizes Brett Ashley differently. With the critical interest in cultural history, she convincingly shows that Hemingway's portrait of Lady Brett was written almost to script from the "new woman" paradigm. The sociological information in Martin's essay, "Brett Ashley as New Woman in *The Sun Also Rises*," provides a way to read the primary characters apart from their romantic bonds. As Martin notes, "One of the important observations about sexual politics in the novel is that masculine eroticism confines women; therefore Hemingway implies that sex and friendship are inversely related. In traditional courtship situations, the woman's power is the power to be pursued; once caught, she forfeits her opportunity to choose . . . by retaining the interest of multiple suitors, Brett keeps her options open, diversifies her investment of social and sexual energy, and thereby maximizes her opportunities." Martin also reads Brett as a powerful woman who breaks off relationships when men attempt to control her (this is her reading of Brett's leaving Romero at the novel's end). What had occurred in literary criticism and scholarship during those thirty years helped to prepare readers for changing assessments of Hemingway's work: both feminist criticism and gender studies offered new strategies, from both French and the American critics, to read anew the existing classics of literature.

Increasingly, readers' interests in sexuality, ethnicity, race, nationality, and the complicated construction of subjectivities fed into the camps of gender and feminist studies. All of this critical energy was abetted, in the case of changing perspectives on Hemingway's works, by the posthumous publication of Hemingway's own writing, beginning with *A Moveable Feast* in 1964 and continuing through the 1986 publication of his controversial *A Garden of Eden* and the recent appearance of *True at First Light* (1999). As the oeuvre of Hemingway's works grew, readers were forced to relinquish some of the simpler explanations for this book or that, or for this character or that. It could be said that what was happening in critical circles brought new life to the study of Hemingway's fiction.

Ira Elliott's 1995 essay, "Performance Art: Jake Barnes and 'Masculine' Signification in *The Sun Also Rises*," would have been impossible to write during the 1980s. Drawing from lesbian and gay theory, as well as gender studies, Elliott uses the scaffolding of biography—that Hemingway remained ambivalent about sexuality and gender throughout his life—to probe into a number of short stories, as well as the novel in question. In Elliott's reading, Jake Barnes is positioned by Hemingway to transgress the "binary law of male/female": "What Jake is unable or unwilling to acknowledge (disclose) is that his relationship to women resembles that of the homosexual." Elliott draws from the work of Jonathan Dollimore as well, stating that " 'the most extreme threat to the true form of something comes not so much from its absolute opposite or its direct negation, but in the form of its perversion. . . . [which is] very often perceived as at once utterly alien to what it threatens, and yet, mysteriously inherent within it.' " Juxtaposing these three essays about Brett, Jake, and "love" in the novel should provide valuable perspectives on the novel and on the essays themselves.

Two essays that interact similarly are Scott Donaldson's (published in 1971) and George Cheatham's 1992 commentary on it. Each ties economic issues to "morality" in the novel; more important, each creates a discourse about love in relation to a character's capacity to spend/pay/trade (all financial terms that often have sexual meanings as well). The limits of language, or—better—the intentional perversity of language, is one theme of both these essays; and that consideration plays a large role in James Hinkle's essay, "What's Funny in *The Sun Also Rises*," which follows. Often anthologized, the Hinkle essay (originally published in 1985) pairs with an excerpt from Keneth Kinnamon's study of the importance of Spanish culture in much of Hemingway's writing, "Hemingway, the *Corrida,* and Spain," published first in 1959.

The three essays that conclude the casebook are new. Each one represents a different direction analysis of Hemingway's works has been taking. Matts Djos's "Alcoholism in Ernest Hemingway's *The Sun Also Rises*: A Wine and Roses Perspective on the Lost Generation," dating from 1995, takes issue squarely with the romanticization of alcohol abuse. His careful reading of each character in terms of the range of psychological patterns for people who abuse substances opens the novel for vastly different insights. Debra A. Moddelmog's "Contradictory Bodies" excerpt (taken from her 1999 book, *Reading Desire: In Pursuit of Ernest Hemingway*) returns to the first cluster of essays, but takes the reader past the conclusions of Martin and Elliott in her more broadly reaching questions about the social definitions of "male" and "female." And Daniel S. Traber's "Whiteness and the Rejected Other," published in the fall of 2000, provides an apt summary of the issues of Hemingway's anti-Semitism, racism, and homophobia, issues that have been discussed before but not in such a theoretical, and comprehensive, way.

Hemingway's *The Sun Also Rises* remains a magnificent novel. Indeed, it may be that the critical controversies that have surrounded it since its publication have only increased its claim to greatness: no matter how energetic, or antagonistic, or questioning, criticism seems to not wear it out—or down. It is as much a part of the American literary scene today as it was in 1926.

Notes

1. Edmund Wilson, "Mr. Hemingway's Dry-Points," *The Dial* 77, no. 4 (Oct. 1924), 340.

2. Claude McKay, "On Hemingway," *A Long Way from Home* (New York: Lee Furman, 1937), 249.

3. Paul Rosenfeld, "Tough Earth," *New Republic* (Nov. 1925), 22.

4. See Michael Reynolds, *Hemingway: The Paris Years* (Cambridge, Mass.: Basil Blackwell, 1989); Linda Wagner-Martin, *"Favored Strangers": Gertrude Stein and Her Family* (New Brunswick, N.J.: Rutgers University Press, 1995), especially 168–78.

5. See Scott Donaldson, *Hemingway vs. Fitzgerald: The Rise and Fall of a Literary Friendship* (Woodstock, N.Y.: Overlook Press, 1999).

6. Ibid., 91–98; see also Frederic Joseph Svoboda, *Hemingway & The Sun Also Rises: The Crafting of a Style* (Lawrence: University Press of Kansas, 1983), 131–37.

7. See Linda Wagner-Martin, "Hemingway's Search for Heroes, Once Again," *Arizona Quarterly* 44, no. 2 (Summer 1988), 58–68.

8. Leonard J. Leff, *Hemingway and His Conspirators: Hollywood, Scribners, and the Making of American Celebrity Culture* (New York: Rowan & Littlefield, 1997), xvi–xvii; see also John Raeburn, *Fame Became of Him: Hemingway as Public Writer* (Bloomington: Indiana University Press, 1984).

9. Donaldson, *Hemingway vs. Fitzgerald,* 70–71.

10. Leff, *Hemingway and His Conspirators,* 37, 44.

11. Robert W. Lewis, Jr., *Hemingway on Love* (Austin: University of Texas Press, 1965), 25.

12. Ibid.

13. Lionel Trilling, "Contemporary American Literature in Its Relation to Ideas," *The American Writer and the European Tradition,* ed. Margaret Denny and William H. Gilman (New York: McGraw-Hill, 1950), 148–49.

14. Richard P. Adams, "Sunrise Out of the Waste Land," *Tulane Studies in English* 9 (1959), 129.

15. Frederic J. Svoboda, "The Great Themes in Hemingway: Love, War, Wilderness, and Loss," *A Historical Guide to Ernest Hemingway,* ed. Linda Wagner-Martin (New York: Oxford University Press, 2000), 168.

16. Michael S. Reynolds, "The Sun in Its Time: Recovering the Historical Context," *New Essays on* The Sun Also Rises, ed. Linda Wagner-Martin (New York: Cambridge University Press, 1987), 46.

17. Reynolds, *Hemingway: The Paris* Years, 327.

18. Marcelline Hemingway Sanford, *At the Hemingways (with 50 Years of Correspondence between Ernest and Marcelline Hemingway)* (Moscow: University of Idaho Press, 1999), 297–98.

An Interview with Ernest Hemingway

GEORGE PLIMPTON

◆ ◆ ◆

HEMINGWAY: You go to the races?
INTERVIEWER: Yes, occasionally.
HEMINGWAY: Then you read the *Racing Form* . . .
there you have the true Art of Fiction.
—Conversation in a Madrid café, May 1954

E RNEST HEMINGWAY WRITES in the bedroom of his home in
the Havana suburb of San Francisco de Paula. He has a special work-
room prepared for him in a square tower at the southwest corner of the
house, but prefers to work in his bedroom, climbing to the tower room
only when "characters" drive him up there.

The bedroom is on the ground floor and connects with the main room
of the house. The door between the two is kept ajar by a heavy volume list-
ing and describing "The World's Aircraft Engines." The bedroom is large,
sunny, the windows facing east and south letting in the day's light on
white walls and a yellow-tinged tile floor.

The room is divided into two alcoves by a pair of chest-high bookcases
that stand out into the room at right angles from opposite walls. A large
and low double bed dominates one section, oversized slippers and loafers
neatly arranged at the foot, the two bedside tables at the head piled seven
high with books. In the other alcove stands a massive flattop desk with two
chairs at either side, its surface an ordered clutter of papers and mementos.
Beyond it, at the far end of the room, is an armoire with a leopard skin
draped across the top. The other walls are lined with whitepainted bookcases from which books overflow to the floor, and are piled on top

amongst old newspapers, bullfight journals, and stacks of letters bound together by rubber bands.

It is on the top of one of these cluttered bookcases—the one against the wall by the east window and three feet or so from his bed—that Hemingway has his "work desk"—a square foot of cramped area hemmed in by books on one side and on the other by a newspaper-covered heap of papers, manuscripts, and pamphlets. There is just enough space left on top of the bookcase for a typewriter, surmounted by a wooden reading board, five or six pencils, and a chunk of copper ore to weight down papers when the wind blows in from the east window.

A working habit he has had from the beginning, Hemingway stands when he writes. He stands in a pair of his oversized loafers on the worn skin of a lesser kudu—the typewriter and the reading board chest-high opposite him.

When Hemingway starts on a project he always begins with a pencil, using the reading board to write on onionskin typewriter paper. He keeps a sheaf of the blank paper on a clipboard to the left of the typewriter, extracting the paper a sheet at a time from under a metal clip which reads "These Must Be Paid." He places the paper slantwise on the reading board, leans against the board with his left arm, steadying the paper with his hand, and fills the paper with handwriting which in the years had become larger, more boyish, with a paucity of punctuation, very few capitals, and often the period marked with an x. The page completed, he clips it face down on another clipboard which he places off to the right of the typewriter.

Hemingway shifts to the typewriter, lifting off the reading board, only when the writing is going fast and well, or when the writing is, for him at least, simple: dialogue, for instance.

He keeps track of his daily progress—"so as not to kid myself"—on a large chart made out on the side of a cardboard packing case and set up against the wall under the nose of a mounted gazelle head. The numbers on the chart showing the daily output of words differ from 450, 575, 462, 1250, to 512, the higher figures on days Hemingway puts in extra work so he won't feel guilty spending the following day fishing on the Gulf Stream.

A man of habit, Hemingway does not use the perfectly suitable desk in the other alcove. Though it allows more space for writing, it too has its miscellany: stacks of letters, a stuffed toy lion of the type sold in Broadway nighteries, a small burlap bag full of carnivore teeth, shotgun shells, a shoehorn, wood carvings of lion, rhino, two zebras, and a warthog—these last set in a neat row across the surface of the desk—and, of course, books. You remember books of the room, piled on the desk, beside tables, jamming the shelves in indiscriminate order—novels, histories, collections of poetry, drama, essays. A look at their titles shows their variety. On the shelf opposite Hemingway's knees as he stands up to his "work desk" are Virginia Woolf's *The Common Reader*, Ben Ames Williams's *House Divided*, *The Partisan Reader*, Charles A. Beard's *The Republic*, Tarlé's *Napolean's Invasion of Russia*, *How Young You Look* by one Peggy Wood, Alden Brook's *Shakespeare and the Dyer's Hand*, Baldwin's *African Hunting*, T. S. Eliot's *Collected Poems*, and two books on General Custer's fall at the battle of the Little Big Horn.

The room, however, for all the disorder sensed at first sight, indicates on inspection an owner who is basically neat but cannot bear to throw anything away—especially if sentimental value is attached. One bookcase top has an odd assortment of mementos: a giraffe made of wood beads, a little cast-iron turtle, tiny models of a locomotive, two jeeps and a Venetian gondola, a toy bear with a key in its back, a monkey carrying a pair of cymbals, a miniature guitar, and a little tin model of a U.S. Navy biplane (one wheel missing) resting awry on a circular straw placemat—the quality of the collection that of the odds and ends which turn up in a shoebox at the back of a small boy's closet. It is evident, though, that these tokens have their value, just as three buffalo horns Hemingway keeps in his bedroom have a value dependent not on size but because during the acquiring of them things went badly in the bush which ultimately turned out well. "It cheers me up to look at them," Hemingway says.

Hemingway may admit superstitions of this sort, but he prefers not to talk about them, feeling that whatever value they may have can be talked away. He has much the same attitude about writing, Many times during the making of this interview he stressed that the craft of writing should not be tampered with by an excess of scrutiny—"that though there is one part of writing that is solid and you do it no harm by talking about it, the other is fragile, and if you talk about it, the structure cracks and you have nothing."

As a result, though a wonderful raconteur, a man of rich humor, and possessed of an amazing fund of knowledge on subjects which interest him, Hemingway finds it difficult to talk about writing—not because he has few ideas on the subject, but rather that he feels so strongly that such ideas should remain unexpressed, that to be asked questions on them "spooks" him (to use one of his favorite expressions) to the point where he is almost inarticulate. Many of the replies in this interview he preferred to work out on his reading board. The occasional waspish tone of the answers is also part of this strong feeling that writing is a private, lonely occupation with no need for witnesses until the final work is done.

This dedication to his art may suggest a personality at odds with the rambunctious, carefree, world-wheeling Hemingway-at-play of popular conception. The point is, though, that Hemingway, while obviously enjoying life, brings an equivalent dedication to everything he does—an outlook that is essentially serious, with a horror of the inaccurate, the fraudulent, the deceptive, the half-baked.

Nowhere is the dedication he gives his art more evident than in the yellow-tiled bedroom—where early in the morning Hemingway gets up to stand in absolute concentration in front of his reading board, moving only to shift weight from one foot to another, perspiring heavily when the work is going well, excited as a boy, fretful, miserable when the artistic touch momentarily vanishes—slave of a self-imposed discipline which lasts until about noon when he takes a knotted walking stick and leaves the house for the swimming pool where he takes his daily half-mile swim.

Interviewer: Are these hours during the actual process of writing pleasurable?

Hemingway: Very.

Interviewer: Could you say something of this process? When do you work? Do you keep to a strict schedule?

Hemingway: When I am working on a book or a story I write every morning as soon after first light as possible. There is no one to disturb you and it is cool or cold and you come to your work and warm as you write. You read what you have written and, as you always stop when you know what is going to happen next, you go on from there. You write until you come to a place where you still have your juice and know what will happen next and you stop and try to live through until the next day when you hit it again. You have started at six in the morning, say, and may go on until noon or be through before that. When you stop you are as empty but filling, as when you have made love to someone you love. Nothing can hurt you, nothing can happen, nothing means anything until the next day when you do it again. It is the wait until the next day that is hard to get through.

Interviewer: Can you dismiss from your mind whatever project you're on when you're away from the typewriter?

Hemingway: Of course. But it takes discipline to do it and this discipline is acquired. It has to be.

Interviewer: Do you do any rewriting as you read up to the place you left off the day before? Or does that come later, when the whole is finished?

Hemingway: I always rewrite each day up to the point where I stopped. When it is all finished, naturally you go over it. You get another chance to correct and rewrite when someone else types it, and you see it clean in type. The last chance is in the proofs. You're grateful for these different chances.

Interviewer: How much rewriting do you do?

Hemingway: It depends. I rewrote the ending to *Farewell to Arms*, the last page of it, thirty-nine times before I was satisfied.

Interviewer: Was there some technical problem there? What was it that had stumped you?

Hemingway: Getting the words right.

Interviewer: Is it the reading that gets the "juice" up?

Hemingway: Rereading places you at the point where it *has* to go on, knowing it is as good as you can get it up to there. There is always juice somewhere.

Interviewer: But are there times when the inspiration isn't there at all?

Hemingway: Naturally. But if you stopped when you knew what would happen next, you can go on. As long as you can start, you are all right. The juice will come.

Interviewer: Thornton Wilder speaks of mnemonic devices that get the writer going on his day's work. He says you once told him you sharpened twenty pencils.

Hemingway: I don't think I ever owned twenty pencils at one time. Wearing down seven No. 2 pencils is a good day's work.

Interviewer: Where are some of the places you have found most advantageous to work? The Ambos Mundos hotel must have been one, judging from the number of books you did there. Or do surroundings have little effect on the work?

Hemingway: The Ambos Mundos in Havana was a very good place to work in. This *finca* is a splendid place, or was. But I have worked well everywhere. I mean I have been able to work as well as I can under varied circumstances. The telephone and visitors are the work destroyers.

Interviewer: Is emotional stability necessary to write well? You told me once that you could only write well when you were in love. Could you expound on that a bit more?

Hemingway: What a question. But full marks for trying. You can write any time people will leave you alone and not interrupt you. Or rather you can if you will be ruthless enough about it. But the best writing is certainly when you are in love. If it is all the same to you I would rather not expound on that.

Interviewer: How about financial security? Can that be a detriment to good writing?

Hemingway: If it came early enough and you loved life as much as you loved your work it would take much character to resist the temptations. Once writing has become your major vice and greatest pleasure only death can stop it. Financial security then is a great help as it keeps you from worrying. Worry destroys the ability to write. Ill health is bad in the ratio that it produces worry which attacks your subconscious and destroys your reserves.

Interviewer: Can you recall an exact moment when you decided to become a writer?

Hemingway: No, I always wanted to be a writer.

Interviewer: Philip Young in his book on you suggests that the traumatic shock of your severe 1918 mortar wound had a great influence on you as a writer. I remember in Madrid you talked briefly about his thesis, finding little in it, and going on to say that you thought the artist's equipment was not an acquired characteristic, but inherited, in the Mendelian sense.

Hemingway: Evidently in Madrid that year my mind could not be called very sound. The only thing to recommend it would be that I spoke only briefly about Mr. Young's book and his trauma theory of literature. Perhaps the two concussions and a skull fracture of that year had made me irresponsible in my statements. I do remember telling you that I believed imagination could be the result of inherited racial experience. It sounds all right in good jolly post-concussion talk, but I think that is more or less where it belongs. So until the next liberation trauma, let's leave it there. Do you agree? But thanks for leaving out the names of any relatives I might have implicated. The fun of talk is to explore, but much of it and all that is irresponsible should not be written. Once written you have to stand by it. You may have said it to see whether you believed it or not. On the question you raised, the effects of wounds vary greatly. Simple wounds which do not break bone are of little account. They sometimes give confidence. Wounds which do extensive bone and nerve damage are not good for writers, nor anybody else.

Interviewer: What would you consider the best intellectual training for the would-be writer?

Hemingway: Let's say that he should go out and hang himself because he finds that writing well is impossibly difficult. Then he should be cut down without mercy and forced by his own self to write as well as he can for the rest of his life. At least he will have the story of the hanging to commence with.

Interviewer: How about people who've gone into the academic career? Do you think the larger numbers of writers who hold teaching positions have compromised their literary careers?

Hemingway: It depends on what you call compromise. Is the usage that of a woman who has been compromised? Or is it the compromise of the statesman? Or the compromise made with your grocer or your tailor that you will pay a little more but will pay it later? A writer who can both write and teach should be able to do both. Many competent writers have proved it could be done. I could not do it, I know, and I admire those who have been able to. I would think though that the academic life could put a period to outside experience which might possibly limit growth of knowledge of the world. Knowledge, however, demands more responsibility of a writer and makes writing more difficult. Trying to write something of permanent value is a full-time job even though only a few hours a day are spent on the actual writing. A writer can be compared to a well. There are as many kinds of wells as there are writers. The important thing is to have good water in the well and it is better to take a regular amount out than to pump the well dry and wait for it to refill. I see I am getting away from the question, but the question was not very interesting.

Interviewer: Would you suggest newspaper work for the young writer? How helpful was the training you had with the *Kansas City Star*?

Hemingway: On the *Star* you were forced to learn to write a simple declarative sentence. This is useful to anyone. Newspaper work will not harm a young writer and could help him if he gets out of it in time. This is one of the dustiest clichés there is and I apologize for it. But when you ask someone old tired questions you are apt to receive old tired answers.

Interviewer: You once wrote in the *transatlantic review* that the only reason for writing journalism was to be well paid. You said: "And when you destroy the valuable things you have by writing about them, you want to get big money for it." Do you think of writing as a type of self-destruction?

Hemingway: I do not remember ever writing that. But it sounds silly and violent enough for me to have said it to avoid having to bite on the nail and make a sensible statement. I certainly do not think of writing as a type of self-destruction though journalism, after a point has been reached, can be a daily self-destruction for a serious creative writer.

Interviewer: Do you think the intellectual stimulus of the company of other writers is of any value to an author?

Hemingway: Certainly.

Interviewer: In the Paris of the Twenties did you have any sense of "group feeling" with other writers and artists?

Hemingway: No. There was no group feeling. We had respect for each other. I respected a lot of painters, some of my own age, others older—Gris, Picasso, Braque, Monet, who was still alive then—and a few writers: Joyce, Ezra, the good of Stein. . . .

Interviewer: When you are writing, do you ever find yourself influenced by what you're reading at the time?

Hemingway: Not since Joyce was writing *Ulysses.* His was not a direct influence. But in those days when words we knew were barred to us, and we had to fight for a single word, the influence of his work was what changed everything, and made it possible for us to break away from the restrictions.

Interviewer: Could you learn anything about writing from the writers? You were telling me yesterday that Joyce, for example, couldn't bear to talk about writing.

Hemingway: In company with people of your own trade you ordinarily speak of other writers' books. The better the writers the less they will speak about what they have written themselves. Joyce was a very great writer and he would only explain what he was doing to jerks. Other writers that he respected were supposed to be able to know what he was doing by reading it.

Interviewer: You seem to have avoided the company of writers in late years. Why?

Hemingway: That is more complicated. The further you go in writing the more alone you are. Most of your best and oldest friends die. Others move away. You do not see them except rarely, but you write and have much the same contact with them as though you were together at the café in the old days. You exchange comic, sometimes cheerfully obscene and irresponsible letters, and it is almost as good as talking. But you are more alone because that is how you must work and the time to work is shorter all the time and if you waste it you feel you have committed a sin for which there is no forgiveness.

Interviewer: What about the influence of some of these people—your contemporaries—on your work? What was Gertrude Stein's contribution, if any? Or Ezra Pound's? Or Max Perkins'?

Hemingway: I'm sorry but I am no good at these post-mortems. There are coroners literary and nonliterary provided to deal with such matters. Miss Stein wrote at some length and with considerable inaccuracy about her influence on my work. It was necessary for her to do this after she had learned to write dialogue from a book called *The Sun Also Rises*. I was very fond of her and thought it was splendid she had learned to write conversation. It was no new thing to me to learn from everyone I could, living or dead, and I had no idea it would affect Gertrude so violently. She already wrote very well in other ways. Ezra was extremely intelligent on the subjects he really knew. Doesn't this sort of talk bore you? This backyard literary gossip while washing out the dirty clothes of thirty-five years ago is disgusting to me. It would be different if one had tried to tell the whole truth. That would have some value. Here it is simpler and better to thank Gertrude for everything I learned from her about the abstract relationship of words, say how fond I was of her, reaffirm my loyalty to Ezra as a great poet and a loyal friend, and say that I cared so much for Max Perkins that I have never been able to accept that he is dead. He never asked me to change anything I wrote except to remove certain words which were not then publishable. Blanks were left, and anyone who knew the words would know what they were. For me he was not an editor. He was a wise friend and a wonderful companion. I liked the way he wore his hat and the strange way his lips moved.

Interviewer: Who would you say are your literary forebears—those you have learned the most from?

Hemingway: Mark Twain, Flaubert, Stendhal, Bach, Turgenev, Tolstoi, Dostoevski. Chekhov, Andrew Marvell, John Donne, Maupassant, the good Kipling, Thoreau, Captain Marryat, Shakespeare, Mozart, Quevedo, Dante, Vergil, Tintoretto, Hieronymus Bosch, Breughel, Patinier, Goya, Giotto, Cézanne, Van Gogh, Gauguin, San Juan de la Cruz, Góngora—it would take a day to remember everyone. Then it would sound as though I were claiming an erudition I did not possess instead of trying to remember all the people who have been an influence on my life and work. This isn't an old dull question. It is a very good but solemn question and requires an examination of conscience. I put in painters, or started to, because I learn as much from painters about how to write as from writers. You ask how this is done? It would take another day of explaining. I should think what one learns from composers and from the study of harmony and counterpoint would be obvious.

Interviewer: Did you ever play a musical instrument?

Hemingway: I used to play cello. My mother kept me out of school a whole year to study music and counterpoint. She thought I had ability, but I was absolutely without talent. We played chamber music—someone came in to play the violin; my sister played the viola, and mother the piano. That cello—I played it worse than anyone on earth. Of course, that year I was out doing other things too.

Interviewer: Do you reread the authors of your list—Twain, for instance?

Hemingway: You have to wait two or three years with Twain. You remember too well. I read some Shakespeare every year, *Lear* always. Cheers you up if you read that.

Interviewer: Reading, then, is a constant occupation and pleasure.

Hemingway: I'm always reading books—as many as there are. I ration myself on them so that I'll always be in supply.

Interviewer: Do you ever read manuscripts?

Hemingway: You can get into trouble doing that unless you know the author personally. Some years ago I was sued for plagiarism by a man who claimed that I'd lifted *For Whom the Bell Tolls* from an unpublished screen scenario he'd written. He'd read this scenario at some Hollywood party. I was there, he said, at least there was a fellow called "Ernie" there listening to the reading, and that was enough for him to sue for a million dollars. At the same time he sued the producers of the motion pictures *North West Mounted Police* and the *Cisco Kid*, claiming that these, as well, had been stolen from that same unpublished scenario. We went to court and, of course, won the case. The man tuned out to be insolvent.

Interviewer: Well, could we go back to that list and take one of the painters—Hieronymus Bosch, for instance? The nightmare symbolic quality of his work seems so far removed from your own.

Hemingway: I have the nightmares and know about the ones other people have. But you do not have to write them down. Anything you can omit that you know you still have in the writing and its quality will show. When a writer omits things he does not know, they show like holes in his writing.

Interviewer: Does that mean that a close knowledge of the works of the people on your list helps fill the "well" you were speaking of a while back? Or were they consciously a help in developing the techniques of writing?

Hemingway: They were a part of learning to see, to hear, to think, to feel and not feel, and to write. The well is where your "juice" is. Nobody knows what it is made of, least of all yourself. What you know is if you have it, or you have to wait for it to come back.

Interviewer: Would you admit to there being symbolism in your novels?

Hemingway: I suppose there are symbols since critics keep finding them. If you do not mind I dislike talking about them and being questioned about them. It is hard enough to write books and stories without being asked to explain them as well. Also it deprives the explainers of work. If five or six or more good explainers can keep going why should I interfere with them? Read anything I write for the pleasure of reading it. Whatever else you find will be the measure of what you brought to the reading.

Interviewer: Continuing with just one question on this line: One of the advisory staff editors wonders about a parallel he feels he's found in *The Sun Also Rises*: between the dramatis personae of the bull ring and the characters of the novel itself. He points out that the first sentence of the book tells us Robert Cohn is a boxer; later, during the *desencajonada*, the bull is described as using his horns like a boxer, hooking and jabbing. And just as the bull is attracted and pacified by the presence of a steer, Robert Cohn defers to Jake who is emasculated precisely as is a steer. He sees Mike as the picador, baiting Cohn repeatedly. The editor's thesis goes on, but he wondered if it was your conscious intention to inform the novel with the tragic structure of the bullfight ritual.

Hemingway: It sounds as though the advisory staff editor was a little bit screwy. Who ever said Jake was "emasculated precisely as is a steer"? Actually he had been wounded in quite a different way and his testicles were intact and not damaged. Thus he was capable of all normal feelings as a *man* but incapable of consummating them. The important distinction is that his wound was physical and not psychological and that he was not emasculated.

Interviewer: These questions which inquire into craftsmanship really are an annoyance.

Hemingway: A sensible question is neither a delight nor an annoyance. I still believe though that it is very bad for a writer to talk about how he writes. He writes to be read by the eye and no explanations nor dissertations should be necessary. You can be sure that there is much more there than will be read at any first reading and having made this it is not the writer's province to explain it or to run guided tours through the more difficult country of his work.

Interviewer: In connection with this, I remember you have also warned that it is dangerous for a writer to talk about a work in progress, that he can "talk it out" so to speak. Why should this be so? I only ask because there are so many writers—Twain, Wilde, Thurber, Steffens, come to mind—who would seem to have polished their material by testing it on listeners.

Hemingway: I cannot believe Twain ever "tested out" *Huckleberry Finn* on listeners. If he did they probably had him cut out good things and put in the bad parts. Wilde was said by people who knew him to have been a better talker than a writer. Steffens talked better than he wrote. Both his writing and his talking were sometimes hard to believe, and I heard many stories change as he grew older. If Thurber can talk as well as he writes he must be one of the greatest and least boring talkers. The man I know who talks best about his own trade and has the pleasantest and most wicked tongue is Juan Belmonte, the matador.

Interviewer: Could you say how much thought-out effort went into the evolvement of your distinctive style?

Hemingway: That is a long-term tiring question and if you spent a couple of days answering it you would be so self-conscious that you could not write. I might say that what amateurs call a style is usually only the un-avoidable awkwardnesses in first trying to make something that has not heretofore been made. Almost no new classics resemble other previous classics. At first people can see only the awkwardness. Then they are not so perceptible. When they show so very awkwardly people think these awk-wardnesses are the style and many copy them. This is regrettable.

Interviewer: You once wrote me that the simple circumstances under which various pieces of fiction were written could be instructive. Could you apply this to "The Killers"—you said that you had written it, "Ten In-dians" and "Today Is Friday" in one day—and perhaps to your first novel *The Sun Also Rises*?

Hemingway: Let's see. *The Sun Also Rises* I started in Valencia on my birth-day, July 21st. Hadley, my wife, and I had gone to Valencia early to get good tickets for the *feria* there which started the 24th of July. Everybody my age had written a novel and I was still having a difficult time writing a para-graph. So I started the book on my birthday, wrote all through the *feria*, in bed in the morning, went on to Madrid and wrote there. There was no *feria* there, so we had a room with a table and I wrote in great luxury on the table and around the corner from the hotel in a beer place in the Pasaje Al-varez where it was cool. It finally got too hot to write and we went to Hen-daye. There was a small cheap hotel there on the big long lovely beach and I worked very well there and then went up to Paris and finished the first draft in the apartment over the sawmill at 113 rue Notre Dame des Champs six weeks from the day I started it. I showed the first draft to Nathan Asch, the novelist, who then had quite a strong accent and he said "Hem, vaht do you mean saying you wrote a novel? A novel huh. Hem, you are riding a trahvel buch." I was not too discouraged by Nathan and rewrote the book, keeping in the travel (that was the part about the fishing trip and Pamplona) at Schruns in the Vorarlberg at the Hotel Taube.

The stories you mention I wrote in one day in Madrid on May 16 when it snowed out the San Isidro bullfights. First I wrote "The Killers," which I'd tried to write before and failed. Then after lunch I got in bed to keep warm and wrote "Today Is Friday." I had so much juice I thought maybe I was going crazy and I had about six other stories to write. So I got dressed and walked to Fornos, the old bullfighters' café, and drank coffee and then came back and wrote "Ten Indians." This made me very sad and I drank some brandy and went to sleep. I'd forgotten to eat and one of the waiters brought me up some bacalao and a small steak and fried potatoes and a bottle of Valdepeñas.

The woman who ran the pension was always worried that I did not eat enough and she had sent the waiter. I remember sitting up in bed and eating, and drinking the Valdepeñas. The waiter said he would bring up another bottle. He said the señora wanted to know if I was going to write all night. I said no, I thought I would lay off for a while. Why don't you try to write just one more, the waiter asked. I'm only supposed to write one, I said. Nonsense, he said. You could write six. I'll try tomorrow, I said. Try it tonight, he said. What do you think the old woman sent the food up for?

I'm tired, I told him. Nonsense, he said (the word was not nonsense). You tired after three miserable little stories. Translate me one.

Leave me alone, I said. How am I going to write it if you don't leave me alone. So I sat up in bed and drank the Valdepeñas and thought what a hell of a writer I was if the first story was as good as I'd hoped.

Interviewer: How complete in your own mind is the conception of a short story? Does the theme, or the plot, or a character change as you go along?

Hemingway: Sometimes you know the story. Sometimes you make it up as you go along and have no idea how it will come out. Everything changes as it moves. That is what makes the movement which makes the story. Sometimes the movement is so slow it does not seem to be moving. But there is always change and always movement.

Interviewer: Is it the same with the novel, or do you work out the whole plan before you start and adhere to it rigorously?

Hemingway: *For Whom the Bell Tolls* was a problem which I carried on each day. I knew what was going to happen in principle. But I invented what happened each day I wrote.

Interviewer: Were the *Green Hills of Africa, To Have and Have Not*, and *Across the River and into the Trees* all started as short stories and developed into novels? If so, are the two forms so similar that the writer can pass from one to the other without completely revamping his approach?

Hemingway: No, that is not true. The *Green Hills of Africa* is not a novel but was written in an attempt to write an absolutely true book to see whether the shape of a country and the pattern of a month's action could, if truly presented, compete with a work of the imagination. After I had written it I wrote two short stories, "The Snows of Kilimanjaro" and "The Short Happy Life of Francis Macomber." These were stories which I invented from the knowledge and experience acquired on the same long hunting trip one month of which I had tried to write a truthful account of in the *Green Hills*. *To Have and Have Not* and *Across the River and into the Trees* were both started as short stories.

Interviewer: Do you find it easy to shift from one literary project to another or do you continue through to finish what you start?

Hemingway: The fact that I am interrupting serious work to answer these questions proves that I am so stupid that I should be penalized severely. I will be. Don't worry.

Interviewer: Do you think of yourself in competition with other writers?

Hemingway: Never. I used to try to write better than certain dead writers of whose value I was certain. For a long time now I have tried simply to write the best I can. Sometimes I have good luck and write better than I can.

Interviewer: Do you think a writer's power diminishes as he grows older? In the *Green Hills of Africa* you mention that American writers at a certain age change into Old Mother Hubbards.

Hemingway: I don't know about that. People who know what they are doing should last as long their heads last. In that book you mention, if you look it up, you'll see I was sounding off about American literature with a humorless Austrian character who was forcing me to talk when I wanted to do something else. I wrote an accurate account of the conversation. Not to make deathless pronouncements. A fair percent of the pronouncements are good enough.

Interviewer: We've not discussed character. Are the characters of your work taken without exception from real life?

Hemingway: Of course they are not. *Some* come from real life. Mostly you invent people from a knowledge and understanding and experience of people.

Interviewer: Could you say something about the process of turning a real-life character into a fictional one?

Hemingway: If I explained how that is sometimes done, it would be a handbook for libel lawyers.

Interviewer: Do you make a distinction—as E. M. Forster does—between "flat" and "round" characters?

Hemingway: If you describe someone, it is flat, as a photograph is, and from my standpoint a failure. If you make him up from what you know, there should be all the dimensions.

Interviewer: Which of your characters do you look back on with particular affection?

Hemingway: That would make too long a list.

Interviewer: Then you enjoy reading over your own books—without feeling there are changes you would like to make?

Hemingway: I read them sometimes to cheer me up when it is hard to write and then I remember that it was always difficult and how nearly impossible it was sometimes.

Interviewer: How do you name your characters?

Hemingway: The best I can.

Interviewer: Do the titles come to you while you're in the process of doing the story?

Hemingway: No. I make a list of titles *after* I've finished the story or the book—sometimes as many as 100. Then I start eliminating them, sometimes all of them.

Interviewer: And you do this even with a story whose title is supplied from the text—"Hills Like White Elephants," for example?

Hemingway: Yes. The title comes afterwards. I met a girl in Prunier where I'd gone to eat oysters before lunch. I knew she'd had an abortion. I went over and we talked, not about that, but on the way home I thought of the story, skipped lunch, and spent that afternoon writing it.

Interviewer: So when you're not writing, you remain constantly the observer, looking for something which can be of use.

Hemingway: Surely. If a writer stops observing he is finished. But he does not have to observe consciously nor think how it will be useful. Perhaps that would be true at the beginning. But later everything he sees goes into the great reserve of things he knows or has seen. If it is any use to know it, I always try to write on the principle of the iceberg. There is seven eighths of it under water for every part that shows. Anything you know you can eliminate and it only strengthens your iceberg. It is the part that doesn't show. If a writer omits something because he does not know it then there is a hole in the story.

The Old Man and the Sea could have been over a thousand pages long and had every character in the village in it and all the processes of how they made their living, were born, educated, bore children, etc. That is done excellently and well by other writers. In writing you are limited by what has already been done satisfactorily. So I have tried to learn to do something else. First I have tried to eliminate everything unnecessary to conveying experience to the reader so that after he or she has read something it will become a part of his or her experience and seem actually to have happened. This is very hard to do and I've worked at it very hard.

Anyway, to skip how it is done, I had unbelievable luck this time and could convey the experience completely and have it be one that no one had ever conveyed. The luck was that I had a good man and a good boy and lately writers have forgotten there still are such things. Then the ocean is worth writing about just as man is. So I was lucky there. I've seen the marlin mate and know about that. So I leave that out. I've seen a school (or pod) of more than fifty sperm whales in that same stretch of water and once harpooned one nearly sixty feet in length and lost him. So I left that out. All the stories I know from the fishing village I leave out. But the knowledge is what makes the underwater part of the iceberg.

Interviewer: Archibald MacLeish has spoken of a method of conveying experience to a reader which he said you developed while covering baseball games back in those *Kansas City Star* days. It was simply that experience is communicated by small details, intimately preserved, which have the effect of indicating the whole by making the reader conscious of what he had been aware of only subconsciously. . . .

Hemingway: The anecdote is apocryphal. I never wrote baseball for the *Star*. What Archie was trying to remember was how I was trying to learn in Chicago in around 1920 and was searching for the unnoticed things that made emotions such as the way an outfielder tossed his glove without looking back to where it fell, the squeak of the resin on canvas under a fighter's flat-soled gym shoes, the gray color of Jack Blackburn's skin when he had just come out of stir and other things I noted as a painter sketches. You saw Blackburn's strange color and the old razor cuts and the way he spun a man before you knew his history. These were the things which moved you before you knew the story.

Interviewer: Have you ever described any type of situation of which you had no personal knowledge?

Hemingway: That is a strange question. By personal knowledge do you mean carnal knowledge? In that case the answer is positive. A writer, if he is any good, does not describe. He invents or *makes* out of knowledge personal and impersonal and sometimes he seems to have unexplained knowledge which could come from forgotten racial or family experience. Who teaches the homing pigeon to fly as he does; where does a fighting bull get his bravery, or a hunting dog his nose? This is an elaboration or a condensation of that stuff we were talking in Madrid that time when my head was not to be trusted.

Interviewer: How detached must you be from an experience before you can write about it in fictional terms? The African air crashes, for instance?

Hemingway: It depends on the experience. One part of you sees it with complete detachment from the start. Another part is very involved. I think there is no rule about how soon one should write about it. It would depend on how well adjusted the individual was and on his or her recuperative powers. Certainly it is valuable to a trained writer to crash in an aircraft which burns. He learns several important things very quickly. Whether they will be of use to him is conditioned by survival. Survival, with honor, that outmoded and all-important word, is as difficult as ever and as all-important to a writer. Those who do not last are always more beloved since no one has to see them in their long, dull, unrelenting, no quarter given and no quarter received, fights that they make to do something as they believe it should be done before they die. Those who die or quit early and easy and with very good reason are preferred because they are understandable and human. Failure and well-disguised cowardice are more human and more beloved.

Interviewer: Could I ask you to what extent you think the writer should concern himself with the sociopolitical problems of his times?

Hemingway: Everyone has his own conscience and there should be no rules about how a conscience should function. All you can be sure about in a political-minded writer is that if his work should last you will have to skip the politics when you read it. Many of the so-called politically enlisted writers change their politics frequently. This is very exciting to them and to their political-literary reviews. Sometimes they even have to rewrite their viewpoints . . . and in a hurry. Perhaps it can be respected as a form of the pursuit of happiness.

Interviewer: Has the political influence of Ezra Pound on the segregationalist Kasper had any effect on your belief that the poet ought to be released from St. Elizabeth's Hospital?[1]

Hemingway: No. None at all. I believe Ezra should be released and allowed to write poetry in Italy on an undertaking by him to abstain from any politics. I would be happy to see Kasper jailed as soon as possible. Great poets are not necessarily girl guides nor scoutmasters nor splendid influences on youth. To name a few: Verlaine, Rimbaud, Shelley, Byron, Baudelaire, Proust, Gide, should not have been confined to prevent them from being aped in their thinking, their manners or their morals by local Kaspers. I am sure that it will take a footnote to this paragraph in ten years to explain who Kasper was.

Interviewer: Would you say, ever, that there is any didactic intention in your work?

Hemingway: Didactic is a word that has been misused and has spoiled. *Death in the Afternoon* is an instructive book.

Interviewer: It has been said that a writer only deals with one or two ideas throughout his work. Would you say your work reflects one or two ideas?

Hemingway: Who said that? It sounds much too simple. The man who said it possibly *had* only one or two ideas.

Interviewer: Well, perhaps it would be better put this way: Graham Greene said in one of these interviews that a ruling passion gives to a shelf of novels the unity of a system. You yourself have said, I believe, that great writing comes out of a sense of injustice. Do you consider it important that a novelist be dominated in this way—by some such compelling sense?

Hemingway: Mr. Greene has a facility for making statements that I do not possess. It would be impossible for me to make generalizations about a shelf of novels or a wisp of snipe or a gaggle of geese. I'll try a generalization though. A writer without a sense of justice and of injustice would be better off editing the yearbook of a school for exceptional children than writing novels. Another generalization. You see; they are not so difficult when they are sufficiently obvious. The most essential gift for a good writer is a built-in, shockproof, shit detector. This is the writer's radar and all great writers have had it.

Interviewer: Finally, a fundamental question: namely, as a creative writer what do you think is the function of your art? Why a representation of fact, rather than fact itself?

Hemingway: Why be puzzled by that? From things that have happened and from things as they exist and from all things that you know and all those you cannot know, you make something through your invention that is not a representation but a whole new thing truer than anything true and alive, and you make it alive, and if you make it well enough, you give it immortality. That is why you write and for no other reason that you know of. But what about all the reasons that no one knows?

Note

1. As this issue went to press a Federal Court in Washington, D.C., dismissed all charges against Pound, clearing the way for his release from St. Elizabeth's. [April 18, 1958—Ed.]

The Death of Love in *The Sun Also Rises*

MARK SPILKA

❖　❖　❖

She turns and looks a moment in the glass,
Hardly aware of her departed lover;
Her brain allows one half-formed thought to pass:
"Well now that's done: and I'm glad it's over."
When lovely woman stoops to folly and
Paces about her room again, alone,
She smoothes her hair with automatic hand,
And puts a record on the gramophone.
　　　　　　　　　—T. S. Eliot, *The Waste Land*

ONE OF THE MOST persistent themes of the 1920s was the death of love in World War I. All the major writers recorded it, often in piecemeal fashion, as part of the larger postwar scene; but only Hemingway seems to have caught it whole and delivered it in lasting fictional form. His intellectual grasp of the theme might account for this. Where D. H. Lawrence settles for the shock of war on the Phallic Consciousness, or where Eliot presents assorted glimpses of sterility, Hemingway seems to design an extensive parable. Thus, in *The Sun Also Rises,* his protagonists are deliberately shaped as allegorical figures: Jake Barnes and Brett Ashley are two lovers desexed by the war; Robert Cohn is the false knight who challenges their despair; while Romero, the stalwart bullfighter, personifies the good life which will survive their failure. Of course, these characters are not abstractions in the text; they are realized through the most concrete style in American fiction, and their larger meaning is implied only by their response to immediate situations. But the implications are there, the parable is at work in every scene, and its presence lends unity and depth to the whole novel.

Barnes himself is a fine example of this technique. Cut off from love by a shell wound, he seems to suffer from an undeserved misfortune. But as most readers agree, his condition represents a peculiar form of emotional impotence. It does not involve distaste for the flesh, as with Lawrence's crippled veteran, Clifford Chatterley; instead Barnes lacks the power to control love's strength and durability. His sexual wound, the result of an unpreventable "accident" in the war, points to another realm where accidents can always happen and where Barnes is equally powerless to prevent them. In Book II of the novel he makes this same comparison while describing one of the dinners at Pamplona: "It was like certain dinners I remember from the war. There was much wine, an ignored tension, and a feeling of things coming that you could not prevent happening." This fear of emotional consequences is the key to Barnes's condition. Like so many Hemingway heroes, he has no way to handle subjective complications, and his wound is a token for this kind of impotence.

It serves the same purpose for the expatriate crowd in Paris. In some figurative manner these artists, writers, and derelicts have all been rendered impotent by the war. Thus, as Barnes presents them, they pass before us like a parade of sexual cripples, and we are able to measure them against his own forbearance in the face of a common problem. Whoever bears his sickness well is akin to Barnes; whoever adopts false postures, or willfully hurts others, falls short of his example. This is the organizing principle in Book I, this alignment of characters by their stoic qualities. But stoic or not, they are all incapable of love, and in their sober moments they seem to know it.

For this reason they feel especially upset whenever Robert Cohn appears. Cohn still upholds a romantic view of life, and since he affirms it with stubborn persistence, he acts like a goad upon his wiser contemporaries. As the narrator, Barnes must account for the challenge he presents them and the decisive turn it takes in later chapters. Accordingly, he begins the book with a review of Cohn's boxing career at Princeton. Though he has no taste for it, college boxing means a lot to Cohn. For one thing, it helps to compensate for anti-Semitic treatment from his classmates. More subtly, it turns him into an armed romantic, a man who can damage others in defense of his own beliefs. He also loves the pose of manhood which it affords him and seems strangely pleased when his nose is flattened in the ring. Soon other tokens of virility delight him, and he often confuses them with actual manliness. He likes the idea of a mistress more than he likes his actual mistress; or he likes the authority of editing and the prestige of writing, though he is a bad editor and a poor novelist. In other words, he always looks for internal strength in outward signs and sources. On leaving Princeton, he marries "on the rebound from the rotten time . . . in college." But in five years the marriage falls through, and he rebounds again to his present mistress, the forceful Frances Clyne. Then, to escape her dominance and his own disquiet, he begins to look for romance in far-off countries. As with most of his views, the source of this idea is an exotic book:

> He had been reading W. H. Hudson. That sounds like an innocent occupation, but Cohn had read and reread "The Purple Land." "The Purple Land" is a very sinister book if read too late in life. It recounts splendid imaginary amorous adventures of a perfect English gentlemen in an intensely romantic land, the scenery of which is very well described. For a man to take it at thirty-four as a guidebook to what life holds is about as safe as it would be for a man of the same age to enter Wall Street direct from a French convent, equipped with a complete set of the more practical Alger books. Cohn, I believe, took every word of "The Purple Land" as literally as though it had been an R. G. Dun report.

Cohn's romanticism explains his key position in the parable. He is the last chivalric hero, the last defender of an outworn faith, and his function is to illustrate its present folly—to show us, through the absurdity of his behavior, that romantic love is dead, that one of the great guiding codes of the past no longer operates. "You're getting damned romantic," says Brett to Jake at one point in the novel. "No, bored," he replies, because for this generation boredom has become more plausible than love. As a foil to his contemporaries, Cohn helps to reveal why this is so.

Of course, there is much that is traditional in the satire on Cohn. Like the many victims of romantic literature, from Don Quixote to Tom Sawyer, he lives by what he reads and neglects reality at his own and others' peril. But Barnes and his friends have no alternative to Cohn's beliefs. There is nothing here, for example, like the neat balance between sense and sensibility in Jane Austen's world. Granted that Barnes is sensible enough, that he sees life clearly and that we are meant to contrast his private grief with Cohn's public suffering, his self-restraint with Cohn's deliberate self-exposure. Yet, emasculation aside, Barnes has no way to measure or control the state of love; and though he recognizes this with his mind and tries to act accordingly, he seems no different from Cohn in his deepest feelings. When he is alone with Brett, he wants to live with her in the country, to go with her to San Sebastian, to go up to her room, to keep her in his own room, or to keep on kissing her—though he can never really act upon such sentiments. Nor are they merely the yearnings of a tragically impotent man, for eventually they will lead Barnes to betray his own principles and to abandon self-respect, all for the sake of Lady Ashley. No, at best he is a restrained romantic, a man who carries himself well in the face of love's impossibilities, but who seems to share with Cohn a common (if hidden) weakness.

The sexual parade continues through the early chapters. Besides Cohn and his possessive mistress, there is the prostitute Georgette, whom Barnes picks up one day "because of a vague sentimental idea that it would be nice to eat with some one." Barnes introduces her to his friends as his fiancée, and as his private joke affirms, the two have much in common. Georgette is sick and sterile, having reduced love to a simple monetary exchange; but like Barnes, she manages to be frank and forthright and to keep an even keel among the drifters of Paris. Together they form a pair of honest cripples, in contrast with the various pretenders whom they meet along the Left Bank. Among the latter are Cohn and Frances Clyne, the writer Braddocks and his wife, and Robert Prentiss, a rising young novelist who seems to verbalize their phoniness: "Oh, how charmingly you get angry," he tells Barnes. "I wish I had that faculty." Barnes's honest anger has been aroused by the appearance of a band of homosexuals, accompanied by Brett Ashley. When one of the band spies Georgette, he decides to dance with her; then one by one the rest follow suit, in deliberate parody of normal love. Brett herself provides a key to the dizzy sexual medley. With a man's felt hat on her boyish bob, and with her familiar reference to men as fellow "chaps," she completes the distortion of sexual roles which seems to characterize the period. For the war, which has unmanned Barnes and his contemporaries, has turned Brett into the freewheeling equal of any man. It has taken her first sweetheart's life through dysentery and has sent her present husband home in a dangerous state of shock. For Brett these blows are the equivalent of Jake's emasculation; they seem to release her from her womanly nature and expose her to the male prerogatives of drink and promiscuity. Once she claims these rights as her own, she becomes an early but more honest version of Catherine Barkley, the English nurse in Hemingway's next important novel, *A Farewell to Arms.* Like Catherine, Brett has been a nurse on the Italian front and has lost a sweetheart in the war; but for her there is no saving interlude of love with a wounded patient, no rigged and timely escape through death in childbirth. Instead she survives the colossal violence, the disruption of her personal life, and the exposure to mass promiscuity, to confront a moral and emotional vacuum among her postwar lovers. With this evidence of male default all around her, she steps off the romantic pedestal, moves freely through the bars of Paris, and stands confidently there beside her newfound equals. Ironically, her most recent conquest, Robert Cohn, fails to see the bearing of such changes on romantic love. He still believes that Brett is womanly and therefore deeply serious about intimate matters. After their first meeting, he describes her as "absolutely fine and straight" and nearly strikes Barnes for thinking otherwise; and a bit later, after their brief affair in the country, he remains unconvinced "that it didn't mean anything." But when men no longer command respect, and women replace their natural warmth with masculine freedom and mobility, there can be no serious love.

Brett does have some respect for Barnes, even a little tenderness, though her actions scarcely show abiding love. At best she can affirm his worth and share his standards and perceptions. When in public, she knows how to keep her essential misery to herself; when alone with Barnes, she will express her feelings, admit her faults, and even display good judgment. Thus her friend, Count Mippipopolous, is introduced to Barnes as "one of us." The count qualifies by virtue of his war wounds, his invariable calmness, and his curious system of values. He appreciates good food, good wine, and a quiet place in which to enjoy them. Love also has a place in his system, but since he is "always in love," the place seems rather shaky. Like Jake and Brett and perhaps Georgette, he simply bears himself well among the postwar ruins.

The count completes the list of cripples who appear in Book I. In a broader sense, they are all disaffiliates, all men and women who have cut themselves off from conventional society and who have made Paris their permanent playground. Jake Barnes has introduced them, and we have been able to test them against his stoic attitudes toward life in a moral wasteland. Yet such life is finally unbearable, as we have also seen whenever Jake and Brett are alone together, or whenever Jake is alone with his thoughts. He needs a healthier code to live by, and for this reason the movement in Book II is away from Paris to the trout stream at Burguete and the bull ring at Pamplona. Here a more vital testing process occurs, and with the appearance of Bill Gorton, we get our first inkling of its nature.

GORTON IS A SUCCESSFUL WRITER who shares with Barnes a love for boxing and other sports. In Vienna he has helped to rescue a splendid Negro boxer from an angry and intolerant crowd. The incident has spoiled Vienna for him, and as his reaction suggests, the sports world will provide the terms of moral judgment from this point onward in the novel. Or more accurately, Jake Barnes's feelings about sports will shape the rest of the novel. For with Hemingway, the great outdoors is chiefly a state of mind, a projection of moral and emotional attitudes onto physical arenas, so that a clear account of surface action will reproduce these attitudes in the reader. In "Big Two-Hearted River," for example, he describes Nick Adams's fishing and camping activities along a trout stream in Michigan. His descriptions run to considerable length, and they are all carefully detailed, almost as if they were meant for a fishing manual. Yet the details themselves have strong emotional connotations for Nick Adams. He thinks of his camp as "the good place," the place where none of his previous troubles can touch him. He has left society behind him, and as the story begins, there is even a burnt town at his back, to signify his disaffiliation. He has also walked miles to reach an arbitrary camp site, and this is one of the ways in which he sets his own conditions for happiness and then lives up to them. He finds extraordinary pleasure, moreover, in the techniques of making coffee and pitching camp, or in his responses to fishing and eating. In fact, his sensations have become so valuable that he doesn't want to rush them: they bring health, pleasure, beauty, and a sense of order which is sorely missing in his civilized experience; they are part of a healing process, a private and imaginative means of wiping out the damages of civilized life. When this process is described with elaborate attention to surface detail, the effect on the reader is decidedly subjective.

The same holds true, of course, for the fishing trip in *The Sun Also Rises.* As Barnes and Gorton approach "the good place," each item in the landscape is singled out and given its own importance. Later the techniques of fishing are treated with the same reverence for detail. For like Nick Adams, these men have left the wasteland for the green plains of health; they have traveled miles, by train and on foot, to reach a particular trout stream. The fishing there is good, and the talk free and easy, and even Barnes is able to sleep well after lunch, though he is usually an insomniac. The meal itself is handled like a mock religious ceremony: "Let us rejoice in our blessings," says Gorton. "Let us utilize the fowls of the air. Let us utilize the produce of the vine. Will you utilize a little, brother?" A few days later, when they visit the old monastery at Roncevalles, this combination of fishing, drinking, and male camaraderie is given an edge over religion itself. With their English friend, Harris, they honor the monastery as a remarkable place, but decide that "it isn't the same as fishing"; then all agree to "utilize" a little pub across the way. At the trout stream, moreover, romantic love is given the same comparative treatment and seems sadly foolish before the immediate joys of fishing:

> It was a little past noon and there was not much shade, but I sat against the trunk of two of the trees that grew together, and read. The book was some-

thing by A. E. W. Mason, and I was reading a wonderful story about a man who had been frozen in the Alps and then fallen into a glacier and disappeared, and his bride was going to wait twenty-four years exactly for his body to come out on the moraine, while her true love waited too, and they were still waiting when Bill came up [with four trout in his bag]. . . . His face was sweaty and happy.

As these comparisons show, the fishing trip has been invested with unique importance. By sticking closely to the surface action, Barnes has evoked the deeper attitudes which underlie it and which make it a therapeutic process for him. He describes himself now as a "rotten Catholic" and speaks briefly of his thwarted love for Brett; but with religion defunct and love no longer possible, he can at least find happiness through private and imaginative means. Thus he now constructs a more positive code to follow: as with Nick Adams, it brings him health, pleasure, beauty and order, and helps to wipe out the damage of his troubled life in Paris.

Yet somehow the code lacks depth and substance. To gain these advantages, Barnes must move to Pamplona, which stands roughly to Burguete as the swamp in "Big Two-Hearted River" stands to the trout stream. In the latter story, Nick Adams prefers the clear portion of the river to its second and more congested heart:

> In the swamp the banks were bare, the big cedars came together overhead, the sun did not come through, except in patches; in the fast deep water, in the half light, the fishing would be tragic. In the swamp fishing was a tragic adventure. Nick did not want it. . . . There were plenty of days coming when he could fish the swamp.

The fishing is tragic here because it involves the risk of death. Nick is not ready for that challenge, but plainly it will test his manhood when he comes to face it. In *The Sun Also Rises* Barnes makes no such demands upon himself; but he is strongly attracted to the young bullfighter, Pedro Romero, whose courage before death lends moral weight to the sportsman's code.[1]

So Pamplona is an extension of Burguete for Barnes: gayer and more festive on the surface, but essentially more serious. The spoilers from Paris have arrived, but (Cohn excepted) they are soon swept up by the fiesta: their mood is jubilant, they are surrounded by dancers, and they sing, drink, and shout with the peasant crowd. Barnes himself is among fellow aficionados; he gains "real emotion" from the bullfights and feels truly elated afterwards. Even his friends seem like "such nice people," though he begins to feel uneasy when an argument breaks out between them. The tension is created by Brett's fiancé, Mike Campbell, who is aware of her numerous infidelities and who seems to accept them with amoral tolerance. Actually he resents them, so that Cohn (the perennial Jewish scapegoat) provides him with a convenient outlet for his feelings. He begins to bait him for following Brett around like a sick steer.

Mike's description is accurate enough. Cohn is always willing to suffer in public and to absorb insults for the sake of true love. On the other hand, he is also "ready to do battle for his lady," and when the chance finally comes, he knocks his rivals down like a genuine knight-errant. With Jake and Mike he has no trouble, but when he charges into Pedro's room to rescue Brett, the results are disastrous: Brett tells him off, the bullfighter refuses to stay knocked down, and no one will shake hands with him at the end, in accord with prep-school custom. When Brett remains with Pedro, Cohn retires to his room, alone and friendless.

This last encounter is the highpoint of the parable, for in the Code Hero, the Romantic Hero had finally met his match. As the clash between them shows, there is a difference between physical and moral victory, between chivalric stubborness and real self-respect. Thus Pedro fights to repair an affront to his dignity; though he is badly beaten, his spirit is untouched by his opponent, whereas Cohn's spirit is completely smashed. From the beginning Cohn has based his manhood on skill at boxing, or upon a woman's love, never upon internal strength; but now, when neither skill nor love supports him, he has bludgeoned his way to his own emptiness. Compare his conduct with Romero's, on the following day, as the younger man performs for Brett in the bull ring:

> Everything of which he could control the locality he did in front of her all that afternoon. Never once did he look up. . . . Because he did not look up to ask if it pleased he did it all for himself inside, and it strengthened him, and yet he did it for her, too. But he did not do it for her at any loss to himself. He gained by it all through the afternoon.

Thus, where Cohn expends and degrades himself for his beloved, Romero pays tribute without self-loss. His manhood is a thing independent of women, and for this reason he holds special attractions for Jake Barnes.

By now it seems apparent that Cohn and Pedro are extremes for which Barnes is the unhappy medium. His resemblance to Pedro is clear enough: they share the same code, they both believe that a man's dignity depends on his own resources. His resemblance to Cohn is more subtle, but at this stage of the book it becomes grossly evident. Appropriately enough, the exposure comes through the knockout blow from Cohn, which dredges up a strange prewar experience:

> Walking across the square to the hotel everything looked new and changed. . . . I felt as I felt once coming home from an out-of-town football game. I was carrying a suitcase with my football things in it, and I walked up the street from the station in the town I had lived in all my life and it was all new. They were raking the lawns and burning leaves in the road, and I stopped for a long time and watched. It was all strange. Then I went on, and my feet seemed to be a long way off, and everything seemed to come from a long way off, and I could hear my feet walking a great distance away. I had been kicked in the head early in the game. It was like that crossing the square. It was like that going up the stairs in the hotel. Going up the stairs took a long time, and I had the feeling that I was carrying my suitcase.

Barnes seems to have regressed here to his youthful football days. As he moves on up the stairs to see Cohn, who has been asking for him, he still carries his "phantom suitcase" with him; and when he enters Cohn's room, he even sets it down. Cohn himself has just returned from the fight with Romero: "There he was, face down on the bed, crying. He had on a white polo shirt, the kind he'd worn at Princeton." In other words, Cohn has also regressed to his abject college days: they are both emotional adolescents, about the same age as the nineteen-year-old Romero, who is the only real man among them. Of course, these facts are not spelled out for us, except through the polo shirt and the phantom suitcase, which remind us (inadvertently) of one of those dreamlike fantasies by the Czech genius, Franz Kafka, in which trunks and youthful clothes are symbols of arrested development. Yet there has already been some helpful spelling out in Book I, during a curious (and otherwise pointless) exchange between Cohn and another expatriate, the drunkard Harvey Stone. After first calling Cohn a moron, Harvey asks him to say, without thinking about it, what he would rather do if he could do anything he wanted. Cohn is again urged to say what comes into his head first, and soon replies, "I think I'd rather play football again with what I know about handling myself, now." To which Harvey responds: "I misjudged you. . . . You're not a moron. You're only a case of arrested development."

The first thought to enter Cohn's mind here has been suppressed by Barnes for a long time, but in Book II the knockout blow releases it: more than anything else, he too would like to "play football again," to prevent that kick to his head from happening, or that smash to the jaw from Cohn, or that sexual wound which explains either blow. For the truth about Barnes seems obvious now: he has always been an emotional adolescent. Like Nick Adams, he has grown up in a society which has little use for manliness; as an expression of that society, the war has robbed him of his dignity as a man and has thus exposed him to indignities with women. We must understand here that the war, the early football game, and the fight with Cohn have this in common: they all involve ugly, senseless, or impersonal forms of violence, in which a man has little chance to set the terms of his own integrity. Hence for Hemingway they represent the kinds of degradation which can occur at any point in modern society—and the violence at Pamplona is our current sample of such degradation. Indeed, the whole confluence of events now points to the social meaning of Jake's wound, for just as Cohn has reduced him to a dazed adolescent, so has Brett reduced him to a slavish pimp. When she asks for his help in her affair with Pedro, Barnes has no integrity to rely on; he can only serve her as Cohn has served her, like a sick romantic steer. Thus, for love's sake, he will allow her to use him as a go-between, to disgrace him with his friend, Montoya, to corrupt Romero, and so strip the whole fiesta of significance. In the next book he will even run to her rescue in Madrid, though by then he can at least recognize his folly and supply his own indictment: "That was it. Send a girl off with one man. Introduce her to another to go off with him. Now go and bring her back. And sign the wire with love. That was it all right." It seems plain, then, that Cohn and Brett have given us a peacetime demonstration, postwar style, of the meaning of Jake's shell wound.

At Pamplona the demonstration continues. Brett strolls through the fiesta with her head high, "as though [it] were being staged in her honor, and she found it pleasant and amusing." When Romero presents her with a bull's ear "cut by popular acclamation," she carries it off to her hotel, stuffs it far back in the drawer of the bed-table, and forgets about it. The ear was taken, however, from the same bull which had killed one of the crowd a few days before, during the dangerous bull-run through the streets; later the entire town attended the man's funeral, along with drinking and dancing societies from nearby communities. For the crowd, the death of this bull was a communal triumph and his ear a token of communal strength; for Brett the ear is a private trophy. In effect, she has robbed the community of its triumph, as she will now rob it of its hero. As an aficionado, Barnes understands this threat too well. These are decadent times in the bull ring, marred by false aesthetics; Romero alone has "the old thing," the old "purity of line through the maximum of exposure": his corruption by Brett will complete the decadence. But mainly the young fighter means something more personal to Barnes. In the bull ring he combines grace, control, and sincerity with manliness; in the fight with Cohn he proves his integrity where skill is lacking. His values are exactly those of the hunter in "Francis Macomber," or of the fisherman in *The Old Man and the Sea*. As one of these few remaining images of independent manhood, he offers Barnes the comfort of vicarious redemption. Brett seems to smash this as she leaves with Pedro for Madrid. To ward off depression, Barnes can only get drunk and retire to bed; the fiesta goes on outside, but it means nothing now: the "good place" has been ruined.

AS BOOK III BEGINS, Barnes tries to reclaim his dignity and to cleanse himself of the damage at Pamplona. He goes to San Sebastian and sits quietly there in a café, listening to band concerts; or he goes swimming there alone, diving deep in the green waters. Then a telegram from Brett arrives, calling him to Madrid to help her out of trouble. At once he is like Cohn again, ready to serve his lady at the expense of self-respect. Yet in Madrid he learns to accept, emotionally, what he has always faintly understood. As he listens to Brett, he begins to drink heavily, as if her story has driven home a painful lesson. Brett herself feels "rather good" about sending Pedro away: she has at least been able to avoid being "one of these bitches that ruins children." This is a moral triumph for her, as Barnes agrees; but he can scarcely ignore its implications for himself. For when Brett refuses to let her hair grow long for Pedro, it means that her role in life is fixed: she can no longer reclaim her lost womanhood; she can no longer live with a fine man without destroying him. This seems to kill the illusion which is behind Jake's suffering throughout the novel: namely, that if he hadn't been wounded, if he had somehow survived the war with his manhood intact, then he and Brett would have become true lovers. The closing lines confirm his total disillusionment:

> "Oh, Jake," Brett said, "we could have had such a damned good time together."
> Ahead was a mounted policeman in khaki directing traffic. He raised his baton. The car slowed suddenly pressing Brett against me.
> "Yes," I said. "Isn't it pretty to think so?"

"Pretty" is a romantic word which means here "foolish to consider what could *never* have happened," and not "what can't happen now." The signal for this interpretation comes from the policeman who directs traffic between Brett's speech and Barnes's reply. With his khaki clothes and his preventive baton, he stands for the war and the society which made it, for the force which stops the lovers' car, and which robs them of their normal sexual roles. As Barnes now sees, love itself is dead for their generation. Even without his wound, he would still be unmanly, and Brett unable to let her hair grow long.

Yet according to the opening epigraphs, if one generation is lost and another comes, the earth abides forever; and according to Hemingway himself, the abiding earth is the novel's hero. Perhaps he is wrong on this point, or at least misleading. There are no joyous hymns to the seasons in this novel, no celebrations of fertility and change. The scenic descriptions are accurate enough, but rather flat; there is no deep feeling in them, only fondness, for the author takes less delight in nature than in outdoor sports. He is more concerned, that is, with baiting hooks and catching trout than with the Irati River and more pleased with the grace and skill of the bullfighter than with the bull's magnificence. In fact, it is the bullfighter who seems to abide in the novel, for surely the bulls are dead like the trout before them, having fulfilled their roles as beloved opponents. But Romero is very much alive as the novel ends. When he leaves the hotel in Madrid, he "pays the bill" for his affair with Brett, which means that he has earned all its benefits. He also dominates the final conversation between the lovers, and so dominates the closing section. We learn here that his sexual initiation has been completed and his independence assured. From now on, he can work out his life alone, moving again and again through his passes in the ring, gaining strength, order, and purpose as he meets his own conditions. He provides no literal prescription to follow here, no call to bullfighting as the answer to Barnes's problems; but he does provide as image of integrity, against which Barnes and his generation are weighed and found wanting. In this sense, Pedro is the real hero of the parable, the final moral touchstone, the man whose code gives meaning to a world where love and religion are defunct, where the proofs of manhood are difficult and scarce, and where every man must learn to define his own moral conditions and then live up to them.

Note

1. Hemingway's preoccupation with death has been explained in various ways: by his desire to write about simple, fundamental things; by his "sadomasochism"; or more fairly and accurately, by his need to efface an actual war wound, or to supplant the ugly, senseless violence. Yet chiefly the risk of death lends moral serious-

ness to a private code that lacks it. The risk is arbitrary; when a man elects to meet it, his beliefs take on subjective weight and he is able to give meaning to his private life. In this sense, he moves forever on a kind of imaginative frontier, where the opposition is always Nature, in some token form, where the stakes are always manliness and self-respect, and where death invests the scene with tragic implications. In *The Sun Also Rises*, Romero lives on such a frontier, and for Barnes and his friends he provides an example of just these values.

Brett Ashley as New Woman in *The Sun Also Rises*

WENDY MARTIN

❖　❖　❖

T H E *Sun Also Rises*, published in the autumn of 1926, became, along with *The Great Gatsby*, published the previous year, the novel that captured the excitement of the jazz age and expatriate glamour as well as the cultural dislocation and psychological malaise that were the legacy of World War I. The emotional upheavals of Jake Barnes and Brett Ashley, and their friends Bill Gorton, Mike Campbell, and Robert Cohn, who live episodically, taking risks and contending with the elation or despair that follows in the wake of their adventures, provide a cartography of the experience of the lost generation.[1] In this novel filled with surface excitement—love, sexual rivalry, café hopping in France, the revelry of the festival of San Fermin in Pamplona, fishing excursions in the Spanish countryside—Brett and Jake emerge as the paradigmatic couple who best represent the shift in the perception of gender following World War I. This redefinition of masculinity and femininity was not an abrupt rift in the cultural landscape but rather a gradual shifting of the ground on which the edifice of Victorian sexual identity was built.

The blending of the polarized spheres that traditionally separated the lives of women and men was, in part, the result of the centrifugal swirl of events following World War I. As Paul Fussell has observed in *The Great War and Modern Memory*, eight million soldiers died in the trenches of Western

Europe in the years 1914–1918, and this massive carnage created a generation of men for whom the concepts of glorious battle, honor, and heroism
became either suspect or a mockery.[2] Hemingway himself said:

> I was an awful dope when I went into the last war, I can remember just
> thinking that we were the home team and the Austrians were the visiting
> team.[3]

Like John Peal Bishop, E. E. Cummings, John Dos Passos, and Dashiell
Hammett, Hemingway joined the ambulance corps, which Malcolm Cowley described as "a college extension course for a generation of writers."[4] In
Italy, Hemingway was wounded in a trench by an Austrian mortar, a man
next to him was killed instantly, and another was wounded critically. This
random, impersonal violence undermined notions of the romance of war
and the belief in the battlefield as the proving ground for courage; Hemingway observed, "There are no heroes in this war. . . . All the heroes
are dead."[5] In *The Sun Also Rises* Hemingway makes it clear that the postwar
sensibility as exemplified by Jake is one of severe loss, emasculation, and
impotence. In contrast to Robert Cohn's anachronistic readiness to fight
to protect his honor or defend his lady from insults, Jake feels tricked by
the war and is dismayed at having been a pawn in an international con
game masterminded by bankers and politicians. Expressing Hemingway's
disillusionment, Frederic Henry observes in *A Farewell to Arms*, published
three years after *The Sun Also Rises*:

> I did not say anything. I was always embarrassed by the words sacred, glori-
> ous, and sacrifice and the expression in vain. We had heard them, sometimes
> standing in the rain almost out of earshot, so that only the shouted words
> came through, and had read them on proclamations that were slapped up
> by billposters over other proclamations, now for a long time, and I had seen
> nothing sacred and the things that were glorious had no glory and the sac-
> rifices were like the stock yards at Chicago if nothing was done with the
> meat except to bury it.[6]

With the loss of the conviction of masculine invincibility and authority
after the war came a stoic attitude that is a compensatory stance for this
new awareness of vulnerability. Hemingway's definition of courage, which
he succinctly phrased as "grace under pressure," is in many respects a startling echo of the Victorian adage to "suffer and be still" that was directed to
women who felt helpless to meet the demands of their sacrificial role. Just
as the true woman was self-effacing in the name of familial and social stability, the ideal man of Hemingway's world consciously suppressed his feel-

ings, thereby neutralizing his response in the name of courage or mastery and the need to protect his country. But the stoicism and willed mastery are seen as an obligation or a challenge to be met consciously rather than as a natural—that is to say, habitual—response. Certainly this form of willed courage is not glorious, nor is it even a prerogative; instead it is necessity born out of the need to conceal masculine vulnerability and loss of certainty.

A further parallel between the psychic cost of the redemptive role of Victorian women and the disequilibrium of the war-weary man of the lost generation can be seen in the extreme in their respective pathologies—hysteria and shell shock. Both are somatic responses to psychological conflicts; hysteria is a female response to the inability to reconcile the need for self-expression and the cultural imperative for self-denial, and shell shock is a parallel response of men who are terrified of combat and death on the battlefield. Interestingly, hysteria is a response to excessive domestic *confinement* and shell shock to excessive *exposure*. Yet both of these extremes produce the same range of symptoms—including exhaustion, confusion, speech defects, blindness, deafness, and paralysis.

In the gap of meaning that opened after World War I, the female role was undergoing a transformation in the popular consciousness from passive, private creature to avid individualist in pursuit of new experiences. The housebound Victorian nurturer was becoming the modern woman of unprecedented mobility and public visibility. Traditionally, women have inhabited private spaces, which are simultaneously protected and claustrophobic. Along with the opportunities created by the dissolution of polarized social spheres came increased vulnerability for women. Because public space is defined as male, women were often seen either as interlopers or as "fair game" undeserving of respect or safety. Frequently a woman who left the sanctity of the home was automatically defined as disreputable or dangerous.

Although the highly glamorized flapper seen dancing, smoking, and drinking in public and consorting with men of her own choice in cafés and dancehalls was largely a media phenomenon, the image of the short-skirted, shimmying, seductive, sleek new woman promised unprecedented freedom for twentieth-century women in general. Emphasis on mobility and active participation in public life for women in the 1920s—the first decade in which women had the vote—seemed to represent a dramatic break with the past; but in fact, the postwar decade actually consolidated the gains that had been achieved by feminists over a period of almost 100 years.

In the late nineteenth century the new women, like the modern woman of the 1920s, was a product of the urban life of the developing industrial cities. She was educated, valued her autonomy, and did not automatically subscribe to the values of the family; frequently, she was single and had a career. No longer did she define herself as a domestic being; openly rebelling against nineteenth-century bourgeois priorities, the new woman rejected traditional feminine ideals of purity, piety, and submission. Instead she insisted on reproductive freedom, self-expression, and a voice in public life. In short, the new woman rebelled against patriarchal marriage and, protesting against a social order that was rooted in female biology, she refused to play the role of the ethereal other. Since her demands for personal fulfillment suggested a need for new emotional arrangements, they were seen as threatening the social order.

The war had given a generation of women like Sylvia Beach an opportunity to test their abilities; service in the nursing or agricultural corps taught women not only that they could work effectively but that their work was valuable. This postwar feminist consciousness was especially evident in Paris in the early 1920s, when there were more than eighty feminist societies with a total of more than sixty thousand members. This emphasis on women's freedom is demonstrated by the 1922 publication of the bestselling novel *Garcon* by Victor Margueritte, about a nineteen-year-old unmarried woman who plans to have a baby and raise it independently of patriarchal society.[7]

The new woman's radical challenge to the traditional social structure is seen in Lady Brett Ashley, who has stepped off the pedestal and now roams the world. Entering the public sphere without apology, she dares to frequent places and events previously off limits to her, such as the bar and the bullfight. Gone are the long skirts, bustles, and constricted waists: New clothes designed by Coco Chanel and Erté are intended for movement. The short skirts and light fabrics of the new fashions for women shocked traditionalists. In the spring of 1925, the *New York Times* reported that a woman wearing a dress with transparent sleeves literally caused a riot in London. When she was arrested for indecent exposure and disturbing the peace, the woman protested that such dresses were the fashion in New York City. Similarly, when Brett appears with bare shoulders in Monotoya's bar in Pamplona, she deeply offends him; her exposed flesh marks her as a fallen woman.

In spite of the fact that Brett tries to break free of patriarchal control, she often vacillates between the extremes of self-abnegation and self-indulgence, and her relationship with her two former husbands, as well as with

Mike Campbell, Robert Cohn, and even Jake, are filled with ambivalence, anxiety, and frequently alienation. Although Brett has the distinction of having married into the British aristocracy, her protected social status has proved to be inversely proportional to her personal satisfaction. As she bitterly observes, "I had such a hell of a happy life with the British aristocracy."[8] As she tries to find her way between the Scylla of social constraint and the Charybdis of chaotic freedom, her search for a new direction is not validated by the social world in which she lives. In spite of Hemingway's sympathetic treatment of Brett, much critical reaction has mirrored traditional values: Allen Tate calls her "hard-boiled"; Theodore Bardake sees her as a "woman devoid of womanhood"; Jackson Benson says that she is "a female who never becomes a woman"; Edmund Wilson describes her as "an exclusively destructive force"; and John Aldridge declares that Brett is a "compulsive bitch."[9] In a somewhat more generous interpretation, Roger Whitlow describes Brett as self-destructive, and Delbert Wylder sees her as a Janus-like character.[10]

Brett's loose disordered relationships reflect the shattered unity and contradictions of the modern world. On the one hand, she is insouciant, careless, a femme fatale—a woman dangerous to men; on the other, she reflexively lapses into the role of redemptive woman by trying to save men through her sexuality. Mike observes that Brett "loves looking after people" (203), and she has an affair with Robert Cohn because she feels sorry for him and hopes that a romantic interlude will lift his spirits. When he persists in playing the knight who wants to rescue his damsel in distress, she scorns him for his inability to accept episodic or casual sex. In many respects, Brett represents Hemingway's idealized rendering of the woman free of sexual repression. Following F. Scott Fitzgerald's advice, Hemingway cut the original fifteen-page opening sequence of *The Sun Also Rises*, in which he made it clear that the novel was about Brett. The original opening of the novel begins: "This is a novel about a lady. Her name is Lady Ashley and when the story begins she is living in Paris and it is spring."[11]

In the 1920s, Freud's theories of repression were used to justify free love.[12] Contradicting traditional theories of sexuality in the 1920s based on male sexual drive and female receptivity, Brett represents the principle of female eros unbounded by patriarchal control; her closest friend and "true love" is a man who is physically impotent due to a war wound. Many critics have equated Jake's sexual disability with Hemingway's fear of inadequacy, but Jake's affliction has more cultural than biographical significance.[13] His sexual impotence is a sign of loss of masculine power and authority and the axiomatic right to exercise social control. Since Jake's war wound has made it impossible for him to make a physical claim on Brett, he is the only man in the novel who does not try to possess her.

One of the important observations about sexual politics in the novel is that masculine eroticism confines women; therefore, Hemingway implies that sex and friendship are inversely related. In traditional courtship situations, the woman's power is the power to be pursued; once caught, she forfeits her opportunity to choose. Here there are parallels with economic processes; by retaining the interest of multiple suitors, Brett keeps her options open, diversifies her investment of social and sexual energy, and thereby maximizes her opportunities.

Interestingly, Brett breaks up her relationships when her lovers attempt to claim her, that is, to exercise authority over her. She even leaves the bullfighter Romero—a man to whom she is overwhelmingly attracted—when he shows signs of wanting to domesticate her: He tells her to give up her mannish felt hat, to let her hair grow long, to wear more modest clothes. But she has rejected the ideal of female dependence and delicacy: "He wanted me to grow my hair out. Me, with long hair. I'd look so like hell" (242).

Brett prides herself on her daring; for example, she is exceptional in her willingness to take sexual risks. Nevertheless, she is still caught between two modes of gender representation: that of the idealized woman on the pedestal and that of the self-reliant modern woman. She is both the idealized other whom men seek as a prize for their prowess and the autonomous woman who tries to make her own decisions. Although she has broken the connection between moral and physical purity, she still plays the redemptive role of trying to save men through her sexuality—the modern counterpart of Victorian feminine spirituality. In spite of the fact that she is no longer confined to the claustrophobic patriarchal house that in nineteenth-century feminist iconography was the place of entrapment, like the jazz age flapper she has not yet (nor have her male counterparts, for that matter) redefined the traditional relationships of sex and money. Brett has some money from her second husband, from whom she has separated; she also depends on her ability to attract men who will pay for her drinks, her dinners, her taxis and trains. And just as she expects men to pay for many of her pleasures, most of the men in the novel are also bound by the traditional code to assume financial responsibility for women in exchange for their attention. If Brett has gained a measure of freedom in leaving the traditional household, she is still very much dependent on men, who provide an arena in which she can be attractive and socially active as well as financially secure.

Brett's lack of financial and psychological independence is clearly stated in the opening paragraph of the novel; Hemingway observes that Brett has a "grand vitality" but that she "has never been very good at being alone." Her lack of judgment about her romantic liaisons is evident in the following paragraph from the unpublished beginning:

> Lady Ashley was born Elizabeth Brett Murray. Her title came from her second husband. She had divorced one husband for something or other, mutual consent; not until after he had put one of those notices in the paper stating that after this date he would not be responsible for any debts, etc. He was a Scotchman and found Brett much too expensive, especially as she had only married him to get rid of him and to get away from home. At present she had a legal separation from her second husband, who had the title, because he was a dipsomaniac, he having learned it in the North Sea commanding a mine-sweeper, Brett said. When he had gotten to be a proper thoroughgoing dipsomaniac and found that Brett did not love him he tried to kill her, and between times slept on the floor and was never sober and had great spells of crying. Brett always declared that it had been one of the really great mistakes of her life to have married a sailor. She should have known better, she said, but she had sent the one man she had wanted to marry off to Mesopotamia so he would last out the war, and he had died of some very unromantic form of dysentery and she certainly could not marry Jake Barnes, so when she had to marry she had married Lord Robert Ashley, who proceeded to become a dipsomaniac as before stated.[14]

In her exchange with men of sexual and psychological attention in return for their financial favors and protection, Brett mirrors both the traditional wife and the prostitute. Yet she will be neither—she will not submit to the authority or the direction of men, nor will she take money in payment for sex because that would be prostitution. In this transition among wife, mistress, and free woman, Brett and the other women in this novel—Frances, Georgette, and Edna—sometimes find themselves in awkward and contradictory roles.[15] Interestingly, radical feminists and prostitutes themselves have argued that marriage is a sanctioned exchange of sex and nurturance for financial protection and social status and that this basic economic transaction is obscured by sentimental ideology, but Brett shields herself from that knowledge. Although she chooses willed ignorance, she does manage to challenge successfully the male control of female eros.

Hemingway gives considerable attention to financial matters in *The Sun Also Rises*; in this novel, money and morality are closely intertwined. Both

Jake and the count, who has been in "seven wars and four revolutions" (60) and has arrow wounds to prove it, share the conviction that the confrontation with death has intensified their appreciation of life. By paying the ultimate price—risking death—they have earned the right to appreciate life. As the Count remarks:

> "You see, Mr. Barnes, it is because I have lived very much that now I can enjoy everything so well. Don't you find it like that?"
>
> "Yes, absolutely."
>
> "I know," said the Count. "That is the secret. You must get to know the values." (60)

Brett, who has less experience, less money, and therefore less control over the circumstances of her life, questions this economic reductionism: "Doesn't anything ever happen to your values?" The count, who is buffered by both his wide experience and his considerable fortune, answers, "No, not any more" (61). His financial and emotional priorities are established, and he has even factored in the cost of falling in love. Aptly titled, the count estimates the cost—psychological as well as economic—of his experiences and consciously decides what price he is willing to pay. So, economic independence and psychological freedom are correlated, and it is the men in this novel who control most of the money.

In an often quoted passage from the novel, Jake articulates his version of this market economy of the emotions, which paradoxically leads him to observe that the financial and social compensation for men and women is dramatically different. Interestingly, this quantification of pleasure yields a new understanding of the double standard, which he comes to realize is like getting a loan with an unspecified repayment date:

> I had been having Brett for a friend, I had not been thinking about her side of it. I had been getting something for nothing. That only delayed the presentation of the bill. The bill always came. That was one of the swell things you could count on.
>
> I thought I had paid for everything. Not like the woman who pays and pays. No idea of retribution or punishment. Just exchange of values. You gave up something and got something else or you worked for something. You paid some way for everything that was any good. I paid my way into things that I liked, so that I had a good time. Either you paid by learning about them or by experience, or by taking chances, or by money. Enjoying living was learning to get your money's worth and knowing when you had it. (148)[16]

In contrast to the Scottish aristocrat Mike Campbell, whose entire existence is sustained by debt financing, Jake believes in fiscal and emotional responsibility. Yet he has miscalculated the cost of Brett's lifestyle, and he must ultimately accept the financial and social compromises necessary for her to survive in a rapidly changing world, as well as her effort to forge an individual identity that includes sexual freedom. Jake understands that to be her friend, he must truly relinquish his desire to control her. Because Jake is able to wrestle with this issue of territoriality and possessiveness and to accept his loss of control, he is the only man in the novel who is able to meet Brett on common ground.

In part, Jake's philosophy represents a wary response to a historical period when credit was available for the first time on a large scale, and when there was a concerted effort by the government and financial institutions to encourage people to consume, not to save. In response to the threat to capitalist values posed by the Russian Revolution of 1917, American banking and business interests made a concerted effort to create easy credit. With this increased availability of money, the consumer market expanded and the stock market soared in response to widespread speculation that the economy would grow even stronger. All classes of people participated in the speculative fire that ignited Wall Street, and when the flames were doused in 1929, margin calls were delivered to chauffeurs and chambermaids along with bankers and brokers.

A profound—if human—exchange between Jake and his friend Bill Gorton underscores the far-reaching implications of this new wave of capitalism that depends on the consumption of manufactured goods produced by the industrial economics of the United States and Western Europe. While strolling the streets of Paris, Bill wants to buy a stuffed dog: "Mean everything in the world to you after you bought it," he tells Jake. "Simple exchange of values. You gave them money. They give you a stuffed dog." When Jake resists, Bill retorts, "All right. Have it your way. Road to hell paved with unbought stuffed dogs. Not my fault" (72–73).

During 1924–1926, while *The Sun Also Rises* was written and published, the dollar value in francs made it possible for American writers to live quite well in France on limited budgets, and the heirs of wealthy American families—Harry and Caresse Crosby, Sara and Gerald Murphy, for example—had an extensive staff of servants, drank the finest wines, and traveled widely. Postwar Paris was a haven not only for American expatriates but for refugees and émigrés from all over the world. The disillusioned as well as the disenfranchised flocked to the City of Light. This period of social upheaval was accompanied by an extraordinary artistic ferment: The dadaists celebrated the sense of absurdity and possibility of these tumultuous times. The cafés and ateliers were filled with artists and intellectuals whose work formed the cornerstone of modern art, including Chagall, Cocteau, Diaghilev, Dos Passos, Fitzgerald, Gurdjieff, James Joyce, Hemingway, Picabia, Ezra Pound, Man Ray, Satie, Stravinsky, and Tzara. The *années folles,* the crazy years, as the French described the decade, were exciting for women as well as for men. Participating in every aspect of artistic life—dance, painting, photography, writing—as well as in politics, many women experienced unprecedented opportunities, among them Bernice Abbot, Josephine Baker, Djuna Barnes, Natalie Barney, Sylvia Beach, Kay Boyle, Nancy Cunard, Isadora Duncan, Janet Flanner, Emma Goldman, Mina Loy, Katherine Mansfield, and Gertrude Stein.

In *The Sun Also Rises*, the emotional challenges of Brett and Jake are antithetical: Jake must learn to accept the discomfort and uncertainty that come with his loss of authority, and Brett must learn to make choices for herself and to take responsibility for those choices. In this reworking of traditional psychological patterns, Jake becomes more nurturing and *responsive*, Brett more decisive and *responsible*. This role reversal reflects the changing definitions of gender in the jazz age. In *The Sun Also Rises*, men cry and women swear; Brett aggressively expresses her sexual desires, while her lovers wait to be chosen; she likes action—noisy public gatherings, large parties, the blood and gore of the bullfight—whereas the men appreciate the pleasure of sipping brandy in a quiet café.

The loss of traditional cultural meaning is accompanied by a loss of certainty about proper feminine and masculine behavior. Since gender is a social construction, new roles represent a response to new realities, and through trial and error, new forms of sexual behavior emerge. New configurations of gender shatter the old frame, and stripped of their traditional roles, the characters in *The Sun Also Rises* are more transparent, that is, more able to express a greater range of feelings.

Although Hemingway is often stereotyped as a machismo writer, he was fascinated with the variability of the human sexual response and its extraordinary range of expression. Even though Hemingway cultivated a traditional masculine personal and literary style—he was called "Poppa" and much of his work focuses on hunting, fishing, boxing, and bullfighting—he also experimented with role reversal in lovemaking with his wives and wrote a novel and short stories emphasizing androgynous behavior.

In "The Garden of Eden," an unpublished novel manuscript now housed in the Kennedy Library, Hemingway explores the variations of gender identity in terms that echo Brett's disagreement with Romero about her short hair and mannish hat. As in Virginia Woolf's *Orlando*, characters reverse roles: Katherine announces that she wants to become a man and cuts her hair short; she urges her lover, David, to become a woman, or at the very least she wants them to become brothers. David is fascinated and frightened by Katherine's insistence on sexual experimentation. Another couple, Nick and Barbara, both grow their hair long and explore their feminine capacities. This 1,214-page manuscript is set in a small fishing village in the south of France where Hemingway and his second wife, Pauline, honeymooned in 1927 and contains numerous references to experimental lovemaking, never specified but described as "shameless."[17]

Another unpublished story, "A Story of a Man Who Always Wanted to Have Long Hair," indicates that Hemingway continued to be interested in androgynous sexuality, as does an observation by his last wife, Mary:

> In our mutual sensory delights we were smoothly interlocking parts of a single entity, the big cogwheel and the smaller cogwheel. . . . Maybe we were androgynous.[18]

In contrast to his private sexual experiments, the public Hemingway represented tough masculinity, so much so that Zelda Fitzgerald told him that nobody could be that masculine. In an essay in the *New Republic* in 1933, Max Eastman derided Hemingway as "wearing false hair on his chest." Enraged by Eastman's remark, Hemingway stormed into the *New Republic*'s office to display his own hairy chest and then ripped open Eastman's shirt to reveal a hairless chest. Although Hemingway responded with fury when anyone dared to impugn his masculinity, he was a nurturing person. According to Sylvia Beach, he was an unusually loving father and did "everything but breastfeed his baby."[19]

In the context of the new cultural openness—with its new range of ontological possibilities—both Brett and Jake believe in *risk* as the measure of the importance of a choice or action. The true risk taker—the aficionado—is one who is willing to walk the line between life and death in the pursuit of meaning. Yet *afición*—passion—also means certain suffering. For Jake, *afición* is a commitment without reservation to the dangers of the bullfight, and for him, Pedro Romero is the heroic exemplar of masculine courage in his willingness to face the bull without reservation, without protection: "Romero had the old thing, the holding of his purity of line through the maximum of exposure" (168). But Romero is a *boy*; he is nineteen and not yet fully aware of the meaning or dangers of the risks he takes. He is protected, in part, by his innocence.

Brett's affairs represent the kind of risk taking for her that the confrontation with the bull represents for Romero; by exercising sexual freedom she risks disease, pregnancy, ostracism. Brett's freedom of choice leads to what I would call an anxiety of opportunity, and her response is regressive. Ironically, in spite of her many options, when she does choose for herself, she selects Romero, a traditional man in the person of a nineteen-year-old bullfighter. Although Brett has chosen Romero for deeply personal reason (she explains to Jake, "I've got to do something I really want to do. I've lost my self-respect" [183]), she recognizes that with this choice comes certain suffering. As she phrases it, "I'm a goner" (183). But this female version of romantic agony is based on the capacity to endure pain. And her final triumph in this scenario of self-denial is to relinquish Romero.

Hemingway's pastoral interludes, in which his male characters seek relief from social tensions, are part of a tradition in American fiction that begins with Cooper and Brackenridge and extends through Hawthorne, Melville, and Twain. In rural settings, fictional characters are free from the demands of horological time and linear consciousness. Hemingway's description of the excursion to the Irati River expresses this sense of harmonious ease; nature is not divided into artificial hierarchical categories and is instead described as an unbroken whole. The fishing trip in *The Sun Also Rises* is a rite of purification for Jake and Bill: It represents a release from social and sexual competition, an anodyne to the stress of café society. Like Huck Finn, who heads for the woods to escape the confinement of the Widow Douglas's drawing room, Bill and Jake go to the country to escape social constraints. Not only is there freedom from schedules—"Wonderful how one loses track of the days up here in the mountains" (127)—there is freedom from the traditional inhibition of masculine emotion: "Listen. You're a hell of a good guy, and I'm fonder of you than anybody on earth. I couldn't tell you that in New York. It'd mean I was a faggot," Bill declares to Jake (116).

The Irati River, where the two men fish for trout, is described in idealized terms:

> The road came out from the shadow of the woods into the hot sun. Ahead was the river valley. Beyond the river was a steep hill. There was a field of buckwheat on the hill. We saw a white house under the trees on the hillside. It was very hot and we stopped under some trees beside the river. (118)

Here nature and civilization harmoniously coexist. No single feature of the landscape dominates; the house nestles into the hillside and does not command the heights. This passage, then, creates a mood of tranquility, of restful stasis. In reality, the event on which this fishing expedition was based was quite different. Hemingway and his friend visited the Irati, only to discover that loggers had dumped debris into the river, leaving it clogged and muddy.[20]

In spite of freedom, however temporary, from emotional and social tensions, Jake and Bill descend from the mountains and return to the fiesta at Pamplona. This celebration provides the same release for the peasants of the area that fishing on the Irati River does for Jake and Bill, but the patterns are reversed: The peasants come to the city to seek relief from working the land, just as Jake and Bill retreat to the country to rest from urban tensions. The pattern recapitulates the larger historical movement from land to city to land again. In both cases, it is a retreat from responsibility and daily cares that is sought.

In contrast to the appeal of pastoral tranquility to the men, Brett knows that it is the urban centers that provide mobility and choices for the new woman, not the country, with its traditionally limited vision of woman as reproductive being. In an emblematic moment when Jake asks Brett, "Couldn't we go off in the country for a while?", she responds, "It wouldn't do any good. I'll go if you like. But I couldn't live quietly in the country. Not with my own true love." Brett is riding a historical wave and Jake responds, "I know" (55).

At moments like this, Jake represents the desire to remain grounded in familiar traditions, established economic and social rituals. He doesn't like credit, debit financing, unusual sexual arrangements. Yet his penchant for risk taking is a psychological representation of an economic mode. Living on the edge is like buying on margin: It is unpredictable, potentially dangerous, exhilarating, frightening. Both margin buying and a risk-oriented life create the possibility of having more resources—whether money or a wealth of experiences—and carry with them the risk of financial collapse like F. Scott Fitzgerald's as described in *The Crack-Up*.[21]

The manuscript of *The Sun Also Rises* indicates that Hemingway identified himself with Jake, who was called Hem or Ernie in the early drafts.[22] During the writing of this novel, Hemingway was financially supported by his wife Hadley, and the considerable anxiety caused by his financial dependence on her is expressed in the character of Jake. Just as Nathaniel Hawthorne, who was supported by his wife Sophia while writing *The Scarlet Letter*, expressed his tensions regarding the limits and responsibilities of gender roles in the characters of Hester and Dimmesdale, so Hemingway expresses the same concerns via Jake and Brett. In both novels, the female protagonists threaten to overpower the men they love; in both novels, the men feel ambivalent about their attraction to these unusual women and sometimes unmanned, demeaned in the face of demands made on them. Hawthorne resolves the tension in *The Scarlet Letter* by returning to tradition: Hester does not escape social constraints and judgment; her role is to counsel future generations of women to avoid her mistakes. Hawthorne tells us that his wife was deeply disturbed by the fact that Hester Prynne was not punished more severely for her transgression, and it is possible that Hawthorne added the final paragraphs of *The Scarlet Letter* to appease Sophia. But Hemingway takes another route; he does not regulate Brett to the domestic realm. By leaving his heroine free and relatively intact both emotionally and physically, he disengages from the tradition of the destruction of the female protagonist in American fiction from *Charlotte Temple* to *The House of Mirth* and *The Awakening*.

Brett's statement at the conclusion of the novel, "we would have had such a damned good time together," and Jake's response, "Isn't it pretty to think so?" (247), have partly biographical, partly historical origins. After concluding *The Sun Also Rises*, Hemingway divorced Hadley in order to marry the very wealthy Pauline Pfeiffer, with whom he went on fishing expeditions and safaris.[23] In sharp contrast to Hawthorne, who needed the protective sanctity of his home and the gentle ministrations of Sophia, Hemingway left his domestic life (and felt *extremely* guilty about doing so) in order to live a more exciting and adventurous existence. The conclusion of *The Sun Also Rises* reflects his conviction that there was no going back for him and, for that matter, no turning back the tide of history for the new woman *and* the new man. Jake and Brett want to want the dream of pastoral simplicity and domestic harmony—but, in fact, they don't.

In spite of the fact that traditional ideals are rejected in this novel, *The Sun Also Rises* concludes with an abatement of tensions between Brett and Jake that is the beginning of genuine friendship. As Jake and Brett toast each other with their "coldly beaded" glasses, they experience the deep mutuality that Bill and Jake share when they drink from the "moisture beaded" wine bottles that had been cooled in the Irati River. Significantly, Brett and Jake do not discover this mutuality in idealized pastoral space; instead they acknowledge each other as emotional equals while enjoying the civility of the bar in the Palace Hotel in Madrid. This sharing of public space signals the possibility of new kinds of relationships for women and men in the twentieth century.

Notes

1. Malcolm Cowley, *Exile's Return: A Literary Odyssey of the 1920s* (New York: Viking, 1951), 39, observes that the World War I years caused his generation to "fear boredom more than death."

2. Paul Fussell, *The Great War and Modern Memory* (New York: Oxford University Press, 1975), 13.

3. Carlos Baker, *Ernest Hemingway, A Life Story* (New York: Scribner's, 1969), 8.

4. Cowley, *Exile's Return*, 13.

5. Baker, *Ernest Hemingway*, 52.

6. Ernest Hemingway, *A Farewell to Arms* (New York: Scribner's, 1929), 184–85.

7. William Wiser, *The Crazy Years: Paris in the Twenties* (New York: G. K. Hall, 1983), 85.

8. Ernest Hemingway, *The Sun Also Rises* (New York: Scribner's, 1926), 203. All subsequent citations of this novel appear in the text itself. Hemingway modeled Brett Ashley on Lady Duff Twysden, who was with his group in Pamplona in the summer of 1925. See, for example, Bertram D. Sarason, "Lady Brett Ashley and Lady Duff Twysden," *Connecticut Review* 2 (1969), 5–13.

9. Allen Tate, "Hard Boiled," *The Merrill Studies in* The Sun Also Rises, ed. William White (Columbus, Ohio: Charles E. Merrill, 1969), 18; Theodore Bardacke, "Hemingway's Women," *Ernest Hemingway: The Man and His Work*, ed. John K. M. McCaffery (New York: Avon, 1950), 309; Jackson Benson, *Hemingway: The Writer's Art of Self-Defense* (Minneapolis: University of Minnesota Press, 1969), 30; Edmund Wilson, *The Wound and the Bow* (Cambridge, Mass.: Houghton Mifflin, 1941), 238; John W. Aldridge, *After the Lost Generation* (New York: McGraw-Hill, 1951), 24.

10. Delbert E. Wylder, "The Two Faces of Brett: The Role of the New Woman in *The Sun Also Rises*," *Kentucky Philological Association Bulletin* (1980), 23–33.

11. Ernest Hemingway, "The Unpublished Opening of *The Sun Also Rises*," *Antaeus* 33 (Spring 1979), 7.

12. Paul Johnson, *Modern Times: The World from the Twenties to the Eighties* (New York: Harper & Row, 1983), 5–10.

13. Philip Young, in *Ernest Hemingway: A Reconsideration* (Philadelphia: University of Pennsylvania Press, 1966), argues that Hemingway's wounded heroes express his pathological preoccupation with death and his recurrent need to discharge his fear of death through vicarious killing and dying.

14. Hemingway, "Unpublished Opening," 7.

15. F. Scott Donaldson, *By Force of Will: The Life and Art of Ernest Hemingway* (New York: Viking, 1977), 25, argues that "it is women like Brett . . . who provide unfair competition to the streetwalkers of Paris."

16. For a discussion of money in the novel, see Richard P. Sugg, "Hemingway, Money, and *The Sun Also Rises," Fitzgerald–Hemingway Annual* (1972), 245–55.

17. Aaron Latham, "Machismo," *New York Times Sunday Magazine,* October 16, 1977, 81.

18. Ibid., 89.

19. Noel Riley Fitch, *Sylvia Beach and the Lost Generation* (New York: Norton, 1983), 166.

20. Frederic Joseph Svoboda, *Hemingway and* The Sun Also Rises: *The Crafting of a Style* (Lawrence: University Press of Kansas, 1983), 215.

21. F. Scott Fitzgerald, *The Crack-Up,* ed. Edmund Wilson (New York: J. Laughlin, 1945).

22. Svoboda, *Hemingway,* 9.

23. For general background on Hemingway's guilt and anxiety about this impending divorce, see *Sara and Gerald: Villa America and After* (New York: Holt, Rinehart & Winston, 1984), 23–25.

Performance Art

Jake Barnes and "Masculine" Signification
in The Sun Also Rises

IRA ELLIOTT

◆　◆　◆

L ESBIANS AND GAY MEN figure in no fewer than eight Hemingway short stories published between 1925 and 1933. The tone of these
stories and their attitudes toward homosexuality fluctuate between outright scorn ("The Mother of a Queen") and apparent acceptance ("A Simple Enquiry").[1] Homosexuals also appear, albeit in lesser roles, in many of
Hemingway's major novels, from his first full-length fiction, *The Sun Also
Rises,* to his posthumously published *Islands in the Stream.* Homosexuality is
also touched upon in *A Farewell to Arms, Death in the Afternoon, To Have and Have
Not,* and *A Moveable Feast.*

Gender categories and gender reversals are, moreover, central thematic
concerns in works as diverse as *The Sun Also Rises, A Farewell to Arms, Islands in
the Stream,* and *The Garden of Eden,* in which the question of gender constitutes
the basis of the story.[2] As Jeffrey Meyers points out, in *A Farewell to Arms, For
Whom the Bell Tolls, Islands in the Stream,* and *The Garden of Eden,* "the lovers ex-
periment in dyeing their hair the same color and cutting it the same
length in order to exchange sexual roles and merge their identities."[3] Hair,
in fact, functions throughout Hemingway's work as the principal image by
which gender is made known. In *The Sun Also Rises,* for instance, Brett Ashley, epitome of the Modern Woman, "wore a slipover jersey sweater and a
tweed skirt, and her hair was brushed back like a boy's. She started all

that." Whatever is meant by "all that," Brett, a "damned fine-looking woman,[4] evokes androgyny and gender ambiguity both in physical appearance (her hair) and attire (her jersey).[5]

In both his life and his work, Hemingway remained ambivalent about sex and gender.[6] While his later work in particular demonstrates, in Sylvia O'Sullivan's words, how his "public and private selves circulate with his hypermasculine and submerged feminine selves,"[7] a great deal of his fiction retreats from the possibility of multiple sexual identities and fluid gender roles even while acknowledging the inherent instability of gender.

Certainly the unexpected reemergence of the theme of androgyny in *The Garden of Eden,* striking with such force and urgency, supports Mark Spilka's assertion that questions of gender play a major and often overlooked role in Hemingway's fiction. It is not difficult to see why the early novels (*The Sun Also Rises* and *A Farewell to Arms*) may rightly be regarded as the place "where the loss of androgynous happiness initially occurs."[8] As American culture undertakes a reevaluation of gender/sexual politics, Hemingway is, as Jerry Varsava suggests, proving to be a "more influential writer than we ever thought he was . . . more influential than he ever *intended* to be" (Varsava's emphasis).[9]

MY PROJECT IS TO CONSIDER the ways in which Jake Barnes's male identity is called into question by the genital wound he suffered during the First World War, and the ways in which his fractured sense of self functions in relation to homosexuality and the homosexual men he observes at a *bal musette* in the company of Brett Ashley. Jake's attitude toward the homosexuals—the way he degrades them and casts them as his rivals—will, I believe, reveal the extent to which sexual categories and gender roles are cultural constructions. Close readings of several key passages in the novel will at the same time uncover the reasons behind Jake's own inability to openly accept, if not fully endorse, the potentialities of gender/sexual mutability.

I take as my starting point the recent work of theorist Judith Butler, whose influential book *Gender Trouble* maintains that "the heterosexualization of desire requires and institutes the production of discrete and asymmetrical oppositions between 'feminine' and 'masculine,' where these are understood as expressive of 'male' and 'female.'"[10] This process suggests that "the gendered body is performative," and, in fact, "has no ontological status apart from the various acts which constitute reality." Insofar as "the inner truth of gender is a fabrication," "genders can be neither true nor false, but are only produced as the truth effects of a discourse of primary and stable identity." The notion of a "primary and interior gendered self" is, therefore, a cultural construction which creates the "illusion" of such a disguised self. That gender is itself a kind of "performance of drag. . . . *reveals the imitative structure of gender itself—as well as its contingency"* (Butler's emphasis).[11]

With respect to the "crowd of young men, some in jerseys and some in their shirt-sleeves" (20) that Jake encounters at the *bal musette,* external signs—that is, behavioral or performative acts—lead Jake to "read" the men as homosexual. The various signs by which their homosexuality is made known are these: their "jerseys" and "shirt-sleeves," their "newly washed, wavy hair," their "white hands" and "white faces," their "grimacing, gesturing, talking" (20). While it may be argued that the idea of performativity ("grimacing, gesturing, talking") is here conflated with the notion of the homosexual as a morphological "type" ("newly washed, wavy hair"; "white hands" and "white faces") created by a congenital condition,[12] I maintain that what may at first seem to be morphological is in fact performative: these men are "types" not owing to natural physical features, but rather because they have created themselves as a "type" in order to enact (perform) the role of homosexual.

Their casual dress and careful grooming suggest a "feminine" preoccupation with physical appearance. Their hair appears to be styled ("wavy"), like a woman's, while their "white hands" suggest delicacy, their "white faces," makeup or powder. Just as the feminized Jew of the novel, Robert Cohn, is mocked for his excessive barbering (99), the homosexuals are scorned for their obvious concern with appearance. Rather than exhibiting the reticence and rigidity associated with masculinity, they are overly and overtly expressive, uninhibited in the use of their bodies and voices. Jake's "diagnosis" is confirmed, his own masculinity momentarily consolidated, by the policeman near the door of the bar, who, in a gesture that bonds the two "real" men and marginalizes the homosexuals as "other," looks at Jake and smiles (20).

But what is it, really, that Jake "reads"? It is not the sexual orientation of the men but rather a set of signs, a visual (and aural) field—the body— upon which is inscribed, and through which is enacted, their otherwise concealed sexuality. The young men have their homosexuality "written" on their faces and on their bodies. They "perform" their sexuality through facial expressions and physical gestures. Just as Jake's wound remains unnamed, so, too, homosexuality is never mentioned; both are instead disclosed through, in the words of Arnold and Cathy Davidson, "sexual and textual absences." The reader, like Jake, "must read the ostensible sexual preference of the young men from the various signs provided and thereby decode covert private sexuality from overt public sociability."[13] Homosexuality is therefore not simply a matter of erotic object choice and same-gender sex. It is also a way of being, for the performativity of the young men indicates—is, in fact, predictive of—their bedroom behavior.

What Jake "reads" is not, therefore, sexuality, but gender. In Butlerian terms, Brett's companions are "imitating" the "wrong" gender. Sexual identity can be determined through careful observation of behavior, and sex and gender collapse into a single "truth" manifest in appearance. The "feminine," regarded as the exclusive province of the female, is seen as inscribed within/on the female body. Its appropriation by the male constitutes a gender transgression which in and of itself becomes the visible sign of homosexuality. The homosexual reveals himself through a performative "error," and, by this logic, the feminine, effeminate, or feminized man is always homosexual.

According to Jonathan Dollimore, the notion that sex and (performative) "truth" are connected leads to the supposition that sexual deviation is a "deviation from the truth . . . [which is] embodied in, and really only accessible to, normality."[14] This in turn implies that "there is something like an 'error' involved in what the [homosexuals] do . . . a manner of acting that is not adequate to reality."[15] This perverse "error" is not only enacted in sex but also in "performance" or self-presentation. Boys will be boys only if boys act like boys; when boys act like girls—that is, do not conform to gender/ed expectations—they are acting, in public or in private, in ways "not adequate to reality."

Jake objects not so much to homosexual behavior (which is unseen) but to "femininity" expressed through the "wrong" body. Gender-crossing is what troubles Jake; the rupture between a culturally determined signifier (the male body) and signified (the female gender) disrupts the male/female binary. But what if the young men had not crossed the gender line, if their behavior were "in accord" with their sex, if they, in short, acted the way Jake expects men to act? He would then have no "signs" of their homosexuality.

The perception that the young men are enacting the "wrong" gender leads to the conclusion that they are inauthentic, that the projection of a "feminine" persona is a parody, a send-up of the female's "proper" role. Just as their presumed sexual deviation is a "deviation from the truth," a behavioral "error," so the way they act in public is a deliberate "deviation" from the "truth" of their gender. Although one could argue that the men are "camping" in order to destabilize the notion of fixed (naturalized) gender characteristics—that theirs is a conscious deployment of gender for strategic political ends—Jake cannot allow for the possibility that they might truly *be* the way they *act*. He cannot believe that these men are *really* like that ("feminine") because they are male.

When Jake sees one of the men dancing with Georgette, the prostitute he picked up earlier in the evening, he describes her "tall blonde" partner as dancing "big-hippily, carrying his head on the side, his eyes lifted as he danced" (20). In other words, he danced like a woman, for "big-hippily" evokes the maternal body—or perhaps the "bump-and-grind" of a "loose" woman who wishes to call attention to her genital area. That his head is carried "on the side" implies that a pose has been struck, that he is unbalanced, somehow "off." His gaze, moreover, is not where it should be—on the female object—but somewhere else, an indication that he is not firmly grounded or well-focused but given to wandering (sexual promiscuity?). "Eyes lifted," he stares dreamily into space, like a screen beauty in a seductive Hollywood photograph. Indeed, Hollywood erotica, magazine "glamour shots," and even Christian iconography depict the female as exposed, inviting, and passive through the position of her head, which is often thrown back in ecstacy/agony. This same receptivity and vulnerability is recalled in the homosexual's dancing, his head tilted to "one side." And when the music stops, "another one of them" asks Georgette to dance, and Jake knows that "they would all dance with her," for "they were like that" (20).

Just what he means by "like that" remains ambiguous; he neither explains nor reflects upon what precisely they are "like" or why they might be that way.[16] I take Jake to mean, however, that homosexuals enjoy flirting with what they perceive as the exotic or marginalized, for the prostitute represents yet another form of "deviant" desire or "perverted" sexuality. She is, moreover, like all women, alien to the homosexual's erotic life, just as the homosexuals are foreign to the conception of manhood expressed in the novel.

Homosexuals, then, enjoy sporting with, or teasing, the "fallen" woman. Her own "corrupted" sexuality provides them with a nonthreatening plaything which they are able to trade among themselves (as they presumably trade sexual partners, hopping from one bed to another). While Georgette is unaffiliated with the homosexual men sexually, she is aligned with them because of her professional promiscuity. What's more, her very name, a feminized version of George (where the masculine is taken for the universal), suggests that she is a feminized man—another "performance of drag" that underscores *male* promiscuity.

Brett uses the homosexuals in a similar manner—"when one's with the crowd I'm with, one can drink in such safety" (20)—and her confidence (perhaps the only wholly unambiguous response to these men, as well as the clearest evidence that they are in fact gay) does not seem to greatly disturb Jake. What offends him is the deployment of the female body as an item of exchange. Georgette is present owing entirely to his transaction with her, but in his case she would be used "properly"—that is, for heterosexual exchange—if only he could do so. Yet the fact that he cannot appropriate her body for the "manly" purpose for which she is intended affiliates Jake with the homosexuals. Although his desire is "normal," his body prevents him from actualizing his "manhood." Jake's inability to perform sexually corresponds to the homosexual's inability to perform his "correct" gender. Jake's sexual inadequacy and the homosexual's gender transgression are therefore conjoined: neither can properly signify "masculinity."

When the men first enter the bar, Jake overhears a part of their conversation which relates to Georgette: "One of them saw Georgette and said: 'I do declare. There is an actual harlot. I'm going to dance with her, Lett. You watch me.' The tall dark one, called Lett, said: 'Don't be rash.' The blonde one answered: 'Don't worry, dear'" (20). Their theatricality and the staginess of the scene itself is underscored by the dramatic presentation of their dialogue, for the colon is a formal device borrowed from the drama (and is employed in the novel only in this instance). Their mannered speech also sounds theatrical and declamatory. The insertion of "do" in "I declare" strikes one as an archaism out of the drawing rooms of the nineteenth century. Reminiscent of the speech of the upper-class, whose diction represents a kind of cultural power, the archaic form of address also recalls the stereotypical southern belle, whose inflection feeds into the construction of the southern woman as artificial and insincere. Like the belle of the Old South, the homosexual affects an aristocratic pose which is arch and pretentious, and both exhibit a "superior, simpering composure" (20). That the blonde "declares" that he sees an "actual" harlot intensifies the split between the "real" and the "feigned," the "true" and the "untrue." Georgette's reality is, in Jakes's mind anyway, a titillation for the men, a contrived danger (like Brett's relationship to the homosexuals) that poses no threat. That which is termed "rash" is "rash" only insofar as it unites the authentic (a "real" female) with the inauthentic (a "false" female—the homosexual). But even this is not a real danger, for both the prostitute and the homosexual are presented as poor copies of an original (authentic) female.

The very existence of the gay man—"feminine" desire expressed through the male body, "feminine" behavior enacted by a man—calls into question not only naturalized sex/gender roles, but also such opposition as seen/unseen, disclosed/undisclosed, real/illusory.[17] That the homosexual appears to hold together "qualities that are elsewhere felt as antithetical: theatricality and authenticity . . . intensity and irony, a fierce assertion of extreme feeling with a deprecating sense of its absurdity,"[18] leads one to entertain the possibility that the contemporary gay man possesses—and this, I believe, is specific to time, place, race, and class—"a heightened awareness and appreciation for disguise, impersonation, the projection and the distinction between instinctive and theatrical behavior."[19] As gay-identified novelist John Rechy put it at the 1991 Out/Write Conference in San Francisco, the so-called gay sensibility "may be marked by its risking of extremes, a duality often revealed within seeming contradictions."[20]

It is also notable that "it is not Brett who elicits Jake's obvious and immediate attraction"[21] when she enters the bar, but rather her homosexual companions: "I was very angry. Somehow they always made me angry. I know they are supposed to be amusing, and you should be tolerant, but I wanted to swing on one, any one, anything to shatter that superior, simpering composure" (20). The urge to physically assault the homosexual man—what we now call "gay bashing," which many theorists argue constitutes an attack on the "feminine" rooted in misogyny—quite clearly derives from Jake's anger; but what, precisely, is he so angry about? The source of his rage is in part his frustration at being unable to categorize the homosexual within the male/female binary. That these men represent and enact gender nonconformity violates the cultural boundaries demarcating appropriate social and sexual behavior. Any attempted remapping of these culturally agreed upon borders exposes the arbitrariness of their frontiers, which in turn calls for a rethinking of the ontological groundwork of sex/gender itself. At the same time, his anger is self-hatred displaced onto the homosexual, for Jake has lost (physically and psychologically) his signifying phallus. What's more, the tolerance he knows he should have for the homosexuals may also be the same tolerance he hopes Brett will have for him and his sexual failing.

In a cultural system that authorizes a single mode of self-presentation for each gender, transgressing the binary law of male/female constitutes a crime. Just as homosexuality is often constructed as "a crime against nature," so, too, this crime, or sin, against naturalized gender performance must be punished: Jake wishes "to shatter that superior, simpering composure" which he sees as a homosexual or "feminine" trait. Robert Cohn's manner is also described as "superior." To whom or what the homosexual is "superior" is not expressed, but Jake apparently believes that they are, or think that they are, "superior" to him. He is also disturbed by their "sim-

pering composure," though one may wonder whether it is their composure itself which troubles Jake, or its simpering nature. In either case, the
ostensibly heterosexual man here feels threatened by the homosexual's acceptance and assertion of his presumably "incorrect" gender behavior. If he
is superior to Jake, then it is axiomatic that Jake is inferior to him, for Jake
himself hopes that he signifies what he is not, namely, the potent and powerful heterosexual male.

What Jake is unable or unwilling to acknowledge (disclose) is that his
relationship to women resembles that of the homosexual. Though for different reasons, both Jake and the homosexual man do not relate to women
in accordance with the demands of a heterosexual/heterosexist culture.
What Jake desires but cannot do is to perform sexually with women, the
same performance rejected by the homosexual. While the homosexual rejects heterosexual performance, he does so in favor of an alternative. Jake,
on the other hand, is bound by a "masculine" signification and desire
which is "untrue"—he cannot *do* what his appearance suggests he can. The
homosexual signifies differently, Jake not at all, and so the homosexual is
seen as "superior."

Jake's body stands, as it were, between himself and his desires; the homosexual's "perverse" desire, however, circumvents the "natural" physical
act. It is therefore not the homosexual's denial or disinterest in women
which offends Jake but the renunciation of naturalized male desire. When
he looks at the homosexual man, what Jakes sees is the body of a male that
does not perform as a "man"; when he regards himself what he sees is the
body of a male that lacks the sign of "manliness." This tends to support
Jonathan Dollimore's observation that "the most extreme threat to the
true form of something comes not so much from its absolute opposite or
its direct negation, but in the form of its perversion. . . . [which is] very
often perceived as at once utterly alien to what it threatens, and yet, mysteriously inherent within it."[22]

For Hemingway, himself something of a "sexual puritan,"[23] "sexual
perversion is inseparable from intellectual and moral corruption."[24] This is
just one instance of how the nineteenth-century "medical model" of homosexuality, which regarded same-gender sex as a "congenital abnormality," absorbed the centuries-old construction of homosexual behavior as "a
sinful and evil practice, . . . [so that] the older conception remained active within the new."[25]

What Judith Sensibar says about John Campton in *A Son at the Front* ap-
plies equally well to Jake Barnes (and Hemingway). She declares that
Wharton's Campton is "a victim of his culture's rigid gender classifications

and patriarchal exchange systems," and that "his refusal to examine his own sexuality is caused partly by his rigid belief in masculinist gender classifications."[26] This is similar to Butler's belief that "institutional heterosexuality both requires and produced the univocity of each of the gendered terms that constitute the limit of gendered possibilities within an oppositional, binary system."[27] Jake can account for the homosexual man only by associating him with aristocratic pretensions or with "femininity," which Jake perceives in the gay man's "superior," southern-belle–like manner—behavior Hemingway elsewhere associates with the "mincing gentry."[28]

In the following chapter (4), Jake's affiliation with the homosexual and with gender reversal is even more pronounced. While undressing for bed, he sees himself in the mirror: "Undressing, I looked at myself in the mirror of the big armoire beside the bed. That was a typically French way to furnish a room. Practical, too, I suppose. Of all the ways to be wounded. I suppose it was funny. I put my pajamas on and got into bed" (30). While the digression concerning the armoire might at first appear to be an attempt to avoid seeing himself or talking about what he sees, it is actually a symbolic corollary of Jake's wound. Just as the armoire represents "a typically French way to furnish a room," so the penis is "typical" of the male body. Whereas the armoire is "practical," however, Jake's member is not (at least in relation to his sex life); rather, it is all "furnishing." In relation to the female, the homosexual's sex is similarly "furnishing." That Jake regards his wound as "funny" recalls his earlier observation that homosexual men "are supposed to be amusing," though clearly neither are a source of much humor. Both are instead ironic objects of derision. What Jake sees in the mirror has come to be mere ornamentation.[29] That which is present signifies absence—not of desire but of ability. The mirror reflects appearance; it does not reveal essence. At the same time, the "external signs" which it presents can, if "read" correctly, provide the clues necessary to apprehend "inner truth." In Jake's case, that "truth" is his fractured sense of masculine identity. In holding the mirror up to himself, what Jake discovers is his close affiliation with the homosexual men.

Inasmuch as Jake considers himself to be heterosexual, the novel posits the site of sexuality in gendered desire rather than sexual behavior. What distinguishes Jake from the homosexual men is gender performance and erotic object choice. By this logic, it follows that sexuality is determined by gender identification rather than sexual activity. Jake's sex can no longer penetrate a woman (and so all sexual relations are apparently ruled out), but he remains heterosexual by virtue of his desire. If the men from the bar discontinued same-gender sex, they would presumably remain homosexual. Sexual identity issues not from the sex act but from covert desire or overt social behavior.

When Jake finally gets into bed, his "head start[s] to work," and he again thinks how his was a "rotten" way to be wounded—and "on a joke front like the Italian" at that—another unfunny joke (31). His wound is an accident which cannot be named, just as homosexuality is the love that dare not speak its name. His "reduced" stature as a man is further signified by his name, a monosyllabic diminutive which suggests that his identity, like his body, has been cut off, foreshortened, reduced. Jake has "given more" (31) than his life, for his manhood has been sacrificed, or al least compromised, and with it the potential for offspring, his link to the future.[30]

The scene continues: "I lay awake thinking and my mind jumping around. Then I couldn't keep away from it, and I started to think about Brett and all the rest of it went away. I was thinking about Brett and my mind stopped jumping around and started to go in sort of smooth waves. Then all of a sudden I started to cry. Then after a while it was better and I lay in bed and listened to the heavy trams go by and way down the street, and then I went to sleep" (31). This is a highly problematic passage not only because of the vagueness of the language (what precisely is "it"?) but also because of the uncertain signification assigned Jake. If we regard these lines as a masturbatory fantasy either for Jake or for a projected male reader, the "it" that he "couldn't keep away from" may be taken to refer to the body itself, the part with which Jake is most preoccupied. Once he has focused his attention on "it"—and nothing suggests that his thoughts alone are what he "couldn't keep away from"—he "started to think about Brett and all the rest of it went away." Now the "it" may be the wound and his reflections on his injury, but he may also be talking about his wounded sex itself, where "sex" is understood to be the male member. That is to say, what "went away" might be the maimed part of himself, leaving Jake free to fantasize that his wound has been healed, his body restored to wholeness, health, and a "correct" masculine morphology. If, on the other hand, what "went away" is the male member itself, then Jake imagines himself in the subject position. In this case, his body has not been restored (even psychologically) but reinscribed.

The trams, a variation on the familiar phallic image of the penis as a powerful forward-moving train, are, like Jake's own maleness, removed from himself, detached and no longer a function of his body, but outside him and "way down the street." Kenneth Lynn goes so far as to suggest that Jake is a man "whose dilemma is that, like a lesbian, he cannot penetrate his loved one's body with his own."[31] While this comparison betrays Lynn's lack of understanding of lesbian sexuality, it is nevertheless an acute observation as it pertains to Jake's ruptured sense of male identity. It remains unclear, however, whether Jake's masculinity is in question because of the lost body part (morphology) or because of his inability to express what is regarded as masculine—that is, heterosexual performativity. This loss is later seen in relation to homosexuality itself, when Jake's wound is directly linked to homosexual identity.

This linkage occurs about midway through the novel, during the fishing trip Jake takes with his friend Bill Gorton before the fiesta. The fishing episode is one of what Wendy Martin calls Hemingway's "pastoral interludes, in which his male characters seek relief from social tensions," part of a tradition in American fiction "that begins with Cooper and Brackenridge and extends through Hawthorne, Melville, and Twain."[32] This "pastoral interlude" is also a "set piece" profoundly colored by the homoerotic element. Like the Arcadian adventures described in more specifically "gay texts"—the fishing trip in Forster's *Maurice,* for example—Jake and Bill's "relief from social tensions" represents "relief" or escape from the bonds of mainstream morality. Maurice's "greenwood" of erotic possibilities has its antithesis in another kind of "set piece" found in Anglo-American literature, the man-to-man combat features two males as signifiers of the "masculine," the most famous example being perhaps the "Gladiatorial" chapter in Lawrence's *Women in Love.* In *The Sun Also Rises* the physical battle between male rivals is most overtly expressed in the bullfight, where two such signifiers are the man and the bull. And just as Jake is a spectator at the bullfight rather than a participant, so, too, he can only look on as other men (Robert Cohn, Mike Campbell, Pedro Romero) compete for the affections of Brett Ashley. The arena where "real" men compete—whether the bullring or the bedroom—is for Jake a foreclosed area of emotional and psychic involvement.

Whether their setting is the "greenwood," bullring, or battlefield, these episodes are intense moments of male bonding, which for Mario Mieli (and I concur) is always an expression of a "paralysed and unspoken homosexuality, which can be grasped, in the negative, in the denial of women."[33] While alone and apart from the world, Bill teases Jake by asking him if he knows what his real "trouble" is: "You're an expatriate [Bill explains]. One of the worst type. . . . You've lost touch with the soil. You get precious. Fake European standards have ruined you. You drink yourself to death. You become obsessed by sex. You spend all your time talking, not working. You are an expatriate, see? You hang around cafés" (115). Jake's association with the old world places him within the shadow of European decadence, which is seen as a performance, a role unbecoming to him. That he has "lost touch with the soil" suggests that Jake is estranged from enduring values, for "the earth abideth forever."[34] Jake has become "precious," "ruined" by "fake European standards," so that his very identity has been compromised, if not corrupted by a foreign object, perhaps a mortar shell. This has in turn transformed his corporeal existence into something foreign or other—not quite a "whole" man but certainly not a woman. Jake has come to inhabit the demi-monde, the world of the outcast, the lost, the homosexual—the decadent other *par excellence*. What's more, like Lawrence's, Hemingway's "anxieties about homosexuality were conjoined with class antagonism"[35]—his antipathy for the rich, the "mincing gentry."

Jake, like the homosexual, is a habitué of cafés, where one "does" very little except talk, and the homosexual, the female, and the Jew are constructed as overly discursive. (Another of Hemingway's fears was that writing—talking—was unmanly, for it is not "doing.") The gay man, however, is like a woman in that he "hangs around" and doesn't work much. His only "work" is nightwork related to sex, just as the "proper" work for woman is to serve her man. Even Brett, the independent Modern Woman, exists only in relation to men—Jake, Mike, Robert, Pedro, Count Mippipopolous, the homosexuals.

Bill goes on to say that Jake doesn't work, after all, and that while some claim he is supported by women, others insist that he's impotent. A man who is supported by women is of course not a "real" man, but what Bill means by "impotent" is ambiguous. He may believe that Jake is sexually impotent or that as a decadent American who has adopted "fake" European standards he is psychically impotent. In either case, the link between non-normative sexuality and decadence is clear. Jake responds to Bill by saying, "I just had an accident." But Bill tells Jake, "Never mention that. . . . That's the sort of thing that can't be spoken of. That's what you ought to work up into a mystery. Like Henry's bicycle" (115). Once again, just as homosexuality is the love that dare not speak its name, so Jake's "accident" should not be discussed. "Henry's bicycle" is a reference to Henry James and the "obscure hurt" he suffered while a teenager—either a physical wound which rendered him incapable of sexual performance or a psychic "hurt," the realization of his homosexuality.[36] The failure to perform in the culturally prescribed way (heterosexually) is therefore figured as "de-masculinizing."

Jake and Bill then banter about whether Henry's wound was suffered while riding a bicycle or a horse, with attendant puns on "joy-stick" and "pedal" (116). When Jake "stands up" for the tricycle, Bill replies, "I think he's a good writer, too." He adds that Jake is "a hell of a good guy":

> I'm fonder of you than anybody on earth. I couldn't tell you that in New York. It'd mean I was a faggot. That was what the Civil War was about. Abraham Lincoln was a faggot. He was in love with General Grant. So was Jefferson Davis. Lincoln just freed the slaves on a bet. The Dred Scott case was framed by the Anti-Saloon League. Sex explains it all. The Colonel's Lady and Judy O'Grady are Lesbians under the skin. (116)

That Jake opts for the tricycle over the horse as the instrument of Henry's "unmanning" implies that the modern world of the machine has had a negative, disruptive effect on traditional male/female roles. When Bill acknowledges that Henry, in spite of his wound, was "a good writer" (could still perform as an artist), he is also reassuring Jake that he can still perform as a good friend and "proper" man—fishing, eating, drinking. Jake will not be banished from the homosocial realm where all "good guys" go to escape from the debilitating influence of women.

WHILE JAKE MAY NOW occupy an uncertain place between the genders, Bill continues to be "fonder" of him than anybody. Defending himself from any potential "charge" of homosexuality, Bill quickly adds that had they been in New York, he wouldn't be able to voice his affection for Jake without being a "faggot"; European decadence makes it possible to speak the unspeakable. Without belaboring Bill's mock history of the Civil War, we should remark that "sex explains it all." The "truth" of the self is revealed, after all, in sex; and homosexuality (in this instance, lesbianism) is inscribed in the body, concealed "under the skin." If we recall that male homosexuality may be "read" in external signs, it appears here that lesbian sexuality is not similarly marked by gender nonconformity, that concealed lesbian identity cannot be discerned through observing performance but only by unmasking what is hidden in the body, under the skin. This seems to suggest that lesbianism is congenital, while male homosexuality is performative.

The novel concludes with the justly famous scene of Jake and Brett together in a cab: "'Oh, Jake,' Brett said, 'we could have had such a damned good time together.' Ahead was a mounted policeman in khaki directing traffic. He raised his baton. The car slowed suddenly pressing Brett against me. 'Yes,' I said. 'Isn't it pretty to think so?'" (247). Earlier in the novel, Georgette pressed against Jake while in a cab (15), and now Brett is thrown against the body of a man who desires more than he can do; he wants not just "pressing" but penetration. Once again the symbolic policeman is present, but this time he isn't smiling; he and Jake are no longer members of the same "club." This time his raised baton is a rebuke. The policeman, a "manly" authority figure, is not only "mounted" (and perhaps "well-mounted") on a horse (suggesting a "stud" or "stallion" while recalling Henry's "accident"), but also a uniformed presence whose "raised" baton is suggestive not only of an erect phallus but also of the baton of a conductor or military officer, two whose role is to orchestrate the performance of others, though Jake can no longer perform.

The sun, almost always figured as "male" (and in most Indo-European languages grammatically of the "male gender"), "ariseth" and "goeth down," as does a male. The earth, a female/maternal signifier, "abideth forever," and "the soil," it will be recalled, is what Jake has "lost touch" with. As Arnold and Cathy Davidson note, "Jake's last words readily devolve into an endless series of counter-statements that continue the same discourse: 'Isn't it pretty to think so?' / 'Isn't it pretty to think isn't it pretty to think so?'" This "negation," as the Davidsons call it, closes the novel and returns us to its title, for "only the earth—not heroes, not their successes or their failures—abideth forever."[37] The use of so "feminine" a word as "pretty" further underscores Jake's mixed gender identification as well as the "feminine" qualities of life which abide forever.

If there is hope for Jake—that is, for those confined by their culture's "rigid gender classifications"—it may be found, paradoxically enough, in the image of the homosexual man and the "feminized" male, in the "possibility of a consciousness integrating both the masculine and feminine," in the recognition that "patriarchy as a cultural phenomenon . . . can destroy a man's ability to develop his fullest potential."[38] Similarly, that Jake and Brett share the public space of the bar may signal "the possibility of new kinds of relationships for women and men in the twentieth century."[39]

Notes

1. Although I here use the designations "lesbians" and "gay men" for the sake of convenience (and at the risk of historical inaccuracy), I elsewhere employ the terms "homosexual" and "gay man" interchangeably. Except where otherwise noted, "homosexual" and "homosexuality" should be understood to refer exclusively to males. The eight stories I have in mind are "Mr. and Mrs. Elliot," "Che Ti Dice la Patria?" "A Simple Enquiry," "A Pursuit Race," The Sea Change," "The Mother of a Queen," "The Light of the World," and "The Last Good Country."

2. For an account of the editing process that led to the published version of *The Garden of Eden,* and for a discussion of the plotlines omitted, see Robert E. Fleming's article, "The Endings of Hemingway's *Garden of Eden,*" *American Literature* 61 (May 1989), 261–70.

3. Jeffrey Meyers, *Hemingway: A Biography* (New York: Harper and Row, 1986), 434.

4. Ernest Hemingway, *The Sun Also Rises* (1926; reprint, New York: Scribner's, 1954), 22. Subsequent references to this novel will be noted parenthetically in the text.

5. The relationship between hair and (sexual) power is of course a common one. In *Wars I Have Seen,* for example, Gertrude Stein notes that girls who "kept company with Germans" during World War II had their heads shaved (London: Batesford, 1945), 160. Hair and barbering are also mentioned in four other places in *The Sun* (83, 97, 101, 150), and Hemingway once wrote an unpublished short story entitled, "A Story of a Man Who Always Wanted to Have Long Hair." See Wendy Martin, "Brett Ashley as New Woman in *The Sun Also Rises,*" in *New Essays on "The Sun Also Rises,*" ed. Linda Wagner-Martin (New York: Cambridge University Press, 1987), 76. [Reprinted in this volume.]

6. Probably the best critical biographies for background on Hemingway's childhood and troubled family life—his relationship to his parents and his androgynous "twinship" (Lynn) with sister Marcelline—are James R. Mellow's *Hemingway: A Life without Consequences* (New York: Houghton Mifflin, 1992), Kenneth Lynn's *Hemingway* (New York: Fawcett Columbine, 1987), and Meyer's *Hemingway: A Biography.*

7. Sylvia O'Sullivan, "Hemingway vs. Hemingway: Femininity and Masculinity in the Major Works" (Ph.D. diss., University of Maryland, 1986), abstract in *Dissertation Abstracts International* 48 (1987), 127A.

8. Mark Spilka, *Hemingway's Quarrel with Androgyny* (Lincoln: University of Nebraska Press, 1990), 4.

9. Jerry A. Varsava, "En-Gendered Problems: Characteral Conflict in Hemingway's *Garden,*" *LIT: Literature Interpretation Theory* 3 (1991), 131.

10. Judith Butler, *Gender Trouble: Feminism and the Subversion of Identity* (New York: Routledge, 1990), 17.

11. Butler, *Gender Trouble,* 136–37.

12. The pallor of the young men evokes the familiar vampiric construction of the gay man and lesbian, figures of the night who prey on innocents and by sucking their blood "convert" them to a "perverted" way of life. The fear of homosexual "contamination" (especially "contamination"/"conversion" of the young) is a typical homophobic strategy that relies on the homosexual's ability to "pass" as heterosexual in mainstream society. The idea of the homosexual as carrier of moral and physical disease was fully deployed during the McCarthy period and during Anita Bryant's antigay "Save Our Children" campaign of the 1970s. Today's so-called

Religious Right follows in the footsteps of such ignoble movements. See Barry D. Adams, *The Rise of a Gay and Lesbian Movement* (Boston: Twayne, 1987); John D'Emilio and Estelle B. Freedman, *Intimate Matters: A History of Sexuality in America* (New York: Harper and Row, 1988); and James Levin, *The Gay Novel in America* (New York: Garland, 1991). For a discussion of the "polluted body," see Mary Douglas, *Purity and Danger: An Analysis of Concepts of Pollution and Taboo* (New York: Praeger, 1966); and, for an examination of how these stereotypes work in relation to the AIDS pandemic, see Cindy Patton, *Inventing AIDS* (New York: Routledge, 1990), and Simon Watney, *Policing Desire: Pornography, AIDS and the Media* (Minneapolis: University of Minnesota Press, 1989). For a recent discussion of the reemergence of the vampire legend in popular culture, see Pat H. Broeske's article in the *New York Times,* "Hollywood Goes Batty for Vampires" (26 April 1992), and, of course, Ann Rice's vampire novels.

13. Arnold E. Davidson and Cathy N. Davidson, "Decoding the Hemingway Hero in *The Sun Also Rises,"* in *New Essays on* The Sun Also Rises, ed. Linda Wagner-Martin (New York: Cambridge University Press, 1987), 89. For a reading of *The Sun* similar to the Davidsons' and my own, though with a different slant from our respective pieces, see Debra A. Moddelmog's excellent article, "Reconstructing Hemingway's Identity: Sexual Politics, the Author, and the Multicultural Classroom," *Narrative* 1 (October 1993), 187–206.

14. Jonathan Dollimore, *Sexual Dissidence: Augustine to Wilde, Freud to Foucault* (Oxford: Oxford University Press, 1991), 69.

15. Michel Foucault, Introduction to *Herculine Barbine: Being the Recently Discovered Memoirs of a French Hermaphrodite,* trans. Richard McDougall (New York: Pantheon, 1980), x–xi.

16. According to Peter Griffin, Hemingway's naturalized conception of homosexuals was based on their "tendency to overreact or, better, to misreact, because their emotions were somehow short-circuited. Usually afraid to let their genuine feelings show, they would either amplify or suppress their response—keeping up a static of excitement or affecting ennui—in order to hide themselves. In speech and writing, everything for them had to be more, or less, that it was" (*Less Than a Treason: Hemingway in Paris* [New York: Oxford University Press, 1990], 50).

17. Such binarisms were suggested to me by Eve Kosofsky Sedgewick's proposition that "many of the major nodes of thought and knowledge in twentieth-century Western culture as a whole are structured—indeed, fractured—by a chronic, now endemic crisis of homo/heterosexual definition" (*Epistemology of the Closet* [Berkeley: University of California Press, 1990], 3).

18. Richard Dyer, *Heavenly Bodies: Film Stars and Society* (London: Macmillan, 1987), 154.

19. Jack Babuscio, "Camp and the Gay Sensibility," in *Gays and Film,* ed. Richard Dyer (London: British Film Institute, 1977), 45.

20. Quoted by Joan Fry in "An Interview with John Rechy," *Poets & Writers* 20 (May/June 1992), 25–34.

21. Davidson and Davidson, "Decoding the Hemingway Hero," 89.

22. Dollimore, *Sexual Dissidence,* 121.

23. Scott Donaldson, *By Force of Will: The Life and Art of Ernest Hemingway* (New York: Viking, 1977), 180.

24. Dollimore, *Sexual Dissidence,* 67.

25. Dollimore, *Sexual Dissidence,* 46.

26. Judith Sensibar, "'Behind the Lines' in Edith Wharton's *A Son at the Front*: Rewriting a Masculinist Tradition," *Journal of American Studies* 24 (1990), 192.

27. Butler, *Gender Troubles,* 22.

28. Ernest Hemingway, *Death in the Afternoon* (1932; reprint, New York: Lyceum-Scribner Library, 1960), 205. Also, see Robert Scholes and Nancy R. Comley, "Hemingway's Gay Blades," *differences: A Journal of Feminist Cultural Studies* 5 (1993), 116–39. Two of the best places to begin further reading on the aristocracy and homosexuality are Susan Sontag's seminal 1964 essay, "Notes on 'Camp,'" in *Against Interpretation* (New York: Delta-Dell, 1966), 275–92; and Eve Kosofsky Sedgwick's equally important *Between Men: English Literature and Homosexual Desire* (New York: Columbia University Press, 1985).

29. Hemingway writes in *A Moveable Feast* (1964; reprint, New York: Bantam 1979): "If I started to write elaborately, or like someone introducing or presenting something, I found that I could cut that scrollwork or ornamentation out and throw it away and start with the first true simple declarative sentence I had written" (12). The "true simple declarative sentence," stripped of "scrollwork" and "ornamentation," because both are seen to be dishonest and excessive, was the aesthetic ideal which would serve equally well in life and literature.

30. Hemingway took great pains in selecting both the titles of his books and the names of his characters. The androgynous names Brett and Frances are no accident. Robert Jordan of *For Whom the Bell Tolls,* whose father, like Hemingway's, committed suicide, has two first names (Jordan can also be a woman's name—for example, the professional golfer Jordan Baker in *The Great Gatsby*). Frederic Henry in *A Farewell to Arms* has two first names as well, which, because there is no patronymic, indicates that the link to the father has been severed. Kenneth Lynn traces the source of both Frederic and Catherine Barkley's names to Barklie Henry, "the husband of a Whitney heiress" whose wife, like Catherine, had "a tough time giving birth to their first child" (239, 297–98). Like the dissatisfied wife in "Cat in the Rain" (1925), Catherine is referred to in *A Farewell* as "Cat"; she is "reborn" in the person of Catherine Bourne in *The Garden of Eden.* As for Jake Barnes, his name may derive from lesbian salon hostess Natalie Barney, writer Djuna Barnes, or the rue Jacob/Hotel Jacob, where many Americans stayed upon first arriving in Paris in the

1920s. Such androgynous names and sources for names recall the various personas Hemingway assumed throughout his life—Papa, Hemingstein, Dr. Hemingstein, Ernie, and so forth.

31. Lynn, *Hemingway,* 323.

32. Martin, "Brett Ashley as New Woman in *The Sun Also Rises,"* 77–78.

33. Mario Mieli, *Homosexuality and Liberation: Elements of a Gay Critique,* trans. David Fernback (London: Gay Men's Press, 1980), 34.

34. The fact that the sun rises but Jake does not suggests not only his "lost manhood" but also the loss of all "masculine" values. He is a member of the "lost generation" in two respects: he is lost in the chaos of a changing world, and lost in terms of nineteenth-century values that no longer abide.

35. Dollimore, *Sexual Dissidence,* 268.

36. See R. W. B. Lewis, *The Jameses: A Family Narrative* (New York: Farrar, Straus and Giroux, 1991), 117.

37. Davidson and Davidson, "Decoding the Hemingway Hero," 103–4.

38. Nancy McCampbell Grace, "The Feminized Male Character in Twentieth-Century Fiction: Studies in Joyce, Hemingway, Kerouac and Bellow" (Ph.D. diss., Ohio State University, 1986), abstract in *Dissertation Abstracts International* 48 (1988), 2334 A.

39. Martin, "Brett Ashley as New Woman in *The Sun Also Rises,"* 81.

Hemingway's Morality of Compensation

SCOTT DONALDSON

◆ ◆ ◆

Books should be about the people you know, that
you love and hate, not about the people you study
up about. If you write them truly they will have all
the economic implications a book can hold.

—Ernest Hemingway

WHILE VOYAGING BACK to the United States in 1833, Ralph
Waldo Emerson puzzled over a definition of morals. His thoughts,
he admitted in his journal, were "dim and vague," but one might obtain
"some idea of them . . . who develops the doctrine in his own experience that nothing can be given or taken without an equivalent." In Emerson's sublime optimism, he weighted the scales of equivalence in favor of
the taker. Only the half blind, as he observes in his essay in "The Tragic,"
had never beheld the House of Pain, which like the salt sea encroached on
man in his felicity. But felicity was man's customary state, for he lived on
the land, not at sea. If pain disturbed him, he could rest in the conviction
that nature would proportion "her defence to the assault" and "that the
intellect in its purity, and the moral sense in its purity, are not distin-
guished from each other, and both ravish us into a region whereinto these
passionate clouds of sorrow cannot rise."

On this issue, Emerson's Concord voice sounds in off-key opposition to
that of Emily Dickinson in western Massachusetts, who wrote of the pri-
macy of pain in the equation of compensation:

For each extatic instant
We must an anguish pay

In keen and quivering ratio
To the extasy

For each beloved hour
Sharp pittances of years—
Bitter contested farthings—
And Coffers heaped with Tears!

For her, the transactions of life have been costly; cosmic usurers demand payments of anguish, at unconscionable interest, for each momentary joy. But it is a debt that *"must"* be paid, however unfair the terms.

Ernest Hemingway, throughout his fiction but especially in *The Sun Also Rises,* sides with Dickinson in this hypothetical quarrel. The cost of joy, ecstasy, or happiness comes high, yet it must be met. Like the poet from Amherst, he expressed his view of compensation in the metaphor of finance—a metaphor which runs through the fabric of his first novel like a fine, essential thread, a thread so fine, indeed, that it has not before been perceived. The classic statement against Hemingway's lack of moral sensitivity in this book was made by James T. Farrell, who described the characters as "people who have not fully grown up" and the moral outlook as amounting "to the attitude that an action is good if it makes one feel good."Among others, even the perceptive Philip Young seems at first (later, he changed his mind) to have read *The Sun Also Rises* in this way: "Jake's disability excepted, always, the book now seems really the long *Fiesta* it was called in the English edition, and one's net impression today is of all the fun there is to be had in getting good and lost." That was not the impression, clearly, that Hemingway meant to convey. Lunching with a group of professors from the University of Hawaii in 1941, he advised against their students reading *A Farewell to Arms.* "That's an immoral book. Let them read *The Sun Also Rises.* It's very moral."

It is Jake Barnes who explicitly states the code of Hemingway's "very moral" novel. Lying awake at Pamplona, Jake reflects that in having Brett for a friend, he "had been getting something for nothing" and that sooner or later he would have to pay the bill, which always came:

> I thought I had paid for everything. Not like the woman pays and pays. No idea of retributions or punishment. Just exchange of values. You gave up something and got something else. Or you worked for something. You paid some way for everything that was any good. I paid my way into enough things that I liked, so that I had a good time. Either you paid by learning about them, or by experience, or by taking chances, or by money.

Enjoying living was learning to get your money's worth and knowing when you had it. You could get your money's worth. The world was a good place to buy in.

It is understandable that Jake, sexually crippled in the war, should think that he has already paid for everything; and it is an index of his maturity, as a man "fully grown up," that he comes to realize that he may still have debts outstanding, to be paid, most often and most insistently, in francs and pesetas and pounds and dollars.

For Jake's philosophical musing is illustrated time and again in the profuse monetary transactions of *The Sun Also Rises.* On the second page of the novel, one discovers that Robert Cohn has squandered most of the $50,000 that his father, from "one of the richest Jewish families in New York," has left him; on the last page of the book, that Jake has tipped the waiter (the amount is unspecified) who has called a taxi for him and Brett in Madrid. Between the beginning and the end, Hemingway specifically mentions sums of money, and what they have been able to purchase, a total of thirty times. The money dispensed runs up from a franc to a waiter to the fifty francs that Jake leaves for his *poule,* Georgette, at the dancings, to the two hundred francs which Count Mippipopolous gives to Jake's concierge, to the $10,000 the count offers Brett for a weekend in her company. Mostly, though, the monetary amounts are small, and pay for the food, drink, travel, and entertainment that represent the good things in life available to Jake.

Hemingway reveals much more about his characters' financial condition and spending habits than about their appearance: the book would be far more useful to the loan officer of a bank than, say, to the missing person's bureau, which would have little more physical information to go on, with respect to height, weight, hair and eye color, than that Brett had short hair and "was built with curves like the hull of a racing yacht" and that Robert Cohn, with his broken nose, looked as if "perhaps a horse had stepped on his face." When Hemingway cut forty thousand words out of the first draft of *The Sun Also Rises* but retained these ubiquitous references to the cost of things, he must have kept them for some perceptible and important artistic purpose.

IN FACT, HE HAD SEVERAL good reasons to note with scrupulous detail the exact nature of financial transactions. Such a practice contributed to the verisimilitude of the novel, denoting the way it was; it fitted nicely with Jake's—and his creator's—obsession with the proper way of doing things; and mainly, it illustrated in action the moral conviction that you must pay for what you get, that you must earn in order to be able to buy, and that only then will it be possible, if you are careful, to buy your money's worth in the world.

In the early 1920s exchange rates in postwar Europe fluctuated wildly. Only the dollar remained stable, to the benefit of the expatriated artists, writers, dilettantes, and party-goers who found they could live for next to nothing in Paris. Malcolm Cowley and his wife lived there the year of 1921 in modest comfort on a grant of $1,000, twelve thousand francs by that year's rate. By the summer of 1924, when Barnes and his companions left for the fiesta at Pamplona, the rate was still more favorable, almost nineteen francs to the dollar. And you could get breakfast coffee and a brioche for a franc or less at the cafés where Hemingway, expatriated with the rest, wrote when the weather turned cold. There were even better bargains elsewhere, and the Hemingways, somewhat strapped once Ernest decided to abandon journalism for serious fiction, found one of the best of them in the winter of 1924–1925, at Schruns in the Austrian Voralberg, where food, lodging, snow, and skiing for the young writer, his wife, and son came to but $28.50 a week. Europe was overflowing with (mostly temporary) American expatriates, living on the cheap. Any novel faithful to that time and that place was going to have to take cognizance of what it cost to live and eat and drink.

Hemingway regarded most of his fellow Americans on the Left Bank as poseurs pretending to be artists, but "nearly all loafers expending the energy that an artist puts into his creative work in talking about what they are going to do and condemning the work of all artists who have gained any degree of recognition." The tone of moral indignation in this dispatch, one of the first that Hemingway sent the *Toronto Star Weekly* from Paris in 1922, is emphasized by the anecdote he includes about "a big, light-haired woman sitting at a table with three young men." She pays the bill, and the young men laugh whenever she does: "Three years ago she came to Paris with her husband from a little town in Connecticut, where they had lived and he had painted with increasing success for ten years. Last year he went back to America alone."

To the writer, single-minded in his dedication to his craft, the time-wasting of café habitués represented the greatest sin of all. It was the work that counted, and talking about art was hardly a satisfactory substitute. As Jake remarks, setting forth an axiom of Hemingway's creed, "You'll lose it if you talk about it." In the posthumously published *A Moveable Feast,* Hemingway laments having accompanied the hypochondriacal Scott Fitzgerald on an unnecessarily drawn-out trip to Lyons. Nursing his traveling companion, he "missed not working and . . . felt the death loneliness that comes at the end of every day that is wasted in your life." Observing the playboys and playgirls of Paris waste their lives on one long hazy binge, Hemingway as foreign correspondent felt much the same disgust that visits Jake after the revels at Pamplona, when he plunges deep into the waters off San Sebastian in an attempt to cleanse himself.

What distinguishes Jake Barnes from Mike and Brett, who at least make no pretenses toward artistic (or any other kind of) endeavor, and from Robert Cohn, a writer who is blocked throughout the novel, is that he works steadily at his regular job as a newspaperman. He is, presumably, unsupported by money from home, and he spends his money, as he eats and drinks, with conspicuous control. Above all, he is thoughtful and conscientious in his spending. Sharing a taxi with two fellow American reporters who also work regularly and well at their jobs but at least one of whom is burdened, as he is not, by "a wife and kids," Jake insists on paying the two-franc fare. He does the right thing, too, by Georgette, the streetwalker he picks up at the Napolitain. Not only does he buy her dinner as a preliminary to the sexual encounter she has bargained for, but upon deserting her for Brett, he leaves fifty francs with the patronne—compensation for her wasted evening—to be delivered to Georgette if she goes home alone. The patronne is supposed to hold the money for Jake if Georgette secures another male customer, but this being France, he will, Brett assures him, lose his fifty francs. "Oh, yes," Jake responds, but he has at least behaved properly, and Jake, like his creator, was "always intensely interested in how to do a thing," from tying flies to fighting bulls to compensating a prostitute. Besides, he shares a double kinship with Georgette: she too is sick, a sexual cripple, and she pursues her trade openly and honestly.

The case is different with Lady Ashley, who acquires and casts off her lovers nearly as casually as Georgette, but does so without thought of the consequences to others. There is a certain irony in Brett's telling Jake that it was wrong of him to bring Georgette to the dance, "in restraint of trade." Surely this is a case of the pot and kettle, for she has arrived in the company of a covey of homosexuals. More to the point, it is women like Brett—and even, to a lesser degree, Cohn's companion Frances Clyne—who provide unfair competition to the streetwalkers of Paris.

After an unsatisfactory time with Brett, Jake Barnes returns to his room, where he immediately goes over his bank statement: "It showed a balance of $2,432.60. I got out my checkbook and deducted four checks drawn since the first of the month, and discovered I had a balance of $1,832.60. I wrote this on the back of the statement." This is a make-work, an attempt to delay thinking about the love for Brett that he cannot consummate. But it is also characteristic of Jake's meticulousness about money. The surprising thing, in fact, is that Jake should have spent as much as $600 in any given month, for he is a man who tries very hard always to get his money's worth. He knows whom to write to secure good bullfight tickets, and he reserves the best rooms in the best hotels at the best price. In Bayonne, he helps Bill buy "a pretty good rod cheap, and two landing-nets," and checks with the tourist-office "to find what we ought to pay for a motor-car to Pamplona": four hundred francs. At Burguete, he bargains to have the wine included in the twelve-pesetas-a-day hotel room he and Bill share, and they make certain at dinner that they do "not lose money on the wine." He is annoyed when Cohn sends a wire of only three words for the price of ten ("I come Thursday"), and takes revenge by answering with an even shorter telegram ("Arriving to-night"). After the fiesta, when a driver tries to overcharge Jake for a ride from Bayonne to San Sebastian, he first works the price down from fifty to thirty-five pesetas and then rejects that price too as "not worth it." Jake is careful to fulfill his obligations, but he will not be taken advantage of. Once, in church, regretting that he is such a rotten Catholic, he even prays that he will "make a lot of money," but here the verb is important, for he next begins thinking about how he might make the money. He does not pray or even hope to *have* a lot of money, or for it to descend upon him from the trees or the deaths of relatives. Robert Cohn and Mike Campbell remind him, often and painfully, of what inherited money, or the promise of it, can do to undermine a man.

THOUGH PHYSICALLY IMPOTENT and mentally tortured, Jake Barnes remains morally sound, while Mike Campbell, Robert Cohn, and Brett Ashley, who are physically whole, have become morally decadent. As Baker observes, *The Sun Also Rises* has "a sturdy moral backbone," deriving much of its power from the contrast between Barnes-Gorton-Romero, who constitute the "moral norm" of the book, and the morally aberrant trio of Ashley–Campbell–Cohn. What has not been observed is that money and its uses form the metaphor by which the moral responsibility of Jake, Bill, and Pedro is measured against the carelessness of Brett, Mike, and Robert. Financial soundness mirrors moral strength.

Bill Gorton is the most likeable of the crew at the fiesta. Modeled upon the humorist Donald Ogden Stewart, Bill regales Jake with topical gags about Mencken, the Scopes trial, literary fashions, and middle-class mores. An enthusiast, he finds every place he visits equally "wonderful." The adjective is a private joke between Barnes and Gorton, for Bill knows as well as Jake that when things are really wonderful, it is neither necessary nor desirable to say so. Thus, hiking through the magnificent woods at Burguete, Bill remarks simply, "This is country." The five days they share at Burguete stand in idyllic contrast to the sickness and drunkenness which characterize both Paris and Pamplona. It is not that Bill and Jake do not drink together on the fishing trip; they drink prodigious quantities of wine. But it is drinking for the pleasure they have earned, both through hard work (in contrast to Cohn, Gorton is a producing writer) and through the rigors of the outdoor life they choose to pursue on vacation. Furthermore, Bill knows when not to drink. After dinner at Madame Lecomte's and a long walk through Paris, Jake proposes a drink. "No," says Bill. "I don't need it."

The first thing Jake says about Bill Gorton is that he is "very happy. He had made a lot of money on his last book, and was going to make a lot more." He has paid for his fiesta, and like all who have earned "the good things," he is careful of the rights of others. In Vienna, he tells Jake, he had gone to an "enormous . . . prize-fight" in which a "wonderful nigger" knocked a local boy cold and aroused the anger of the crowd. People threw chairs into the ring, and not only was the victorious fighter deprived of payment (he had agreed not to knock out the local fighter), but his watch was stolen. "Not so good, Jake. Injustice everywhere," as Gorton remarks. Conscientious about money matters, he is disturbed by a world where fights are fixed and debts go unpaid. So, though tight and on holiday, Bill lends the cheated fighter clothes and money and tries to help him collect what's owed to him.

Bill's comic determination to purchase stuffed animals foreshadows Jake's serious reflections on compensation. Passing a Paris taxidermist's, Bill appeals to Jake to buy

> "Just one stuffed dog. I can take 'em or leave 'em alone. But listen, Jake. Just one stuffed dog."
>
> "Come on."
>
> "Mean everything in the world to you after you bought it. Simple exchange of values. You give them money. They give you a stuffed dog."

His affinity for spending money on the ridiculous emerges again at Pamplona, when he buys Mike eleven shoeshines in a row. "Bill's a yell of laughter," Mike says, but Jake, who unlike them has not had much to drink, "felt a little uncomfortable about all this shoe-shining." Still, Bill's expenditures buy amusement for himself and others (including, of course, the reader), and these otherwise merely amusing incidents serve to illustrate the principle of exchange of values: to obtain stuffed dogs, shoe-shines, or drinks, you must deliver payment.

ROBERT COHN, FOR WHOM GORTON conceives an immediate dislike, does not belong with the party at Pamplona. A romantic, he is understandably unable at first to conceive that his weekend with Brett at San Sebastian has meant nothing to her, but he forfeits any claim to sympathy by his subsequent stubborn and violent unwillingness to accept that obvious fact. Terribly insecure, he takes insult after insult from Frances and Mike without retaliation, though he is ready enough, anachronistically, to fight with his "best friend" Jake over what he construes as insults to Brett. A Jew in the company of Gentiles, he is a bore who takes himself—and his illusions—far too seriously. Unlike Jake, he has not "learned about" things. He does not know how to eat or drink or love. It is no wonder that Harold Loeb, unmistakably recognizing himself in Hemingway's portrait of Cohn, "felt as if he had developed an ulcer" and, decades later, attempted to vindicate himself in his autobiography.

Still, it would be possible to pity Cohn for his dominant malady (is not romantic egotism a less unlovely illness than nymphomania or dipsomania?) were it not for his callous and opportunistic use of the money he has not earned. His allowance ($300 a month, from his mother) comfortably stakes him to his period of expatriation. He has written a novel which has been "accepted by a fairly good publisher," but it is not, clearly, a very good novel, and now the well has run dry. In his idleness, he hangs around Jake's office, disturbing his work, and even proposes to pay Jake's way as his companion on a trip to South America, a continent he invests with an aura of romance. How Hemingway felt about such proposals was later made clear in *A Moveable Feast,* when he reflected, in connection with the trip to Lyons with Fitzgerald, that he "had been a damned fool to accept an invitation for a trip that was to be paid for by someone else." But biographical evidence is hardly necessary to make the point that Cohn, whose money comes to him through no effort of his own but fortuitously because of the accident of his birth, does not understand the proper way of spending it: the point is made implicitly by a number of incidents in *The Sun Also Rises.*

Having inherited a great deal of money, he has wasted nearly all of it on a little magazine—and in maintaining the prestige that came to him as its editor. He is consistently lucky in gambling, but that does him more harm than good. What comes too easily has a pernicious effect on him as a person. While he was in New York to see his publisher, for example, several women had been nice to him as a budding novelist.

> This changed him so that he was not so pleasant to have around. Also, playing for higher stakes than he could afford in some rather steep bridge games with his New York connections he had held cards and won several hundred dollars. It made him rather vain of his bridge game, and he talked several times of how a man could always make a living at bridge if he were ever forced to.

Cohn wins a 100-peseta bet with Gorton that Mike and Brett will not arrive as scheduled at Pamplona, but the bet costs him any possibility of friendship with Bill. Gorton wagers, in fact, only because Cohn's arrogance in parading inside knowledge of Brett's and Mike's habits makes him angry. Furthermore, when the wager has been agreed on, Cohn first does Bill the indignity of asking Jake to remember it, and then, to make amends after he has won, pretends that it really does not matter.

What most damns Cohn, however, is his habit of buying his way out of obligations to women. Frances Clyne, one of the bitchiest women in Hemingway's fiction, reveals this practice of Cohn's in a devastating scene. Flat broke and not so young or attractive as she once was, Frances is being packed off to England so that her paramour may see more of the world—and, he surely hopes, of Lady Ashley:

> "Robert's sending me. He's going to give me two hundred pounds [about a thousand dollars] and then I'm going to visit friends. Won't it be lovely? The friends don't know about it, yet."
>
> She turned to Cohn and smiled at him, He was not smiling now.
>
> "You were only going to give me a hundred pounds, weren't you, Robert? But I made him give me two hundred. You're really very generous. Aren't you, Robert?"

"I do not know," Jake reflects, "how people could say such terrible things to Robert Cohn." But Frances can say them, and get away with it, because they are absolutely true. Cohn, in fact, has disposed of another girl, his "little secretary on the magazine," in just the same way, except cheaper. It is in his attempt to buy his way out of entanglements, without expending anything of himself, that Robert Cohn most viciously breaks the moral code of compensation.

Furthermore, there are suggestions in the book that Cohn is tightfisted with his money. He has, apparently, tried to bargain with Frances. He directs Jake to buy him a double-tapered fishing line, but says he will pay later instead of now. After unleashing a stream of insults against Cohn ("Don't you know you're not wanted?"), Mike Campbell tells Bill Gorton, who is about to remove Cohn from the slaughter, to stay. "Don't go," Mike said. "Robert Cohn's about to buy a drink." The clear implication is that Robert Cohn rarely buys drinks.

Mike, on the other hand, is more than willing to buy drinks, whenever—which means rarely—he has any money. Hemingway reveals a good deal about Mike's financial condition and habits, as he does of all the other major characters in the book. Brett, Jake tells Robert, is going to marry Mike Campbell. "He's going to be rich as hell some day." Cohn refuses to believe that Brett will marry Mike—and indeed, the matter remains in doubt at the end of the novel—but there is no question about Mike's potential wealth. He is trying, Brett says, to get his mother to pay for her divorce so they can be married. "Michael's people have loads of money." But for the moment, he makes do on a rather skimpy allowance and is not even allowed to write checks. When he needs funds, he must "send a wire to the keeper."

Mike Campbell is held under strict financial control for the best of reasons: he is totally irresponsible about money. With his anticipated future wealth serving as a promissory note, he sponges off everyone in sight and simply does not pay his debts. After suffering a business collapse, he has had to resort to bankruptcy, an ungentlemanly if legal way of evading creditors. It is, as Brett realizes when she introduces him, one of the two most important and typical things about the man she intends to marry. The other is that he drinks too much: "This is Bill Gorton. This drunkard is Mike Campbell. Mr. Campbell is an undischarged bankrupt."

Mike is no more conscientious about the settling of his debts to friends than to his former business "connections." Yet he possesses a certain self-deprecatory wit, and Bill Gorton, especially, is drawn to him. Bill likes Mike so much, in fact, that it is very difficult for him to admit that Mike does not meet his obligations. One night in Pamplona, Mike, Bill, and Bill's girl Edna are thrown out of a bar by the police. "I don't know what happened," Bill says, "but some one had the police called to keep Mike out of the back room. There were some people that had known Mike at Cannes. What's the matter with Mike?" "Probably he owes them money," Jake says. "That's what people usually get bitter about." The next morning Bill remembers the incident more clearly: "There was a fellow there that had helped pay Brett and Mike out of Cannes, once. He was damned nasty." The night before, Bill had emphatically defended his friend: "They can't say things like that about Mike." But in the light of dawn, he modifies the statement: "Nobody ought to have a right to say things about Mike. . . . They oughtn't to have any right. I wish to hell they didn't have any right." Bill's own loyalty to Mike finally crumbles when, after the fiesta, another incident makes it clear *why* they have the right.

Jake, Bill, and Mike have hired a car together and stop at "a very Ritz place" in Biarritz where they roll the dice to see who will pay for the drinks. Mike loses three times in a row, but cannot pay for the third round:

> "I'm so sorry," Mike said. "I can't get it."
> "What's the matter?"
> "I've no money." Mike said. "I'm stony. I've just twenty francs. Here, take twenty francs."
> Bill's face sort of changed.

He had had just enough money for his hotel bill in Pamplona, Mike explains, though it turns out that Brett has given him all of her cash to pay his bill. Neither can Mike help pay for their car, and his promise to send Jake what he owes is hardly reassuring.

Mike continually banters about his bankruptcy, as if making light of the obligations might somehow cause them to disappear. "I'm a tremendous bankrupt," he remarks. "I owe money to everybody." He will not go down into the ring after the running of the bulls because "it wouldn't be fair to my creditors." As Mike observes, "One never gets anywhere by discussing finances," but he is unable to resist touching the wound by discussing his own. There is the story, for example, of the medals and Mike's tailor. Invited to "a whopping big dinner" in England where medals are to be worn, Mike prevails upon his tailor to supply him with some medals which had been left by another customer for cleaning. When the dinner fizzles out, he goes to a nightclub and passes the medals around. "Gave one to each girl. Form of souvenir. They thought I was hell's own shakes of a soldier. Gave away medals in a night club. Dashing fellow." The story delights his audience, but it had not seemed so funny to his tailor. If it was foolish to set too great store by military medals, as did the chap who had left them with the tailor, it was quite wrong to propose to wear medals that one had not earned. Mike has fought in the war, and "must have some medals." but he does not know which ones and has never sent in for them. He is careless about them, quite as willing to don other people's ribbons as he is to spend other people's money.

Brett shares with Mike a carelessness of personal behavior which stems from a lifetime of having things done for her. Her room in Madrid, for example, "was in the disorder produced only by those who have always had servants." She makes appointments and does not keep them. She accepts the generosity of others as if it were her due. The Paris homosexuals, one feels certain, were paying her way. Count Mippipopolous finances her champagne binge. "Come on," she says at Pamplona. "Are these poisonous things paid for?" In the bar of the Palace Hotel in Madrid, she asks Jake, "*Would* you buy a lady a drink?" She has been given, she admits, "hell's own amount of credit" on her title. And, of course, she and Mike had jointly run up the bills they could not settle at Cannes. Moreover, she satisfies her demanding sexual appetites at the expense of others, effectively turning Robert into a steer, Mike into a swine, and Jake into a pimp. She is clearly not what Madame Duzinell, Jake's concierge, calls her after the bribe of 200 francs from the count, "trés, trés gentille."

Oddly, though, Brett observes a strict code in connection with her sexual activity. She will not accept money for her favors. Thus she rejects the count's offer of "ten thousand dollars to go to Biarritz [or Cannes, or Monte Carlo] with him." She pays Mike's way, not vice versa, out of the Hotel Montoya. Though Romero pays the hotel bills in Madrid, she will take nothing else from him. "He tried to give me a lot of money, you know. I told him I had scads of it. He knew that was a lie. I couldn't take his money, you know." In sending Romero away, against the urgings of the flesh, she has done the right thing at the cost of real personal anguish. She will be neither a whore nor "one of those bitches that ruins children."

Furthermore, Brett's apparent nymphomania can be at least partly excused by the unhappy circumstances of her past life. She has lost one man she loved in the war, and married another ("Ashley, chap she got the title from") who has returned quite mad from serving as a sailor. "When he came home," Mike explains, "he wouldn't sleep in a bed. Always made Brett sleep on the floor. Finally, when he got really bad, he used to tell her he'd kill her. Always slept with a loaded service revolver. Brett used to take the shells out when he'd gone to sleep. She hasn't had an absolutely happy life." Like Jake, she still suffers from war wounds. Like him, too, she articulates her awareness of the law of compensation. If she has put chaps through hell, she's paying for it all now. "Don't we pay for all the things we do, though?"

Brett's case is far more ambiguous than that of Robert Cohn or Mike Campbell. If she recklessly imposes nearly insupportable burdens on others, she carries an even heavier burden herself. Morally, she is neither angel nor devil, but somewhere, rather fascinatingly, in between. It is almost as if Hemingway himself were alternately attracted to and repelled by Brett. In Carlos Baker's biography there is a strong implication that Hemingway either had, or wanted to have, an affair with Duff Twysden, the prototype for Brett. In the fall of 1925, Duff sent Hemingway a note asking for a loan: "Ernest my dear, forgive me for this effort but can you possibly lend me some money? I am in a stinking fix but for once only temporary and can pay you back for *sure*. I want 3,000 francs—but for God's sake lend me as much as you can." In the novel, as if to protect Duff, Hemingway transfers her behavior to Mike Campbell: it is he and not Brett who asks, repeatedly, for loans.

HEMINGWAY'S INSISTENCE on the need to earn, and to pay for, what you get is in no way a statement in support of materialism, for it is accompanied by disgust with the crooked and corrupting values of the commercial world. Eager to line their pockets, the merchants of Pamplona double prices during fiesta. Away go the cafés' marble-topped tables and comfortable white wicker chairs, to be replaced by cast-iron tables and severe folding chairs: "The café was like a battleship stripped for action." The warship's objective, of course, is to relieve peasants and tourists alike of their cash. At the start of the fiesta, the peasants confine their drinking to the outlying shops, where wine sells for 30 centimes a liter. "They had come in so recently from the plains and the hills that it was necessary that they make their shifting in values gradually. . . . Money still had a definite value in hours worked and bushels of grain sold. Late in the fiesta it would not matter what they paid, nor where they bought." When the peasants reach the stage of heedlessness (epitomized by the futile death of one of them during the running of the bulls), they will have lost any sense of the dignity of labor, of hours worked and bushels sold.

The cancer of commercialism also threatens to infect bullfighting. Romero is forced to face a dangerously bad bull, who cannot see well the lure of the cape, because the promoters have paid for the bull and "don't want to lose their money." The crowd sends a volley of cushions, bread, and vegetables into the ring where Belmonte, ill and more cautious than he once had been, is performing his art. "Belmonte was very good. But because he got thirty thousand pesetas and people had stayed in line all night to buy tickets to see him, the crowd demanded that he should be more than very good." His greatness had been "discounted and sold in advance," and nothing he could do would satisfy those who watched him do it.

Montoya, an aficionado who represents bullfighting's conscience, puts up all the good toreros at his hotel and keeps in his room framed photographs of the bullfighters he "really believed in." The pictures of the commercial bullfighters, though, are consigned first to a desk drawer and then to the wastebasket. Montoya welcomes Jake, a fellow aficionado, and is grateful for his advice not to deliver to Romero his invitation from the American ambassador. "People take a boy like that," the hotel-keeper explains. "They don't know what he's worth. . . . They start this Grand Hotel business, and in one year they're through." Montoya is even inclined to forgive Jake his friends, but that tolerance dissolves when he sees "Pedro Romero with a big glass of cognac in his hand, sitting laughing between me [Jake] and a woman with bare shoulders, at a table full of drunks. He did not even nod." When Jake and his companions check out, Montoya does "not come near" them.

Romero, however, remains immune to the disease of commercialism—and the caution unto cowardice it is likely to breed. He wants and expects to make money as a bullfighter: when Brett reads in his hand that there are thousands of bulls in his future, "Good," he replies, and in an aside to Jake in Spanish, "At a thousand duros apiece." But he has not yet begun to compromise his bullfighting, as Belmonte has, by insisting on manageable bulls with smallish horns. And Hemingway invokes the metaphor of profit and loss in comparing Pedro's afternoon of triumph to the jeers that had greeted Belmonte: "Pedro Romero had the greatness. He loved bull-fighting, and I think he loved the bulls, and I think he loved Brett. Everything of which he could control the locality he did in front of her all that afternoon. . . . But he did not do it for her at any loss to himself. He gained by it all through the afternoon." His willingness to take chances, one of the ways, as Jake reflected, in which you could pay "for everything that was any good," gives the bullfight, his relationship with Brett, and the fiesta itself a kind of dignity.

It hardly matters that "the Biarritz crowd" does not appreciate what he has accomplished, with either his bad bull or his good one. Hemingway obviously regards the rich English and American tourists from Biarritz, come for one day of the quaint fiesta at Pamplona, with undisguised scorn. Those who buy false wares, like the secretly manipulated boxer toys hawked on the streets of Paris, deserve no more than they get.

The depth of this contempt can be measured against the sympathetic portrayal of Wilson-Harris, the Englishman who fishes and plays three-handed bridge with Jake and Bill at Burguete. When his companions must leave, Harris (as the Americans call him) insists on buying them a bottle of wine apiece. The atmosphere is one of warm camaraderie, punctuated by Harris's regret that Bill and Jake must leave. As they board the bus for Pamplona, Harris presses still another gift upon each of them: a dozen flies that he has tied himself. "They're not first-rate flies at all," he insists. "I only thought if you fished them some time it might remind you of what a good time we had." It has been a good time indeed, so that Jake first wishes Harris were coming along to Pamplona but then reflects that, "You couldn't tell how English would mix with each other, anyway." But you can tell: a man who spends his holiday trout fishing in the Pyrenees and who behaves so generously would not have mixed at all well with the perpetually carousing crew at the fiesta.

Hemingway's major characters in the novel are all, with the exception of Romero, English and American, and each is easily distinguishable from the others. The foreigners, though, he tends to stereotype. Most of the Europeans in the book are, of course, French or Spanish, and these two nationalities are characterized almost solely on the basis of their attitude toward money. French standards of value are epitomized by Jake's concierge, who will not admit shabbily dressed friends of Jake to his quarters and who conveniently changes her mind about Brett—from "a species of woman" to "a lady . . . of very good family"—on the strength of a bribe. In *The Sun Also Rises,* Frenchmen always have their hands out, like the dining-car conductor who pockets ten francs but does nothing to earn them. In an interior monologue, Jake dissects the French national character. He has just overtipped a waiter in Bayonne: "Everything is on such a clear financial basis in France. It is the simplest country to live in. No one makes things complicated by becoming your friend for any obscure reason. If you want people to like you you have only to spend a little money. I spent a little money and the waiter liked me. He appreciated my valuable qualities." Repetition and the pun on "valuable qualities" underscore the heavy irony of this passage. For Jake obviously prefers Spain to France, just as he prefers bullfighting, a sport which cannot be fixed, to Viennese prizefights and French and Belgian bicycle-racing where the contestants "had raced among themselves so often that it did not make much difference who won. . . . The money could be arranged."

Spaniards, unlike Frenchmen, were likely to be friendly for no good financial reason at all. The Basques, for example, share a crowded bus with Bill and Jake, and all share their wine, the Americans from the bottles they have just bought, the Spanish from their wineskins. When the bus stops at a *posada* in a small town, Bill and Jake each have an *aguardiente,* at twenty centimes apiece. "I gave the woman fifty centimes to make a tip, and she gave me back the copper piece, thinking I had misunderstood the price." Two of the Basques join them, and the cost of the drinks is split equally between them. On the opening day of the fiesta at Pamplona, Spanish peasants in a wine-shop will not let Jake and his friends pay for wine and food. They will accept in return only "a rinse of the mouth from the new wine-bag" Jake has bought, at the "lowest price," because the shopkeeper discovers he intends to drink out of it, not resell it in Bayonne. Spanish peasants, with their ethic of sharing, display a dignity and readiness for fellowship not to be thought of among the French.

The minor character who best exemplifies the morality of compensation is the Greek Count Mippipopolous. It is possible to regard him solely as the sort of aging voluptuary that he appears, on the surface, to be. But to do so is to miss the point. It "means any amount to him" to buy fine champagne directly from Baron Mumms. All he wants out of wines, he says, is to enjoy them. When Brett objects to his ordering a bottle of 1811 brandy, he reprimands her in his customary tough English:

> "Listen, my dear. I get more value for my money in old brandy than in any other antiquities."
>
> "Got many antiquities?"
>
> "I got a houseful."

It is the same with food, and with women: the count can enjoy them properly because he has a sense of values acquired through long and painful experience. Count Mippipopolous has been involved in seven wars and four revolutions. In Abyssinia when he was twenty-one, two arrows went clean through his body: he shows Brett and Jake the scars. He is "one of us," as she remarks after this demonstration, because like them he has paid in suffering for the pleasures he now pursues. The temptation to judge the count by puritanical standards (Jake last sees him at Zelli's, surrounded by three girls he has just picked up) is tempered by an awareness that he has earned his pleasure, and that generosity and loyalty, as well as hedonism, form facets of his code.

AFTER DELIVERING HIMSELF of his thoughts on the need to pay for the good things, Jake Barnes concludes rather cynically, "It seemed like a fine philosophy. In five years . . . it will seem just as silly as all the other fine philosophies I've had." Hemingway, however, did not abandon the code of compensation Jake had enunciated, but continued to regard the rich—and the lure of easy money—as threats to artists in general and himself in particular. "Money," he wrote John Dos Passos in 1929, "had been the ruination of too many of their friends." Don Stewart had taken up with Jock Whitney, to say nothing of selling his soul to Hollywood for a $25,000 contract. John Bishop's career had been spoiled by his wife's munificent income. The search for eternal youth had clearly sunk the Fitzgeralds. In *Green Hills of Africa,* he cited money as the first way in which American writers were destroyed. When they have made some money, they "increase their standard of living and they are caught. They have to write to keep up their establishments, their wives, and so on, and they write slop."

For his own part, as becomes clear in *A Moveable Feast,* he quite specifically blamed the demise of his idyllic first marriage on the predatory rich who had followed Hadley, Bumby, and himself to the Voralberg:

> When you have two people who love each other, are happy and gay and really good work is being done by one or both of them, people are drawn to them. . . . Those who attract people . . . do not always learn about the good, the attractive, the charming, the soon-beloved, the generous, the understanding rich who have no bad qualities and who give each day the quality of a festival and who, when they have passed and taken the nourishment they needed, leave everything deader than the roots of any grass Attila's horses hoofs have ever scoured.

Especially in the long story *The Snows of Kilimanjaro,* Hemingway excoriated himself, in the guise of the writer-narrator Harry, for drinking and playing with the rich and letting his talent erode through idleness. "It was strange, too, wasn't it," Harry thinks, "that when he fell in love with another woman, that woman should always have more money than the last one." That was exactly the case with Pauline, Hemingway's second wife, and as Philip Young has divined, the story is partly "a special and private . . . analysis of his past failures as a writer of prose fiction, as of 1936." He had not published a first-rate book since *A Farewell to Arms,* seven years before, and like Harry, contemplated with despair all the stories he had not written. Though it was not really his wife's fault, though he had destroyed his talent himself, still it was her money that gave him the chance to spend what he had not earned and was not paying for. Perhaps it was not coincidental that in his other major fiction of the 1930s, Hemingway depicted his most coolly vicious female characters of all in Margot Macomber and Helene Bradley, the rich, writer-collecting adventuress of *To Have and Have Not.*

But the morality of compensation found expression not only in the fiction of the 1930s, but throughout Hemingway's works. Both in *A Farewell to Arms* (1929) and *Across the River and into the Trees* (1950), his protagonists are virtually obsessed with their obligations. After making his "separate peace" with the war, a totally justifiable escape, Frederic Henry nonetheless feels "damned lonely" and tortures himself with recurring thoughts that he has deserted in a conventional way. Colonel Cantwell, facing his certain death, carefully discharges his outstanding debts: he sends ducks to the waiter at the Gritti Palace Hotel, returns his girl's emeralds and her portrait, and makes her a gift of the shotguns that have served him so well. All of Hemingway's major protagonists share this sense of obligation—to political belief (Robert Jordan), to craft (Santiago as well as Romero), to wife and family (Harry Morgan). Though Hemingway himself was divorced three times, his heroes never cast off commitments. They pay their bills in full, sometimes at the cost of their lives.

A teacher in Oak Park, Illinois, an upper-middle-class suburb noted for nothing so much as its respectability, once wondered "how a boy brought up in Christian and Puritan nurture should know and write so well of the devil and the underworld." But Ernest Hemingway carried with him always an inheritance from the community where he grew up, a faith in the efficacy and staying power of certain moral values. Strongest among these was the axiom that you had to earn your happiness, though the price might come exceedingly high, with its corollary that easy money could ruin a man. In his first novel, Hemingway imposed this standard on the expatriate world of the early 1920s. At the end of the last book he wrote, looking back on those years as an idyll when he had worked hard and loved well and taken nothing without making full payment, his nostalgia found expression in the same metaphor which runs through *The Sun Also Rises:* "Paris was always worth it and you received return for whatever you brought to it. But this is how it was in the early days when we were very poor and very happy."

"Sign the Wire with Love"

The Morality of Surplus in The Sun Also Rises

GEORGE CHEATHAM

◆ ◆ ◆

Bill gorton's mocking words as Jake Barnes returns from digging worms for trout fishing offer an interesting point of entry into *The Sun Also Rises*:

> "I saw you out the window," [Bill] said. "Didn't want to interrupt you. What were you doing? Burying your money?"
>
> "You lazy bum!"
>
> "Been working for the common good? Splendid. I want you to do that every morning." (113)

For Bill's joke foregrounds Jake's middle-class obsession with money—with working to make it and with spending it efficiently for his own pleasure. The ironically Marxist joke figures a distinction between surplus and exactitude, subtly undercutting Jake's repeatedly professed desire for the latter, and so calls into question the orthodoxy, I suppose it is, of what Scott Donaldson has called a "morality of compensation" in the novel.

Donaldson explains this morality of compensation as the "code" of the whole novel, which Jake explicitly states:

> Just exchange of values. You gave up something and got something else. Or you worked for something. You paid some way for everything that was any

good. I paid my way into enough things that I liked, so that I had a good time. Either you paid by learning about them, or by experience, or by taking chances, or by money. Enjoying living was learning to get your money's worth and knowing when you had it. You could get your money's worth. The world was a good place to buy in. (148)

This code, Donaldson explains, pervades the novel through the metaphor of finance which illustrates the moral strength or weakness of the novel's various characters:

> Though physically impotent and mentally tortured, Jake Barnes remains morally sound, while Mike Campbell, Robert Cohn, and Brett Ashley, who are physically whole, have become morally decadent. . . . Money and its uses form the metaphor by which the moral responsibility of Jake, Bill, and Pedro is measured against the carelessness of Brett, Mike, and Robert. Financial soundness mirrors moral strength. (77)

Well, certainly, to an extent. But Donaldson's thesis raises at least two basic questions which I wish to explore. First, isn't such an analysis rather too pat, rather too much like an equation which can be rather too easily problematized. And, second, isn't such an explicit exposition as that in Jake's meditations rather uncharacteristic of Hemingway, whose usual technique is to explore central concerns indirectly, through apparent trifles?

First, Donaldson's thesis is clear: Jake, Bill, and Pedro = financial and thus moral responsibility; Brett, Mike, and Robert = financial and thus moral carelessness; financial soundness = moral strength. But the entire pattern is undercut by Bill's joke, for example, which briefly foregrounds the miserly ("Burying your money?") and selfish (Bill, finally, doesn't use the worms) tinge to what Donaldson approvingly calls Jake's "meticulousness about money" and so, however subtly, aligns Jake with Robert Cohn, the stereotyped "Jew," and against Bill Gorton.

Certainly, as Donaldson says, Cohn is apparently "tightfisted with his money" (80).

But isn't Jake somewhat tightfisted as well? What else can one infer from this exchange with Cohn about the bus trip to Burguette:

> "I'm not going up to-day." [Cohn said]. "You and Bill go on ahead."
>
> "I've got your ticket."
>
> "Give it to me. I'll get the money back."
>
> "It's five pesetas."
>
> Robert Cohn took out a silver five-peseta piece and gave it to me. (100)

By this time in the story, of course, Jake, "blind, unforgivingly jealous" (99) of the affair with Brett, hates Cohn and probably demands his five pesetas out of spite. Even so Jake's understated insistence is notable. That his hatred manifests itself financially, even if only to cover his emotions, is telling. Cohn's "wonderful quality of bringing out the worst in everybody" (98) brings out of Jake a sense of rigid exactitude in financial matters. It brings out an undertone of miserliness to Jake's desire, his obsession, to "get his money's worth" which connects him, ironically, with Cohn and so clouds Donaldson's equation.

Jake's quibbling with the hostess in Burguete, although Donaldson cites it approvingly as part of Jake's trying "very hard always to get his money's worth" (76), is similar. Jake first balks at the high price of the lodging, twelve pesetas, but he accepts it when his and Bill's wine is included in that price:

> The girl brought in a big bowl of hot vegetable soup and the wine. We had fried trout afterward and some sort of a stew and a big bowl full of wild strawberries. We did not lose money on the wine, and the girl was shy but nice about bringing it. The old woman looked in once and counted the empty bottles. After supper we went up-stairs and smoked and read in bed to keep warm. Once in the night I woke and heard the wind blowing. It felt good to be warm. (110–11)

I quote this passage at some length to show the jarring note of Jake's concern about money. The bounty of the meal and comfort of the bed anticipate the understated spiritual goodness of the entire Burguete episode, typified by Bill's mock sermon of the next day:

> We should not question. Our stay on earth is not for long. Let us rejoice and believe and give thanks. . . . Let us rejoice in our blessings. Let us utilize the fowls of the air. Let us utilize the product of the vine. (122)

Framed in such a context, Jake's thought, however fleeting, that he is drinking enough wine to get his money's worth, and thereby financially besting the old woman, seems at best petty, at worst blasphemous, depending on how seriously one takes Bill's preaching. At least to a degree Jake is drinking for the wrong reason, not joyfully but commercially. The unpleasant undertone of miserliness here and elsewhere, subtle though it is, is enough to call into question Donaldson's thesis, according to which even such minor tremors in the metaphor of finance would threaten the whole moral structure of the novel.

Many of Bill Gorton's expenditures, on the other hand, are marked by a certain lavishness which disturbs Jake but aligns Bill with the financial carelessness of Brett and Mike rather than the meticulousness of Jake, further vexing Donaldson's division. The redundant shoe-shines Bill buys Mike, for example, make Jake "a little uncomfortable" (173). And Bill's stuffed animals, which are similar to the shoe-shines, bring up the second question I started with: Isn't such an explicit morality of compensation as that in Jake's meditations rather uncharacteristic of Hemingway, whose usual technique is to explore central concerns indirectly, through apparent trifles? The central concerns in this case seem more properly called the morality of surplus than the morality of compensation, and it's explored indirectly through the apparent trifle of Bill's stuffed dogs rather than directly in Jake's meditations.

Bill, in fact, not Jake, first introduces what Donaldson calls the "code" of the novel—the concept of "exchange of values":

> "Here's a taxidermist's," Bill said. "Want to buy anything? Nice stuffed dog?"
>
> "Come on," I said. "You're pie-eyed."
>
> "Pretty nice stuffed dogs," Bill said. "Certainly brighten up your flat."
>
> "Come on."
>
> "Just one stuffed dog. I can take'em or leave'em alone. But listen, Jake. Just one stuffed dog."
>
> "Come on."
>
> "Mean everything in the world to you after you bought it. Simple exchange of values. You give them money. They give you a stuffed dog."
>
> "We'll get one on the way back."
>
> "All right. Have it your own way. Road to hell paved with unbought stuffed dogs. Not my fault." (72–73)

Bill introduces the concept in such a context, though, that Jake's unqualified echoing of it seems at least a little odd. A stuffed dog is so superfluous, so gratuitously nonutilitarian, as to mock in advance Jake's notion of exchange as equivalence.

The two continue their conversation:

> "How'd you feel that way about dogs so sudden?" [Jake asked.]
>
> "Always felt that way about dogs. Always been a great lover of stuffed animals."
>
> We stopped and had a drink.
>
> "Certainly like to drink." Bill said. "You ought to try it sometime, Jake."
>
> "You're about a hundred and forty-four ahead of me."

"Ought not to daunt you. Never be daunted. Secret of my success. Never been daunted. Never been daunted in public." (73)

Jake, though, seems to be daunted. That is, he seems to draw back from, even to fear, both here and throughout the novel, the sort of loss of control, the sort of risk, the sort of financial and moral inexactitude, exemplified by Bill's drunken excess. Such superfluity as Jake fears, however, such inexactitude of exchange, is essentially human. It is natural for humans to transcend their own limits. What we call culture or history is, after all, an open-ended transformation of fixed boundaries, a transcendence of mere appetite, a rich surplus over precise measure. It is this capacity for a certain lavish infringement of exact limit which distinguishes humankind (Eagleton).

Surplus, however, is radically ambivalent. And this creative tendency to exceed oneself is also the source of destructiveness. Hence Jake's fear. He's literally and figuratively gun shy. For the war, on a large scale, pervasively figures the destructive use of surplus throughout *The Sun Also Rises*. A colossal cultural over-reaching into too much—too much wealth, power, greed, rhetoric, patriotism—that "dirty war" has in some way wrecked the lives of a generation. The war has stripped away its excess in self-destruction leaving a kind of nothingness at its center, a lack—figured most clearly in Jake's wound. And as a defensive response to both the war's excess and the threat of that nothingness, Jake embraces exactitude. A world stripped clean of excess is an exact one, one in which a person can precisely balance both his financial and moral checkbook, as it were, one in which a person can precisely know the values, one in which, as Jake asserts, "You could get your money's worth."

The talkative waiter probably knows how to get his money's worth. He's probably daunted too. He certainly shares if not Jake's fear of destructive excess at least Jake's sense of the waste of it. Following the death of the peasant gored during the encierro, the waiter, himself not an aficionado, denounces bullfighting:

> "Badly cogido through the back," he said. He put the pots down at the table and sat down in the chair at the table. "A big horn wound. All for fun. Just for fun. What do you think of that? . . . Muerto. Dead. He's dead. With a horn through him. All for morning fun. Es muy flamenco." (197–98)

This waiter, of course, will never run the bulls. But, for that matter, Jake doesn't run them either. He only watches, and he barely manages to do that. Jake describes two encierros, both of which he almost misses by oversleeping. One he watches—significantly, I think—from the balcony of Cohn's room, where he's slept, wearing Cohn's coat; the other he almost misses, hung over and groggy from the previous night's drunken fight with Cohn.

But although he doesn't face the bulls himself, Jake, unlike the waiter, at least recognizes the value deriving from such confrontations. And he recognizes further, with some trepidation, that it's not just bullfighters who must work either in or out of the terrain of the bull. "In bull-fighting," says Jake, "they speak of the terrain of the bull and the terrain of the bull-fighter. As long as a bull-fighter stays in his own terrain he is comparatively safe. Each time he enters into the terrain of the bull he is in great danger" (213). The terrain of the bull specifically and the whole fiesta generally figure that tenuous ground between too much and nothing where creative excess resides. Jake, however, after the destruction of the war, alternately fears and desires this excess, and the novel maps his alternate advances into and retreats from this tenuous ground, into and from the terrain of the bull.

The road to hell doesn't traverse this tenuous ground, of course, and it is, as Bill Gorton says, paved with unbought stuffed dogs. That is, crass, utilitarian quantifying of experience, of life, of whatever is damning. And whatever sort of salvation or redemption there is lies in surplus, in the exceeding of exact equivalence. Experiences, for example, exceed the sort of valuation that Jake, in his night-time meditations, would like to give them:

> We walked on and circled the island. The river was dark and a bateau mouche went by, all bright with lights, going fast and quiet up and out of sight under the bridge. Down the river was Notre Dame squatting against the night sky. We crossed to the left bank of the Seine by the wooden foot-bridge from the Quai de Bethune, and stopped on the bridge and looked down the river at Notre Dame. Standing on the bridge the island looked dark, the houses were high against the sky, and the trees were shadows.
>
> "It's pretty grand," Bill said. "God, I love to get back." (77)

Notions of equivalence, of exact valuation, are radically vexed by such moments as this one on the bridge—like stuffed dogs which, mysteriously, mean "everything in the world" to you after you buy them (72). Or like Brett, who by any equitable standard of valuation clearly isn't worth what Jake pays to indulge her selfish desire for Romero. As Michael Reynolds says,

By pimping for Brett, [Jake] has cancelled his membership in the select club of aficionados. Montoya may have once forgiven him his drunken friends, but he will never forgive him for assisting in Pedro Romero's corruption. The novel's most understated passage occurs when Jake pays his hotel bill. He tells us: "Montoya did not come near us." This, the cruelest line in the book, goes without comment. . . . Jake, who started with so few assets, now has even fewer to get him through the night. If the novel "is such a hell of a sad story," as Hemingway said it was, the sadness resides in Jake's loss. (132)

Yet somehow Jake's morality is mirrored in this very loss, not, as Donaldson says, in his financial soundness. For by returning to Brett, Jake re-enters—decisively, I think—the terrain of the bull, that tenuous ground between too much and nothing:

> That was it. Send a girl off with one man. Introduce her to another to go off with him. Now go and bring her back. And sign the wire with love. That was it all right. (239)

Such forgiveness simply doesn't add up, to use Donaldson's metaphor. Has Jake paid for Brett with Montoya? Is she then his? Must he now pay again? Is he getting his money's worth? Unlike Jake's checkbook, the relationship just doesn't balance. Nor should it, for the relationship involves a simple exchange of values. When introducing the concept of exchange of values, we remember, Bill Gorton says,

> Mean everything in the world to you after you bought it. Simple exchange of values. You give them money. They give you a stuffed dog. (73)

When echoing this concept, however, Jake makes a subtle but deeply significant revision:

> Just exchange of values. You gave up something and got something else. (148)

Both phrases—simple exchange of values and just exchange of values—are radically ambiguous. Just exchanges are mere exchanges, sure, but they are also equitable exchanges, legal, correct, proper, exact, accurate, uniform exchanges. Simple exchanges, on the other hand, are mere exchanges as well, but they are also artless, open, guileless, innocent, humble, wretched, pitiful, silly, foolish exchanges. This understated trifle, the distinction between *just* and *simple,* is perhaps the moral center of the novel.

No, Jake's rescue of Brett doesn't add up. For Jake, having lost his penis in the war, will not be, as it were, stuffing Brett. Hemingway probably intended such a sexual implication, since the stuffed and probably mounted dogs are part of a series of such images, most obviously the final mounted policeman with his raised baton. Were Jake able to have intercourse, he and Brett would fit, match, balance, in the conventional sexual equation $1 + 1 = 1$. Without a penis, however, with this nothing in the middle caused by the destructive excess of the war, Jake no longer fits. Hence his fear and its attendant risk, nothingness. And hence his obsession with balance, with exactitude. But only in such a wretched, pitiful, and foolish imbalance as that of his relationship with Brett does Jake's humanity, his morality, reside. His simple forgiveness of Brett exceeds exact equivalence. It is a gratuitous excess of the strict requirements of justice, a kind of nothing, a refusal to calculate debt, out of which something may come.

Works Cited

Donaldson, Scott. "Hemingway's Morality of Compensation," *Ernest Hemingway's* The Sun Also Rises. Ed. Harold Bloom. New York: Chelsea House, 1987, 71–90. [Reprinted in this volume.]

Eagleton, Terry. *William Shakespeare*. Oxford: Blackwell, 1986.

Hemingway, Ernest. *The Sun Also Rises*. New York: Scribner's, 1970.

Reynolds, Michael. "False Dawn: *The Sun Also Rises* Manuscript," *Ernest Hemingway's* The Sun Also Rises. Ed. Harold Bloom. New York: Chelsea House, 1987. 117–32.

What's Funny in *The Sun Also Rises*

JAMES HINKLE

◆　◆　◆

> "Hemingway, why do you always come here drunk?"
> "I don't know, Miss Stein, unless it's to see you."
> —quoted in John Atkins,
> *The Art of Ernest Hemingway*

> "Uh, it was a joke then."
> "Yes. To laugh at."
> —*The Sun Also Rises*, 18

READERS HAVE COME UP with many reasons for admiring *The Sun Also Rises* but no one, so far as I know, has made much of the jokes in the novel. The free-associating banter of Bill Gorton, the fractured English of Count Mippipopolous, occasional sardonic comments by the narrator, Jake Barnes, have of course been noted. But jokes in *The Sun Also Rises?* What jokes? Most readers seem to find the book no funnier than did Harold Loeb, prototype of *The Sun Also Rises's* humorless Robert Cohn: "I do not remember that Hem was much of a spoofer as a young man. Perhaps he developed a taste for it as age overtook him."[1] The prototype of Bill Gorton, Donald Ogden Stewart, a professional humorist himself, said flatly that "written humor was not his [Hemingway's] dish."[2]

Yet I propose to point to about sixty submerged jokes in *The Sun Also Rises*—if by "jokes" I can be understood to mean all of the various kinds of plays on words whose effect is incongruous or funny once they are recognized. Few of them will make anyone roll in the aisle, but they have their moments. My aim is not to defend Hemingway's sense of humor or to sort his jokes into categories. My aim is simply to identify his jokes—to demonstrate by example that there are many more of them in *The Sun Also Rises* than we have realized. Playing with the multiple meanings inherent in words is a pervasive feature of Hemingway's writing.

Most readers have approached Hemingway with serious expectations, and these expectations have determined and limited much of what they have found. But Hemingway always claimed to be at least a part-time humorist. He is consistently unsympathetic to those who looked down on him when he himself "committed levity":

> [L]ots of criticism is written by characters who are very academic and think it is a sign you are worthless if you make jokes or kid or even clown.[3]
>
> The bastards don't want you to joke because it disturbs their categories.[4]
>
> "Joke people and you make enemies. That's what I always say." (*The Sun Also Rises*, 58)

Anyone who has read through Hemingway's letters must have been struck by his persistent reliance on humor. Even when he is most serious he often develops his argument in an ironic or flippant or mocking tone. We know from his letters that he thought the first draft of *The Sun Also Rises* was funny. *The Torrents of Spring,* clearly intended as a funny performance, he wrote between finishing the first draft of *The Sun Also Rises* and before starting the revision. And in an inscribed copy of the printed *The Sun Also Rises* Hemingway called the novel a "little treatise on promiscuity including a Few Jokes."[5]

I want to present my sixty *The Sun Also Rises* jokes roughly in order of their difficulty, moving from relatively obvious examples to more subtle or ingenious or likely-to-be overlooked ones. Begin with a simple pun whose effect is mild humor:

> Everything is on such a clear financial basis in France. . . . If you want people to like you you have only to spend a little money. I spent a little money and the waiter liked me. He appreciated my valuable qualities. (233)

But that is not a typical *The Sun Also Rises* pun, because it calls attention to itself. Most of Hemingway's puns are less insistent:

> Brett was radiant. . . . The sun was out and the day was bright. (207)

That should be a clear example. Here is another:

> for six months I never slept with the electric light off. That was another bright idea. (148)

Sometimes a pun is introduced and then played with:

> The publishers had praised his [Cohn's] novel pretty highly and it rather went to his head. (8)

Where else except up would high praise go? This is followed on the next page by adding "steep" to the pun on "high":

> playing for higher stakes than he could afford in some rather steep bridge games. (9)

Another example:

> In the dark I could not see his face very well.
> "Well," I said, "see you in the morning." (195)

That is a variation of:

> There is no reason why because it is dark you should look at things differently from when it is light. The hell there isn't! (148)

The narrator, Jake Barnes, is not the only one in the book who is alive to puns. On the evening Bill Gorton arrives in Paris Jake asks him:

> "What'll we do to-night?"
> "Doesn't make any difference. Only let's not get daunted. Suppose they got any hard-boiled eggs here?"

"Hard-boiled" eggs to guard against becoming daunted. The meaning of "hard-boiled" we already know from Jake:

> It is awfully easy to be hard-boiled about everything in the daytime, but at night it is another thing. (34)

Sometimes the pun depends on the reader knowing at least something of a foreign language. After Cohn and Jake have their first near-fight:

> we walked up to the Café de la Paix and had coffee. (40)

At least one pun in *The Sun Also Rises* is based on a catch phrase of the day. When Jake leaves Cohn at the end of the first chapter he says:

> "I'll see you to-morrow at the courts." (7)

He means the tennis courts, but his sentence is a play on "See you in court."

Sometimes *The Sun Also Rises*'s words make a statement that is literally true in more ways than the presumably intended one. While the effect of these second meanings is usually funny, that is not always the case. Consider the scene when Jake learns from Brett that it was Robert Cohn she had gone to San Sebastian with:

> "Who did you think I went down to San Sebastian with?"
> "Congratulations," I said . . .
> We walked along and turned a corner. (83)

Their relationship at that moment did indeed turn a corner. Jake can't keep back his bitterness after Brett explains that she rather thought the experience would be good for Cohn:

> "You might take up social service."
> "Don't be nasty." (84)

Shortly after Jake has helped set up Brett with Romero, Cohn comes looking for her:

> "Where's Brett?" he asked.
> "I don't know."
> "She was with you."
> "She must have gone to bed." (190)

Yes, that is exactly where she is—in bed, with Romero.

When Brett and Jake approach the Café Select after reaching a romantic impasse in a Paris cab:

> On the Boulevard Raspail, with the lights of Montparnasse in sight, Brett said: "Would you mind very much if I asked you to do something?"
> "Don't be silly."
> "Kiss me just once more before we get there."
> When the taxi stopped I got out and paid. (27–28)

The last is quite a line. Literally it means that Jake gives the taxi driver five or ten francs. But it also means that Jake has an emotional price to pay for his hour in the cab close to Brett. He leaves the Select shortly afterward, walks to his apartment alone, thinks of his wound and of Brett, and then cries himself to sleep.

Mike sees that Brett has a new hat:

> "Where did you get that hat?"
> "Chap bought it for me. Don't you like it?" (79)

Doesn't he like what? The hat or the idea that a man bought it for her? The first is probably what Brett intended but the second has more meaning for the novel.

Brett makes a remark to Romero that the reader can (and probably should) take in more than one way:

"The bulls are my best friends . . ."

"You kill your friends?" she asked.

"Always," he said in English, and laughed. "So they don't kill me." He looked at her across the table.

"You know English well." (186)

There are three meanings in Brett's last comment: first, she could be simply complimenting Romero on his ability to speak English; second, she could be saying that his sure manner, his way of looking at her, show that he knows very well how to make himself attractive to a English lady; third, and more ominous, she could be saying that he knows English people very well if he realizes that English friends could kill him. This last meaning is supported by several other passages: Mike says it was his friends, false friends, that did him in. Montoya says about Romero: "Any foreigner can flatter him. They start this Grand Hotel business, and in one year they're through" (172). Jake has already told us that "any foreigner was an Englishman" (31), and Brett says in Madrid after she had sent Romero away, "I'd have lived with him if I hadn't seen it was bad for him" (243), and she hopes it is true when she says "I don't think I hurt him any" (241).

Religion is put in its place by one brief comment:

That afternoon was the big religious procession, San Fermim was translated from one church to another. . . .

"Isn't that the procession?" Mike asked.

"Nada," some one said. "It's nothing." (155, 158)

Jake goes to confession several times in Pamplona. Brett would like to go with him but Jake tells her:

not only was it impossible but it was not as interesting as it sounded, and, besides, it would be in a language she did not know. (151)

Jake's minor joke here is that his confession would not be likely to interest Brett because he does not have any sexual items to report. A more significant meaning concerns the language Brett would not understand. Confessions in a Spanish church would be in Spanish. But in the following sentence we learn that Brett has her fortune told at a gypsy camp, and that too would be in Spanish, and there is no mention then of her not being able to understand what was said. Nor does she have any trouble understanding and being understood by Romero, or the other Spanish men who use her as an image to dance around or to sing to in their hard Spanish voices. The point seems to be that it is the language of the church that

Brett doesn't know and it makes no difference whether one takes that to be Spanish or Latin. As she says herself, "I'm damn bad for a religious atmosphere. I've the wrong type of face" (208).

At the end of the book Brett suggests that the satisfaction resulting from decent behavior might substitute for the consolation of religion. Jake is not so sure, so he gently proposes a pain-killer more in line with her temperament:

> "You know it makes one feel rather good deciding not to be a bitch.
> . . . It's sort of what we have instead of God."
> "Some people have God," I said. "Quite a lot."
> "He never worked very well with me."
> "Should we have another Martini?" (169)

Mike obviously has reached the same conclusion concerning Brett:

> "These bull fights are hell on one," Brett said. "I'm limp as a rag."
> "Oh, you'll get a drink," Mike said. (169)

The most frequent kind of joke in *The Sun Also Rises* is the peculiarly literal one that results when someone (the narrator or one of the other characters) understands (or pretends to understand) a word in a different sense (usually a more literal one) than might reasonably have been expected. This pattern is easier illustrated than described. "The Snows of Kilimanjaro" has a pure example:

> "I don't see why that had to happen to your leg. What have we done to have that happen to us?"
> "I suppose what I did was to forget to put iodine on it when I first scratched it. Then I didn't pay any attention to it because I never infect. Then, later, when it got bad, it was probably using that weak carbolic solution when the other antiseptics ran out that paralyzed the minute blood vessels and started the gangrene." He looked at her. "What else?"
> "I don't mean that."[6]

Frank O'Connor tells a story of an evening when he was James Joyce's guest:

> [I] touched the frame of a picture on the wall.
> "What's this?"
> "Cork."
> "Yes, I see it's Cork. I was born there. But what's the frame?"

"Cork."

Some time later, in conversation with Yeats, [I] told him about the picture and its frame. Yeats sat up straight.

"That is mania. That is insanity."[7]

Mania it may be, but it is also funny.

Words deliberately taken as words are the basis of much of the humor in *The Sun Also Rises.* The simplest form of this basic joke in *The Sun Also Rises* can be seen when Jake tries to get by difficult moments with Brett by responding literally to her words rather than to their intended meaning:

"Don't look like that, darling."
"How do you want me to look?" (56)

"What did you say that for?"
"I don't know. What would you like me to say?" (83)

"Darling, don't let's talk a lot of rot."
"All right. Talk about anything you like." (181)

"I was in school in Paris, then. Think of that."
"Anything you want me to think about it?" (244)

Sometimes the literal joke is buried in a seemingly innocent remark. After Cohn knocks Jake out, Jake reluctantly goes to Cohn's room and finds Cohn feeling sorry for himself"

"Now everything's gone. Everything."
"Well," I said, "so long. I've got to go." (194–95)

and:

"You were the only friend I had. . . ."
"Well," I said, "so long." (194)

One time Cohn drops by Jake's Paris office and wants to talk. When it becomes apparent Cohn isn't going to leave, Jake invites him downstairs for a drink:

"Aren't you working?"
"No," I said. (11)

Literally that is an accurate response. Jake isn't working; he is at the moment talking with Cohn. But he wants to work and is maneuvering to get rid of Cohn so he can get back to work.

"Hell" is the subject of several instances of unexpected literalness. In one, Jake has just told Cohn that Brett is a drunk and is going to marry Mike Campbell: "I don't believe it." . . .

> "You asked me what I knew about Brett Ashley."
> "I didn't ask you to insult her."
> "Oh, go to hell."
> He stood up from the table his face white, and stood there white and angry behind the little plates of hors d'oeuvres.
> "Sit down," I said. "Don't be a fool."
> "You've got to take that back."
> "Oh, cut out the prep-school stuff."
> "Take it back."
> "Sure. Anything. I never heard of Brett Ashley. How's that?"
> "No. Not that. About me going to hell."
> "Oh, don't go to hell," I said. "Stick around. We're just starting lunch."
> (39)

Jake suggests the crowded condition of hell when he is talking with Cohn about going to South America:

> "Well, why don't you start off?"
> "Frances."
> "Well," I said, "take her with you."
> "She wouldn't like it. That isn't the sort of thing she likes. She likes a lot of people around."
> "Tell her to go to hell." (37–38)

An interesting use of hell occurs after Jake has helped set up Brett with Romero and then Cohn comes looking for her:

> "Tell me where Brett is."
> "I'll not tell you a damn thing."
> "You know where she is."
> "If I did I wouldn't tell you."
> "Oh, go to hell, Cohn," Mike called from the table. "Brett's gone off with the bull-fighter chap. They're on their honeymoon."
> "You shut up."
> "Oh go to hell!" Mike said languidly.
> "Is that where she is?" Cohn turned to me.
> "Go to hell!"

"She was with you. Is that where she is?"

"Go to hell!" (190)

It is hard to say whether Cohn's "Is that where she is?" refers primarily to "honeymoon" or "hell"—if the two are not indeed the same thing, for when Jake gets to Madrid to rescue Brett from her "honeymoon" she reports: "I've had such a hell of a time" (241), and earlier she had said about being in love: "I think it's hell on earth" (27).

Sometimes someone (usually Jake) deliberately and perversely misunderstands what is said to him:

"Would you like to go to South America, Jake?"

"No."

"Why not?"

"I don't know. . . . You can see all the South Americans you want in Paris anyway."

"They're not the real South Americans."

"They look awfully real to me." (9)

Sometimes Jake deliberately misunderstands but doesn't expect his off-center response to be picked up. Romero is asking about Mike:

"What does the drunken one do?"

"Nothing."

"Is that why he drinks?"

"No. He's waiting to marry this lady." (176)

Sometimes someone misunderstands unintentionally:

"You never come here any more, Monsieur Barnes," Madame Lecomte said.

"Too many compatriots."

"Come at lunch-time. It's not crowded then." (76)

Jake's objection, of course, is not to the number of customers at the restaurant but to the fact that most of them are American tourists.

Sometimes the twisting of meaning is intended by the speaker to be recognized as a joke. Mike tries it:

"How did you go bankrupt?" Bill asked.

"Two ways," Mike said. "Gradually and then suddenly." (136)

and Brett:

> "Here come the gentry," Bill said.
> They were crossing the street. . . .
> "Hello, gents!" said Bill (165)

and Bill:

> "Well," I said, "the saloon must go."
> "You're right there, old classmate," Bill said. "The saloon must go and I will take it with me." (123)

and Jake:

> I found Bill up in his room. He was shaving. . . .
> "How did you happen to know this fellow, anyway?"
> "Don't rub it in."
> Bill looked around, half-shaved, and then went on talking into the mirror while he lathered his face. (101)

It would be easy to read right over that passage without realizing that Jake has made a small joke with "Don't rub it in" and that Bill, by interrupting his lathering and turning around, acknowledges that he understands it.

Sometimes the joke is a seemingly innocent throwaway line that goes along with a conversation:

> "I can't stand it any more."
> He lay there on the bed. (195)
> "All my life I've wanted to go on a trip like that," Cohn said. He sat down. . . . "But I can't get started." (10)
> "Don't just sit there. . . . Don't sit there looking like a bloody funeral." . . .
> "Shut up," Cohn said. He stood up. (141–42)
> "I'm just low, and when I'm low I talk like a fool."
> I sat up, leaned over, found my shoes beside the bed and put them on. I stood up. (56)

The last example tells us quite a bit about Jake. Only to a person with an enormous regard for words would it ever occur to think of standing up as a remedy for feeling low.

Sometimes words trigger a bizarre train of thought. A waiter asks:

> "Shrimps?"
> "Is Cohn gone?" Brett asked. (206)

Sometimes an expression is acted out:

"Ask her if she's got any jam," Bill said. "Be ironical with her."

"Have you got any jam?"

"That's not ironical" . . .

The girl brought in a glass dish of raspberry jam . . .

"Poor," said Bill. "Very poor. You can't do it." (114)

Bill and the waitress in different ways give Jake the raspberry.

Brett comes to Jake's room and wakes him up at half-past four in the morning. Jake makes drinks and listens while Brett talks on about her evening with Count Mippipopolous: "Offered me ten thousand dollars to go to Biarritz with him. . . . Told him I knew too many people in Biarritz." Brett laughs but Jake doesn't.

"I say, you are slow on the up-take," she said. I had only sipped my brandy and soda. I took a long drink.

"That's better. Very funny." (33)

Jake's taking a long drink is not simply a clever response to Brett's saying he is "slow on the uptake." It is also his way of indicating he had understood earlier when Brett had acted out one meaning of being "one of us" by taking a drink:

"The count? Oh, rather. He's quite one of us."

"Is he a count?"

"Here's how." . . . She sipped at her glass. (32)

Occasionally a passage needs to be read aloud for us to realize what is funny. Brett first appears in the book at a *bal musette* with a group of flamboyant male homosexuals. We recognize them by how they talk when they see Georgette:

"I do declare. There is an actual harlot. I'm going to dance with her, Lett. You watch me."

The tall dark one, called Lett, said: "Don't you be rash."

The wavy blond one answered: "Don't you worry, dear." And with them was Brett. (20)

Hemingway and Jake do not care for homosexuals. In this scene, when Jake returns to the *bal* Mrs. Braddocks brings up a young man and introduces him as Robert Prentiss. If we continue reading aloud we discover that Prentiss too must have been part of Brett's entourage:

He was from New York by way of Chicago, and was a rising new novelist. He had some sort of an English accent. I asked him to have a drink.

"Thanks so much," he said. "I've just had one."

"Have another."

"Thanks, I will then." . . . "You're from Kansas City, they tell me," he said.

"Yes."

"Do you find Paris amusing?"

"Yes."

"Really?" . . .

"For God's sake," I said, "Yes. Don't you?"

"Oh, how charmingly you get angry," he said. "I wish I had that faculty." (21)

When Jake hears that last speech, he gets up and walks away again. Mrs. Braddocks follows:

"Don't be cross with Robert," she said. "He's still only a child, you know."

"I wasn't cross," I said. " I just thought perhaps I was going to throw up."

Robert Cohn wants to be a writer, but listen to his first words in the book:

"For God's sake, why did you say that about that girl in Strasbourg for?" (6)

Can anyone who can say a sentence like that ever become a decent writer?

Sometimes in order to see that is funny the reader has to do more than read aloud: he has to follow up on implied instructions. Consider this passage taken from Jake's and Bill's first morning at Burguete:

As I went down-stairs I heard Bill singing, "Irony and pity. When you're feeling . . . Oh, Give them Irony and Give them Pity. Oh, give them Irony. When they're feeling . . . Just a little irony. Just a little pity . . ." He kept on singing until he came down-stairs. The tune was: "The Bells are Ringing for Me and My Gal." (114)

There is nothing funny here when we simply read the words, although we do quickly figure out what the rhyme word for "pity" is—the word that caused Maxwell Perkins to insist on three spaced periods.[8] But see what happens if we try to sing Bill's words to the tune of "For Me and My Gal." We discover there is no way Bill's words can be made to fit that tune. This tells us that Bill must be splendidly rhythm-deaf, and this leads us to understand funny meanings for several other passages—when the Spaniard beats time on Bill's back while trying to teach him a song and Jake comments that Bill "wasn't getting it," and what it must have sounded like when Bill plays the piano to keep warm at the inn at Burguete. As the old advertising slogan put it: "They laughed when I sat down at the piano, but then I started to play . . ."

Some of Hemingway's jokes are like syllogisms with the middle term unstated and which the reader must use his ingenuity to supply. Jake takes the train at Irun and "after forty minutes and eight tunnels I was at San Sebastian." Surely "forty" and "eight" are meant to suggest the wartime 40 and 8 military transport cars (40 hommes/8 chevaux) and represent Jake's comment on the primitive Spanish rail accommodations of the 1920s. This has to be Hemingway's purpose in the passage, for the manuscript of *The Sun Also Rises* shows "forty minutes and six tunnels" and Hemingway later changed it to 40 and 8.[9]

One of Hemingway's funniest and most obscure jokes is in Bill's comment about Robert Cohn's telegram to Burguete:

> The telegram was in Spanish: "Vengo Jueves Cohn."
> I handed it to Bill.
> "What does the word Cohn mean?" he asked. (127)

Bill is just learning Spanish. Among the first phrases one picks up in any language (after "yes," "no," "where is," and "how much") is "I come." So Bill presumably has gotten far enough in Spanish to understand "Vengo." But "Jueves" (Spanish for "Thursday") he apparently hasn't learned yet and the appearance of the word gives him no help. "Jueves" is J-U-E-V-E-S. What does that look like or suggest to an American who doesn't know Spanish? Jew. And thus Bill's comment: Why add Cohn? His point is that the message already says "I come, Jew." What other Jews does Cohn think we might be expecting?—This joke is no doubt objectionable now but in the 1920s it was one of the ways the game was played.

We recognize Mike's less than rigorous thinking when he says:

> "I gave Brett what for, you know. I said if she would go about with Jews
> and bullfighters and such people, she must expect trouble." (203)

Jews and bullfighters and such people? What kind of category is that? I suppose he means people who are not "one of us," but it would be hard to imagine a more vague way of defining that group.

When Jake takes the prostitute Georgette to join his literary friends for coffee after dinner, he introduces her as his "fiancée, Mademoiselle Georgette Leblanc." This is Jake's attempt at a mild joke. The girl is obviously a prostitute, his friends know he has no fiancée, and Georgette Leblanc was the name of a well-known real person—the ex-mistress of Maeterlinck, an actress, singer, and past-middle-aged eccentric who regularly bicycled around Paris in a flowing medieval robe of gold-flowered velvet. The men at the table go along with Jake's joke and all stand up. But Mrs. Braddocks, "a Canadian [with] all their easy social graces" (Hemingway didn't think much of Canada and Canadians), understands nothing of what is happening. She takes Jake's introduction seriously and talks "cordially" with Georgette. When it finally gets through to her that Jake's introduction is not entirely accurate, she calls down the table to her husband to report what she considers an amusing discrepancy: "Did you hear that, Henry? Mr. Barnes introduced his fiancée as Mademoiselle Leblanc, and her name is actually Hobin." At which point Braddocks makes his joke—for the benefit of the others at the table. Proud of his innocent wife and secure in knowing she will not see anything amiss in his saying he knows a prostitute, he says: "Of course, darling. Mademoiselle Hobin. I've known her for a very long time" (18).

Brett's jokes are usually more worldly. Count Mippipopolous drives to the far side of Paris to bring back a basket of champagne for Brett and Jake:

> "I think you'll find that's very good wine," he add. "I know we don't get much of a chance to judge good wine in the States now, but I got this from a friend of mine that's in the business."
>
> "Oh, you always have some one in the trade," Brett said.
>
> "This fellow raises the grapes. He's got thousands of acres of them."
>
> "What's his name?" asked Brett. "Veuve Cliquot?"
>
> "No," said the count. "Mumms. He's a baron." (56–57)

There are two jokes here—one intended by Brett and a second possible only for Jake and Hemingway. Brett knows the count is interested in women, since he had already offered her ten thousand dollars to go with him to Biarritz or Cannes or Monte Carlo. So when he says he has a friend in the champagne business Brett adds up what she knows and makes her joke: "What's his name? Veuve Cliquot?" Her guess has a kind of oblique logic, since "Veuve Clicquot" is the name of one of France's four great champagnes. Her point is that "Veuve Clicquot" *means* something in French that seems to her to fit the situation—"the widow Clicquot." In fact Veuve Clicquot champagne is called in British slang "the merry widow." Thus, if the count says he knows a champagne grower, Brett is suggesting it would probably be the merry widow. Hemingway's joke is that Brett simply picked the wrong brand. The count actually *does* know one of the great French champagne producers—Baron Mumm.

Earlier in the book Brett makes a joke that Hemingway specifically identifies as a joke, but readers seem not to have bothered to try to make sense of it. Jake and Brett are sitting in a taxi at night, moodily discussing how Jake's wound has made impossible what might have been a satisfying relationship. Brett says:

> "When I think of the hell I've put chaps through. I'm paying for it all now."
>
> "Don't talk like a fool," I said. "Besides, what happened to me is supposed to be funny. I never think about it."
>
> "Oh, no. I'll lay you don't."
>
> "Well, let's shut up about it."
>
> "I laughed about it too, myself, once. A friend of my brother's came home that way from Mons. It seemed like a hell of a joke. Chaps never know anything, do they?" (26–27)

What seemed like a hell of a joke? Answer: Not just to be wounded in the groin but to be wounded in the groin at Mons. Mons was, of course, a major battlefield of World War I, but "mons" is also the "mons veneris" which, as anyone who has had a high school course in sex education knows, is the polite term for a woman's pubic mound. For a man to have an encounter at "mons" and come away with damaged sexual apparatus does indeed act out the ancient female threat of "vagina dentata"—vagina with teeth. As Brett says, "It seemed like a hell of a joke."

Mike shouts drunkenly to Jake: "Tell him [Romero] Brett is dying to know how he can get into those pants." "Pipe down," someone says. Yes, pipe down. If Joyce in *Ulysses* can make a joke out of "U-P up," Hemingway in *The Sun Also Rises* can explain to anyone who doesn't already know that bullfighters fit into their tight pants "pipe down" (176)

Near the beginning of the book Jake watches a red and green stop-and-go traffic signal. At the end he sees a traffic policeman raise his baton, forcing the cab Jake is riding in with Brett to a sudden halt. Between these two scenes we find a number of references to people waving things—the drummer waving his drumstick, Bill waving a chicken drumstick, Marshal Ney waving his sword, "the inventor of the semaphore engaged in doing same." All seem to prepare us for the policeman's raised baton of the final page. It would be hard to imagine a more explicit symbolic acting out of a reminder of the reason Jake cannot satisfy Brett.

I am not the first, of course, to have noticed the sexual overtones of the policeman's raised baton, but I am not aware that anyone has spelled out how the details of the scene work. The baton is a twelve-inch white club. When not being used—when it is at rest—it dangles from the policeman's waist. The policeman is a "mounted" policeman. "Mounted" is itself a sexual word. Presumably here it means that he is riding a horse[10]—thus in the saddle, an easy rider—and this takes us back to Bill's "puts a man on her horse" which is in turn based on "puts lead in your pencil." The policeman is wearing Khaki. That suggests a military uniform and is a reminder of the reason Jake cannot now go ahead. But khaki (rhymes with "tacky") is a relatively recent and specifically American pronunciation. In the 1920s in Europe it was "cock-ee" which has an unavoidable sexual suggestion. Add to this that a few minutes earlier Jake had trouble entering Brett's hotel because he could not make "the elevator" work,[11] and then he was told that the personages of her establishment were "rigidly selectioned." The policeman's raised baton forces Jake to confront the fact that he will never qualify for admission to Brett, since "making the elevator work" and a selection process involving "rigid" represent for him impossible requirements.

Jake's jokes (and thus Hemingway's in *The Sun Also Rises*) are all in the ironic mode—variations on Bill's "Give them Irony and Give them Pity." Surely, taken together, and at the very least, the jokes represent one possible and reasonably effective defensive stance for someone who has been wounded in a rotten way on a joke front—which, less literally, seems to have been the situation of almost all young men and women of feeling after World War I.

Notes

1. Bertram D. Sarason, *Hemingway and the Sun Set* (Washington, D.C.: NCR, 1972), 115.

2. Donald Ogden Stewart, "Recollections of Fitzgerald and Hemingway," *Fitzgerald/Hemingway Annual, 1971*, 184.

3. Carlos Baker, *Ernest Hemingway: Selected Letters, 1917–1961* (New York: Scribner's, 1981), 767.

4. Letter from Hemingway to Arnold Gingrich, 3 April 1933, in the substantial private Hemingway collection of Maurice Neville, Santa Barbara, California. Quoted with the kind permission of Mr. Neville.

5. Matthew J. Bruccoli and C. E. Fraser Clark, Jr., *Hemingway at Auction 1930–1973* (Detroit: Bruccoli-Clark, 1973), 42.

6. *The Short Stories of Ernest Hemingway* (New York: Scribner's, 1987).

7. L. A. G. Strong, *The Sacred River: An Approach to James Joyce* (New York: Pellegrini and Cudahay, 1951), 144–45.

8. At no time—not in manuscript nor in typescript—had Hemingway written "shitty." He used long dashes instead. Perkins insisted the dashes could not stand, but why he thought the three spaced periods he substituted would be less offensive is hard to understand.

9. In 1950 I took the train from Irun to San Sebastian to see how many tunnels there were then. Six or eight or even twenty could be an accurate count, depending on what one wants to consider a tunnel. The roadbed ran through cliffs along the shore and there were many semi-tunnels of twenty-or-so feet which could or could not be counted. The present train route from Irun to San Sebastian is farther inland and has almost no tunnels.

10. Both the French and Spanish translations of *The Sun Also Rises* take "mounted" to mean mounted on a horse. Because that meaning may be right and because it fits the argument of my paragraph, I go along with it here. Really, however, I suspect "mounted" means standing on a raised platform in the center of the intersection. That would have been a better position from which to direct traffic and it corresponds to 1950s Madrid practice and to 1920s photos of at least Paris traffic policemen.

11. Jake tells us he was wounded while flying on the Italian front. The "elevator" was the name for the control on World War I planes that made them climb and kept them from plunging. Perhaps the reason Jake is forever unavailable to Brett is that also on an earlier day in 1917 or 1918 he could not make the elevator work.

Hemingway, the *Corrida,* and Spain

KENETH KINNAMON

◆　◆　◆

O N   D E C E M B E R   8 ,   1 9 2 1 ,   E R N E S T   H E M I N G W A Y   and his first
wife sailed for Paris. At the age of twenty-two he had already decided
to become a writer, and Paris offered a better environment for his apprenticeship than Kansas City, Toronto, or Chicago.[1] Instead of the customary
landing at Cherbourg, however, he followed the longer route to Spain and
then north to Paris by rail. As he had not had an opportunity to visit Spain
while in Europe during World War I, he was now seeing it for the first time.
His reaction was immediate and intense. Soon after his arrival in Paris, he
wrote back to Sherwood Anderson in Chicago, "You ought to see the
Spanish coast. Big brown mountains looking like tired dinosaurs slumped
down into the sea."[2] Shortly afterward he used the same simile in a dispatch to the Toronto *Star Weekly* describing Vigo, the town where he had
landed. In terms of his later literary production, it seems appropriate that
he should have landed in Spain when he came to Europe to begin his serious career.

Of Hemingway's seven novels to date, four have had in whole or in part
Spanish or Spanish-American settings. *The Sun Also Rises* takes place both in
France and in Spain, but the emotional center of the book is in the section
dealing with the fiesta in Pamplona; indeed, the British title is *Fiesta*. It is
true that Key West and the Gulf of Mexico form more of the background

of *To Have and Have Not* than does Cuba; but Cuban revolutionary activity and intrigue, if not quite a vital thematic element, certainly provide important counterpoint both to the predicament of Harry Morgan and the "have-nots" and to that of Richard Gordon and the "haves." *For Whom the Bell Tolls,* of course, is set entirely in Spain. Finally, *The Old Man and the Sea* returns to the Cuban scene and has for protagonist a Cuban fisherman. In addition to these novels—three of which are certainly among Hemingway's best four—the Spanish or Spanish-American scene has been treated in his book on *tauromaquia, Death in the Afternoon,* in roughly twenty-five percent of his published short stories, including such important ones as "The Undefeated" and "A Clean, Well-Lighted Place," and in much of his miscellaneous journalism. If one judges by quantity alone, then, it is obvious that for almost the whole of his artistic career Hemingway has been fascinated by the scene and character of Spain and parts of Spanish America.

Surprisingly little effort has been made to isolate and examine the Spanish influence on Hemingway. The neglect is surprising because this influence has penetrated deep into the origins of his art and his world view; far deeper than most critics have noticed or been willing to allow. The Spanish background in Hemingway has more important functions than merely to serve as a playground for lost generation wastrels, a laboratory for the study of civil war and revolution, or a fishing resort. Hemingway has so completely assimilated certain aspects of the Spanish temperament that they have become—perhaps unconsciously on his part—a determining factor in his conception of morality (at best idiosyncratic and at worst vulgar or barbaric to many non-Spanish readers), his theory of tragedy, and the characteristic type of his hero. An account of the effects of his contacts with the Spanish environment and character on his work should clarify the crucial result of his expatriation—that it has involved, to a remarkable degree, alienation from American and assimilation of Spanish values.

Hemingway saw his first bullfights in the summer of 1922, but he did not begin his serious study of the *corrida* until the following summer. At first his purpose was simply to provide himself with an appropriate subject for his apprenticeship; as he later recalled in *Death in the Afternoon,* he "was trying to learn to write commencing with the simplest things, and one of the simplest things of all . . . is violent death." And he took with him to Spain a stereotyped preconception of what he was going to see: "I thought they would be simple and barbarous and cruel and that I would not like them, but that I would see certain definite action which would give me the feeling of life and death that I was working for." But he quickly discovered the inadequacy of his preconceptions and the mistake he had made in choosing the bullfight as one of "the simple things" to write about: "I found the definite action; but the bullfight was so far from simple and I liked it so much that it was much too complicated for my then equipment for writing to deal with and, aside from four very short sketches, I was not able to write anything about it for five years—and I wish I would have waited ten."[3]

Actually, Hemingway wrote about the bullfight almost immediately. In October 1923, he sent two articles to the Toronto *Star Weekly*. The title of the first, "Bullfights not sport but tragedy," shows that he had already divested himself of the basic misconception about the spectacle that the uninitiated American holds. In addition to these two pieces of journalism, Hemingway also put the bullfight to artistic use in his second published volume, *in our time,* which appeared in the spring of 1924. Six, not four as he later remembered, of the eighteen short sketches in this volume are about the bullfight. All but one of these deal with the least attractive aspects of the *fiesta brava*—gorings of men and horses, cowardly bulls, prolonged and messy kills, a bullfighter drunk the morning before a fight, and the death of a bullfighter. But the sketches also introduce two *toreros* who were among Hemingway's favorites, Nicanor Villalta, whose magnificent kill is the subject of the only sketch showing the bullfight as art, and Maera, who was later eulogized in *Death in the Afternoon* and became a prototype of the Hemingway hero. The sketches as a whole are remarkable for the close accuracy of the descriptions by an *aficionado* of such short standing and for the concentration on sequence of event with the accompanying eschewal of overtly expressed emotion that marks much of Hemingway's best writing.

But the bullfight had become more for Hemingway than merely a subject for literary finger exercises. It had become a profound spiritual experience, perhaps the most profound of all. In the late spring of 1924, he wrote sardonically in the *transatlantic review,* "Since seeing his first bull-fight, Mr. William Bird, the publisher, no longer finds it necessary to read the cabled base-ball reports from New York."[4] Later in the same year, he quoted approvingly a remark made by Picasso to Donald Ogden Stewart, "You know it's absolutely the only thing left in the world. Bul [*sic*] fighting that is." Hemingway's interest, however, had no missionary leanings. Initiation into the brotherhood of *afición* seemed to entail a conspiracy toward the exclusion of the merely curious, and he feared that an invasion of tourists would spoil the fiesta at Pamplona. Therefore, he reasoned, "the more people that think it is terrible, brutal degrading relic of etc. the better."[5]

This cultistic tendency of Hemingway as *aficionado* also receives explicit statement in *The Sun Also Rises* (1926), his first serious novel:

> He [the hotel owner, Montoya] always smiled as though bullfighting were a very special secret between the two of us; a rather shocking but really very deep secret that we knew about. He always smiled as though there were something lewd about the secret to outsiders, but that it was something that we understood. It would not do to expose it to people who would not understand.

The acceptance of Jake Barnes as a colleague by Spanish *aficionados* is not an easy process; it even involves a ritualistic tactile confirmation:

> They were always very polite at first, and it amused them very much that I should be an American. Somehow it was taken for granted that an American could not have aficion. He might simulate it or confuse it with excitement, but he could not really have it. When they saw that I had aficion, and there was no password, no set questions that could bring it out, rather it was a sort of oral spiritual examination with the questions always a little on the defensive and never apparent, there was this same embarrassed putting the hand on the shoulder, or a "Buen hombre." But nearly always there was the actual touching. It seemed as though they wanted to touch you to make it certain.[6]

The almost mystical, certainly spiritual, fellowship of *afición* for the bull-fight was the bond which cemented Jake's relationship with Spain, and we are justified by Jake's role in the novel as well as by the biographical facts of this period of the novelist's life in assuming that the same bond cemented Hemingway's early relationship with Spain. In considering his later Spanish themes, it is extremely important to remember that the bullfight was the first center of Hemingway's Spanish world.

The only completely admirable character in *The Sun Also Rises* is the young matador, Pedro Romero, whom Hemingway patterned after the contemporary Niño de la Palma and named for a great eighteenth-century matador. Thus the bullfighter had become a prototype of the Hemingway hero very early. The moral stature of Romero is most vividly pointed up by the rivalry between him and Robert Cohn for Lady Brett Ashley. The rivalry culminates in a fist fight in which Cohn, although the physical victor, suffers complete moral defeat. And it is Romero who is responsible at least passively for Brett's only moral victory, which is achieved when she renounces him in order not to be "one of these bitches that ruins children." Furthermore, Romero is admirable because he is an artist with a brilliant future in the bull ring, a man with a métier, in contrast to Cohn, Brett, Mike, and even Jake himself, people either without a métier or unsuccessful in it and with no future at all. Finally, Romero is heroic because his way of living is extremely intense; he telescopes experience in much the same way that Robert Jordan was later to do in *For Whom the Bell Tolls.* As Jake tells Cohn early in the novel, "Nobody ever lives their life all the way up except bull-fighters." Cohn, however, whose own abnormality lies in his constant but unsuccessful quest for experience, replies, "I'm not interested in bull-fighters. That's an abnormal life."[7] The irony of this dialogue is that for Jake and Hemingway the life of the *torero* is not abnormal but supernormal, for it is the only one in which a man can be an artist through the exertion of skill and physical and moral courage in the face of what Hemingway himself was later to call the ultimate reality, death.

A great deal of Romero's stature, however, is due to his youth and his innocence. Like Paco of "The Capital of the World," he is, as the Spanish phrase has it, "full of illusions." Also, he is a *torero* before the first goring, and thus largely an unknown quantity. The case is very different for the *torero* in the first story of Hemingway's next book, *Men without Women* (1927). In this story the matador is Manuel García, whose name is the same as that of the actual matador called Maera mentioned above. "The Undefeated" discloses some of the seamiest sides of bullfighting—the ruthless and mercenary promoter, the contemptuous waiters in cheap restaurants, the bored and supercilious critic, the unsympathetic and insulting crowd. The central figure, Manuel García, is a matador long past his prime but compelled to continue fighting by his sense of honor, his pride in his profession, and his illusory rationalization that he is still capable of making a comeback. After wangling a contract to appear as a substitute at a nocturnal *corrida,* he engages the services of a skillful old picador, Zurito. Understanding his friend's compulsion to return to the ring, the old picador agrees to appear with him on the condition that he will give up the profession if the *corrida* is not successful. Manuel's work in the ring is valiant and supremely honest, although he does not maintain full control of the bull and has lost most of his art. When he tries to make the kill, four times the sword strikes bone and fails to penetrate.[8] Although each time he goes in over the horn well and his lack of success is attributable simply to bad luck, the crowd unjustly begins to throw things from the stands. Along with the usual cushions, these things include his own sword, which had rebounded into the crowd after his last attempt at the kill, and an empty champagne bottle, evidently thrown by the bored bullfight critic. On the fifth attempt Manuel is gored. Afterwards in the infirmary Zurito, according to their

agreement, starts to cut off Manuel's *coleta,* the small pigtail that bullfighters wear on the back of their heads as a badge of the profession. Manuel
feels that he must keep his *coleta* intact in order to maintain his honor and
self-respect, and Zurito, understanding his friend's feeling, says, "I won't
do it. I was joking."[9] On the operating table from which he will not arise,
Manuel continues to insist that he "was going good" in the ring before the
goring, maintaining to the end his honor and refusing to accept defeat. It is
in this sense that he is "The Undefeated."

Very early Hemingway was fascinated by the Spanish characteristic of
refusing to accept defeat in a situation justifying surrender and by that refusal achieving a kind of victory. The first example of this characteristic in
action was Pedro Romero's fist fight with Robert Cohn in *The Sun Also Rises.*
The latest example is that of Santiago in *The Old Man and the Sea.* Hemingway's treatments of this theme appear throughout almost the whole
course of his literary career, and the theme itself provides us with an
important key to an understanding of his interpretation of the Spanish
character.

Another story in *Men without Women* is of major importance in indicating
the shift away from American and toward Spanish values which had begun
to take place in Hemingway beginning in 1922. This is "Banal Story." On
one level it represents a reversion to Hemingway's satirical talent, which
had been prominently manifested in his high-school journalism as well as
in *The Torrents of Spring.* The early satirical novel has little connection with
Spain except for one curious parallel. The epigraph to Chapter 1 is the following quotation from Fielding's preface to *Joseph Andrews:* "The only
source of the true Ridiculous (as it appears to me) is affection."[10] Hemingway may or may not have been aware that this quotation is in a direct line
of descent from an epigram by Spain's greatest writer, Cervantes: "Toda
afectación es mala." At any rate, the point of Hemingway's satire in "Banal
Story" on Americans who try to "live the full life of the mind" by seeking
romance and intellectual stimulation in the escapist world of such magazines as *The Forum* is that they are guilty of affectation and insincerity. But in
sharp dramatic contrast to these Americans, "stretched flat on a bed in a
darkened room in his house in Triana, Manuel García Maera lay with a
tube in each lung, drowning with the pneumonia. . . . Bull-fighters
were very relieved he was dead, because he did always in the bull-ring the
things they could only do sometimes."[11] It is evident that Maera had become a prototype of the undefeated Hemingway hero.

Maera is given extended treatment in *Death in the Afternoon.* A *banderillero*
in the *cuadrilla* of the great Juan Belmonte, Maera left Belmonte and be-

came a matador when he was refused an increase in salary.[12] After a close analysis of the development of Maera's style and an assessment of the final achievement of his art, Hemingway relates an incident very similar to that of Maera's fictional projection in "The Undefeated." Maera dislocates his wrist in attempting to make the kill, but after several more unsuccessful efforts he finally succeeds, although all the while the pain in his arm has been almost unbearable. He also dies a Hemingwayesque death:

> Anyway he died that winter in Seville with a tube in each lung, drowned with pneumonia that came to finish off the tuberculosis. When he was delirious he rolled under the bed and fought with death under the bed dying as hard as a man can die. I thought that year he hoped for death in the ring but he would not cheat by looking for it. You would have liked him, Madame. Era muy hombre.

This is one of the few times that Hemingway speaks Spanish to his old lady in *Death in the Afternoon*. For Hemingway, "era muy hombre" is the supreme compliment, and it could only be expressed in Spanish. When the old lady asks him if Maera had been "mean about money," as Belmonte had, the author replies,

> He was not. He was generous, humorous, proud, bitter, foul-mouthed and a great drinker. He neither sucked after intellectuals nor married money. He loved to kill bulls and lived with much passion and enjoyment although the last six months of his life he was very bitter. He knew he had tuberculosis and took absolutely no care of himself; having no fear of death he preferred to burn out, not as an act of bravado, but from choice.

This catalog of virtues, together with "a valor that was so absolute and such a solid part of him that it made everything easy that he understood,"[13] comprises those most important for a Hemingway hero. Maera's death, which occurred in 1924, continued to haunt Hemingway for a long time afterward. It is necessary to emphasize the year, for only *Three Stories and Ten Poems* and *in our time* appeared before it. Thus Hemingway's contact with Maera came exactly when the writer was developing the values and attitudes which would appear in his fiction as well as in *Death in the Afternoon*. Maera did in fact exert a strong formative influence on these values and attitudes.

Death in the Afternoon is, in part, exactly what the author wrote he intended it to be in a bibliographical note at the end of the book: "It is intended as an introduction to the modern Spanish bullfight and attempts to explain that spectacle both emotionally and practically." Also, Hemingway wrote, it "is not intended to be either historical or exhaustive."[14] We need only to glance at a work that is historical and exhaustive, José María de Cossío's monumental study in three huge volumes, *Los toros: Tratado técnico e histórico*, to realize that the brief period of ten years from 1922 to 1932, filled as it was with other activities and other writing, was much too short for Hemingway to gain a really sound scholarly knowledge of all aspects of the complex subject. But as an introduction to the *fiesta brava* for the non-Spanish reader, *Death in the Afternoon* is excellent, much better than any other book of similar intention in English, including the many that have followed it and borrowed from it.

Hemingway knew the bullfight from the inside as well as from the stands. In addition to his friendship with Maera and other bullfighters as well as with Spanish *aficionados*, and in addition to his own brief attempts at amateur bullfighting, which included the celebrated *quite* that saved John Dos Passos a serious goring, Hemingway was a close personal friend of the American matador, Sidney Franklin, whom he met early in August, 1929. Franklin in his autobiography gives a humorous and engaging account of their friendship. On first meeting Hemingway, he suspected that the unkempt writer was a tramp looking for a handout. Even after Hemingway introduced himself, Franklin did not recognize the name; indeed, the bullfighter did not learn of the writer's fame until after a month of constant companionship, and then only from a common friend. But from the first meeting Franklin was highly impressed by Hemingway's modesty, his knowledge of wines, his insistence on paying his own way, and, most of all, his knowledge of the bullfight. "As we chatted," Franklin writes of their first meeting,

> I realized that this fellow had a choice selection of English terms for bullfighting which up until then I had been at a loss to translate. And he used them very casually, as though it were old stuff with him. . . . He was the first person who spoke to me in American English who appeared to have a deep understanding of the business. . . . I drew our conversation into channels which would show me just how much he knew about bullfighting. And, little by little, he amazed me. He was familiar with events and instances which only a deep sincere student of the subject could know about.

Hemingway accompanied Franklin and his *cuadrilla*, living in the same hotel suites with them, for the remainder of the 1929 season and all of the 1930 season. Hemingway and Franklin even worked out a system of signals whereby Hemingway gave the bullfighter instructions from behind the *barrera*. Franklin later generously commented, "This direction from him was the cause of my meteoric rise."[15] The experience was extremely valuable to Hemingway, for it gave him an even deeper insight into the psychology of bullfighters and added to his large store of practical information about the bullfight.

It has been necessary to emphasize the intensity of Hemingway's personal interest in the bullfight, his close association with the institution, and his careful study of the art for almost ten years before the publication of *Death in the Afternoon*, because critics have seldom been willing to accept the book on its own terms. This reluctance is part of the larger question of the difference between Hispanic and Anglo-Saxon culture, for the *fiesta brava* has never been successful outside of Spanish-speaking countries. This is also to say that the emotions and temperament of a non-Hispanic *aficionado* have to some degree been Hispanicized. This statement is notably true in the case of Hemingway. As a result, the condemnations of *Death in the Afternoon* by non-Hispanic critics who are not *aficionados* have been largely on moral grounds. These critics have usually ignored the problem of whether the book succeeds in its primary aim of introducing "the modern Spanish bullfight . . . both emotionally and practically." A notorious example is Max Eastman in his article, "Bull in the Afternoon." There have even been critics who have attempted to imply that Hemingway's reaction to the bullfight is that of a vulgar American rather than a Spaniard. Thus Harry Levin, in an otherwise excellent essay on Hemingway's style, writes,

> Where are his limitations? What are his values? We may well discover that they differ from our assumptions, when he shows us a photograph of a bullfighter close to a bull, and comments: "If there is no blood on his belly afterwards you ought to get your money back." We may be ungrateful to question such curiosity. . . . it may well spring from the American zest of the fan who pays his money to reckon the carnage. When Spain's great poet, García Lorca, celebrated the very same theme, averting his gaze from the spilling of the blood, his refrain was "Que no quiero verla!" ("I don't want to see it!").[16]

The picture Mr. Levin refers to is one of Nicanor Villalta in a *derechazo* pass with the *muleta* in which the bull passes so closely that it brushed blood from its bleeding shoulder onto the unharmed body of the bullfighter. The poem in which Mr. Levin says García Lorca "celebrated the very same theme" is "Llanto por Ignacio Sánchez Mejías," an elegy on the death of a famous matador killed by a goring in the ring. What García Lorca did not want to see was not the blood of the bull on the man as evidence of a close pass, but rather "la sangre / de Ignacio sobre la arena") "the blood / of

Ignacio on the sand"), hardly, one would think, "the very same theme" as that of Hemingway, who many times in *Death in the Afternoon* explicitly insists that the bullfight is an artistic and emotional failure when a bullfighter is gored.

But Mr. Levin very rightly implies that Hemingway's values are different from "ours." They are different precisely in that they are Hispanicized. The truth of this statement is evident on almost every page of *Death in the Afternoon*, but nowhere, perhaps, is it more so than in those parts which discuss death:

> Some one with English blood has written: "Life is real; life is earnest, and the grave is not its goal." And where did they bury him? and what became of the reality and the earnestness? The people of Castille have great common sense. They could not produce a poet who would write a line like that. They know death is the unescapable reality, the one thing any man may be sure of; the only security; that it transcends all modern comforts and that with it you do not need a bathtub in every American home, nor, when you have it, do you need the radio. They think a great deal about death and when they have a religion they have one which believes that life is much shorter than death. Having this feeling they take an intelligent interest in death and when they can see it being given, avoided, refused and accepted in the afternoon for a nominal price of admission they pay their money and go to the bull ring.[17]

That Hemingway has had exactly the same kind of interest in death is obvious from the biographical facts, although to call this interest an obsession is to state the case much too strongly, and to construe his career as a deliberate quest for death, as was done after the African airplane crashes, is ridiculous.

Paradoxically, perhaps, this awareness of the inevitability of death in the end for man is, together with the creation of plastic beauty, what provides the supreme emotional appeal of bullfighting culminating in the death of the bull. Hemingway describes this appeal extremely well:

> Now the essence of the greatest emotional appeal of bullfighting is the feeling of immortality that the bullfighter feels in the middle of a great *faena* and that he gives to the spectators. He is performing a work of art and he is playing with death, bringing it closer, closer, closer, to himself, a death that you know is in the horns because you have the canvas-covered bodies of the horses on the sand to prove it. He gives the feeling of his immortality, and,

as you watch it, it becomes yours. Then when it belongs to both of you, he proves it with the sword.[18]

The perfect bullfight is thus one in which death in the form of a brave bull is conquered artistically and valiantly, thereby allowing the bullfighter and, vicariously, the spectators to make a gesture of defiance at their own ultimate fate, even a temporary victory over it. In this way a perfect bullfight provided a norm around which Hemingway developed his idea of the morally undefeated. It cannot be emphasized too strongly that the idea developed from a Spanish ritual.

Among the most enlightening of the many disgressions in *Death in the Afternoon* are those which deal with Spanish painting. Goya, Velázquez, and El Greco comprise the great trio of painters whom Hemingway admires and evaluates. He has a vast admiration for each of them, although Goya is clearly the favorite. Although made a bit uneasy by his suspicion that El Greco was a homosexual, Hemingway is not speaking ironically when he says that the painter should redeem for the tribe the various types of perversion represented by Gide, Wilde, and Whitman.[19] Velázquez draws Hemingway's special attention because of the importance the painter gave to his art per se. But Goya receives Hemingway's highest praise, probably because his artistic aims were very much like the novelist's own:

> Goya did not believe in costume [unlike Velázquez] but he did believe in blacks and in grays, in dust and in light, in high places rising from plains, in the country around Madrid, in movement, in his own cojones, in painting, in etching, and in what he had seen, felt, touched, handled, smelled, enjoyed, drunk, mounted, suffered, spewed-up, lain-with, suspected, observed, loved, hated, lusted, feared, detested, admired, loathed, and destroyed. Naturally no painter has been able to paint all that but he tried.[20]

Thus Goya is an ideal example of what Hemingway thinks the artist must be, a man who puts into his art what he knows and "the way it was." But Goya is also, like Maera, a type of the Hemingway hero, especially in his appetite for experience. Furthermore, Hemingway is attracted to Goya because two of the painter's basic themes, bullfighting and war, are the writer's own.

One of the articles of Goya's faith, Hemingway asserts, was a belief in his own *cojones*. Why, one wonders, would not the words "heart" or "guts" describe the concept just as well? The answer is not only that Hemingway wanted to stress the quality of masculinity as a major component of courage, but also that he had come to formulate his basic attitudes in Spanish terms; indeed, his attitudes from 1922 to 1932 were becoming progressively more Hispanicized. According to Spanish folklore, which Hemingway accepts in this respect, human courage resides in the *cojones*. In the explanatory glossary at the end of *Death in the Afternoon*, he says of *cojones* that "a valorous bullfighter is said to be plentifully equipped with these."[21] The protagonists of each subsequent Hemingway novel are all plentifully equipped by the novelist with *cojones*.

It is important to note that *Death in the Afternoon* is filled with many of the abstract words which had been so odious to Frederic Henry in *A Farewell to Arms*. Spain, as it were, has restored Hemingway's faith in the reality of the qualities that these abstract words signify, a faith that had been lost after World War I because the qualities did not seem real in a non-Spanish setting and among people who were not Spanish-speaking. "In Spain," Hemingway writes, "honor is a very real thing. Called pundonor, it means honor, probity, courage, self-respect and pride in one word. Pride is the strongest characteristic of the race and it is a matter of pundonor not to show cowardice." Hemingway is completely convinced of the reality of the quality, and he realizes the difficulty of conveying the reality to his non-Spanish audience, among whom honor is only a word: "This honor thing is not some fantasy that I am trying to inflict on you. . . . I swear it is true. Honor to a Spaniard, no matter how dishonest, is as real a thing as water, wine, or olive oil. There is honor among pickpockets and honor among whores. It is simply that the standards differ."[22] And although their standards often differ from conventional ones, Hemingway's heroes all have a strong sense of honor.

Hemingway's most famous use of a Spanish word, of course, is that of *nada* in "A Clean, Well-Lighted Place," which appeared in the March 1933 issue of *Scribner's Magazine* only a little more than five months after the publication of *Death in the Afternoon*. The critics have rightly considered this story central to Hemingway's world view, and a few of them have pointed out the important idea of *cojones* as man's defense against *nada*. Robert Penn Warren, for example, gets to the heart of the matter when he writes, "The violent man is the man taking an action appropriate to the realization of the fact of nada. He is, in other words, engaged in the effort to discover human values in a naturalistic world."[23] And while it is true that the *nada*-concept is a compelling symbol of the emptiness and anarchy of life in the twentieth century, the critics have not sufficiently emphasized that the concept takes its rise from a specific Spanish setting and is expressed by a Spanish word. . . .

Notes

1. For a suggestive discussion of Hemingway's reasons for going to Paris, see Charles A. Fenton, *The Apprenticeship of Ernest Hemingway* (New York: Farrar, Straus & Young, 1954), 115–17.

2. Quoted in Fenton, *The Apprenticeship*, 118–19.

3. *Death in the Afternoon* (New York: Scribner's, 1932), 2, 3.

4. "And to the United States," 1 (1924), 377.

5. "Pamplona Letter," *transatlantic review* 2 (1924), 302.

6. *The Sun Also Rises* (New York: Scribner's, 1926), 135, 136.

7. Ibid., 254, 10.

8. In *Death in the Afternoon* Hemingway recounts a similar incident that happened to Manuel Garcia Maera. This fact and the fact that the names are the same indicate fairly certainly that Hemingway patterned his fictional character after the real matador.

9. *The Fifth Column and the First Forty-nine Stories* (New York: P. F. Collier, 1938), 363.

10. *The Hemingway Reader*, ed. Charles Poore (New York: Scribner's, 1953), 25.

11. *The Fifth Column and the First Forty-nine Stories*, 459.

12. Hemingway's vast admiration for Maera, a personal friend, seems to have led him to distort the facts. Actually, Maera had been a matador before he joined Belmonte's *cuadrilla*, although he did not reach the highest rank in his profession until after he had left Belmonte, having acquired by that time a vast knowledge of bulls and bullfighting. See José Maria de Cossio, *Los Toros: Tratado técnico e histórico*, 3 (Madrid: Espasa-Calpe, 1943), 343.

13. *Death in the Afternoon*, 82, 82–83, 78.

14. Ibid., 517.

15. *Bullfighter from Brooklyn* (New York: Scribner's, 1942), 173–79.

16. "Observations on the Style of Ernest Hemingway," *Kenyon Review* 13 (1951), 606.

17. *Death in the Afternoon*, 266.

18. Ibid., 213.

19. Hemingway is quoted as follows on El Greco's "View of Toledo": "This is the best picture in the Museum for me, and Christ knows there are some lovely ones." See Lillian Ross, "How Do You Like It Now, Gentlemen?" *New Yorker* 26 (May 13, 1950), 58.

20. *Death in the Afternoon*, 205.

21. Ibid., 428.

22. Ibid., 91, 92.

23. "Hemingway," *Literary Opinion in America*, ed. Morton Dauwen Zabel (New York: Harper, 1951), 448.

Alcoholism in Ernest Hemingway's
The Sun Also Rises
A Wine and Roses Perspective on the Lost Generation

MATTS DJOS

◆   ◆   ◆

*T*HE SUN ALSO RISES is a remarkable portrait of the pathology of the disease of alcoholism. As a description of the alcoholic mentality, it has none of the high drama and tragic despair of works like *Days of Wine and Roses* or *Under the Volcano*, but this makes the story all the more realistic and compelling. Indeed, like the disease of alcoholism itself, the plot may be quite deceptive because it presents no images of addictive self-destruction on a grandiose scale.

The novel describes how Jake Barnes and his expatriate friends spend a good deal of time in Paris drinking and talking about drinking, how some of them make a hectic trip over the Pyrennees to Pamplona to go fishing and watch the bullfights, and how, after an astonishing series of affairs, foul-ups, and misunderstandings, they straggle back to Paris to talk some more and do some more drinking. A great deal of the novel is focused on liquor, discussions about liquor, hangovers, drunkenness, and finding more liquor (Gelderman, 12). The following remarks are drawn from just five pages of *The Sun Also Rises*:

> "You were quite drunk my dear."
> "I say, Jake, *do* we get a drink?"
> "He loves to go for champagne."

"Let's have a drink, then. The count will be back."

"You know he's extraordinary about buying champagne. It means any amount to him."

"I think you'll find that's very good wine, . . . we don't get much of a chance to judge good wine. . . ."

"This is a hell of a dull talk. . . . How about some of that champagne?"

"You're always drinking, my dear. Why don't you just talk?"

"I like to drink champagne from magnums. The wine is better but it would have been too hard to cool."

"There, my dear. Now you enjoy that slowly, and then you can get drunk."

"She is the only lady I have ever known who was as charming when she was drunk as when she was sober."

"Drink your wine." (54–59)

It might be assumed that at least three of the characters—Jake Barnes, Brett Ashley, Mike Campbell—are only heavy drinkers; but there is a considerable difference between heavy drinking and the kind of self-destructive, alcoholic drinking that we read about in the novel. Indeed, Hemingway himself may have felt obliged to acknowledge the alcoholic focus of the story. When asked about its libationary focus, he appears to have grudgingly conceded that it was a "book about a few drunks" (Dardis, 163); but, as Tom Dardis notes in his excellent discussion of the writer's alcoholism, the drinking behavior described in *The Sun Also Rises* was pronounced and addictive, regardless of the motives (163). Hemingway may have thought that imbibing on such a monumental scale simply classified the inebriate as a sort of generic "rummy," but, as Dardis writes, he was ignorant of the fact that "alcoholism breeds its own kind of pressure, that of alcoholic depression" (163).

Of course, in defining Mike, Brett, and Jake as practicing alcoholics, we ought to consider exactly what it is that fleshes out the portrait of someone who is alcohol-dependent; that is, we might want to consider what it is that characterizes someone whose life is dominated by an obsession with liquor.

Most social scientists have concluded that alcoholics have a higher level of anxiety, dependence, and defensiveness. This is sometimes reflected in a remarkable degree of moodiness, impulsivity, hostility, and distrust (see, for example, Ward, 168 and Weston, 39–40).[1] A good number of studies have also concluded that alcoholics have lower self-esteem, are more goal-oriented, strive more for a superficial feeling of achievement, and consistently exhibit an intense need for personal power (see, for example, Ward, 169). Such problems may be manifested by the development of façades suggesting a great deal of uncertainty regarding sexual identity (Ward, 176).

If we critique *The Sun Also Rises* with these criteria in mind, it should come as no surprise that Jake, Brett, Mike, and even Robert Cohn and Bill Gorton match the alcoholic profile in no small measure. Regardless of the setting or scene, the bars and the bottles are omnipresent and serve as a focal point for the bullfights, the eating, the peregrinating, the flirting and seducing, the fisticuffs, and even the fishing. Between Paris, Pamplona, and Burguete, Jake gets very drunk at least three times; Brett is known to get drunk twice; Mike is drunk everytime we see him; Bill is rarely sober; even Cohn spends a great deal of time in his cups—and all of this happens during the two weeks or so that we as readers follow the story. Drinking on this kind of scale cannot even begin to resemble normalcy and is most certainly a substantive foundation for addiction and obsessive dependence. Of course, as with most alcoholics, any talk about abuse is usually focused on "other" people in the group, or it is jokingly discounted as the "right" kind of drinking supporting the jolly, good nature of the inner circle.

A key aspect of the alcoholic temperament is the desire for control. There is hardly a single, major character in *The Sun also Rises* who is not a compulsive manipulator. This passion for orchestrating circumstances in conformity with certain, willful desires is well described in *Twelve Steps and Twelve Traditions*, a major publication of Alcoholics Anonymous:

> When we habitually try to manipulate others to our own willful desires, they [family, friends, society at large] revolt and resist us heavily. Then we develop hurt feelings, a sense of persecution, and a desire to retaliate. As we redouble our efforts at control, and continue to fail, our suffering becomes acute and constant. (53)

Jake and his companions are terrified that fate and circumstance might shatter their façade of civilized deference. Sometimes, they barely make it from day to day; sometimes, they appear to be trying to just make it through the next hour, a common enough problem among a great many alcoholics. These people lack the skills and the sanity to break their addiction to self-sufficiency and their destructive loop of unmanageability. Instead, they seek refuge in broken relationships, in changes of scene, in drunkenness and the illusion that, however meager, they can find some pleasure in their brief interludes of time and place. There is a great deal of fear here, fear of self-understanding, fear of emotional and physical inadequacy, and—very important—fear of each other.

Jake is the terminal man. Having been emasculated in the war, he has gotten tangled up in a vicious cycle of emotional self-mutilation. Regardless of whether he is alone or in company, he is resigned to the belief that he is powerless to change anything. So he secludes himself in a mantle of self-pity and hopelessness, chooses to withdraw into a Faustian tragedy of self-denial, and consigns himself to hopeless despair rather than do anything about his problem.

Jake has found a perverse kind of sainthood in the conviction that he is unique (a trait common among unrecovered alcoholics). His suffering has qualified him for a rather peculiar dementia which is likely to be manifested in bleak moods of social hatred and self-pity. Jake is something of a masochist, and his emotional starvation may well be a corollary of low self-esteem. As a consequence, he in inclined to discount his own worth and his right to any substantive fulfillment or happiness, and this may well account for his catastrophic perspective on his relationship with Brett. More often than not, he gets drunk or ends up alone in a hotel room or in his flat, staring at the ceiling while grousing about the hopelessness of his condition and the impossibility of establishing any kind of enduring connection with Brett. Thus, in his refusal to break out of his self-destructive loop, he persists in remaining self-condemned before the fact:

> My head started to work. The old grievance. Well, it was a rotten way to be wounded and flying on a joke front like the Italian. In the Italian hospital we were going to form a society. It had a funny name in Italian. . . . That was where the liaison colonel came to visit me. . . . he made that wonderful speech: "you, a foreigner, an Englishman" (any foreigner was an Englishman) "have given more than your life." What a speech! I would have like[d] to have it illuminated to hang in the office. He never laughed. He was putting himself in my place, I guess. "Che mala fortuna! Che mala fortuna!"
>
> I never used to realize it, I guess. I try to play it along and just not make trouble for people. Probably I never would have had any trouble if I hadn't run into Brett when they shipped me to England. I suppose she only wanted what she couldn't have. Well, people were that way. To hell with people. The Catholic Church had an awfully good way of handling all that. Good advice, anyway. Not to think about it. Oh, it was swell advice. Try and take it sometime. Try and take it. I lay awake thinking and my mind jumping around. Then I couldn't keep away from it. . . . I was thinking about

Brett and my mind stopped jumping. . . . Then all of a sudden I started
to cry. (31)

Like many alcoholics, Jake is convinced that his self-imposed martyrdom is
terminal. He has set down the terms of his life with uncompromising
severity because he is convinced that his wound is different, his front was a
"joke," and he has given "more" than his life for Italy. So he feels hopeless
about Brett, tries to resign himself to circumstance, and thinks about not
thinking.

Like Jake, Brett is self-victimized by her catastrophic thinking and her
remarkable penchant for charades and seduction. She discounts her title—
Lady Brett Ashley—but seems to parade it at every opportunity. She is a
voluptuary of prodigious dimensions who has learned well the game of
disguising her fear of womanhood in the sexual control of men. And
through it all, she canonizes herself as noble and self-sacrificing. It is a
pretty little game she plays, but her strategies are riddled with drunken
fakery. If viewed from a psychological-addictive perspective, Brett personifies the generic female alcoholic with a remarkable prejudice for manipulation and orchestration. She seduces; she complains; she plays the kitten;
and then she runs. She targets the emotions of any man who will have
anything to do with her, hopeful that he will somehow restore the integrity of her womanhood. And she knows no boundaries in her hunt. Just
about anything male is fair game; any assertion of power might affirm that
she is not a victim of circumstances herself. If seduction can lead to a trophy, she will seduce; if abandonment can lead to an assurance of her skill at
breaking hearts, she will abandon; and if sheer, mind-boggling mental tor-
ture will do the job, then tempt and attack she will.

Mike is a masochist and village clown. He uses his money and his connections to control others, to martyr himself, and to confirm that, after
all, he is little more than a drunk. If he is given a chance and enough
liquor, he will attack anyone weaker than himself, a typical enough behavior of any fear-ridden alcoholic. Then, if parried too strongly, he will shake
off the bully boy image and be a "good fellow." Mike has failed at just about
everything—his prospects for marriage, work, sex—and he knows it and
even seems rather proud of it. He adopts the pose of an idle playboy and
jolly intoxicant. In truth, he is neither interested in sobering up nor skilled
enough to break away from himself or his surroundings. His title and what
little money he has left are sufficient to keep him mildly functional despite
his drinking; his self-esteem is meager enough to keep him from even
thinking about sobering up and making any real changes.

Although Cohn does not at first appear to have some of the drinking problems of his more bibulous companions, it is ironic that he provides a vivid example of some of the capricious personality flaws that are commonly perceived in the standard profile of a practicing alcoholic. Indeed, because of his insufferable emotionalism, his addiction to self-pity, and his codependent proximity to Jake's retinue, he seems to manifest the standard characteristics of a "dry drunk" or "prealcoholic" personality (see, for example, Ward, 181–82). Such individuals are commonly recognized around alcoholic circles because they behave like practicing alcoholics, even though they do not appear to have an addiction to or an obsessive need for liquor, as such. Indeed, they provide a striking example of the fundamental distinction between people who are "dry" and people who are "sober."[2]

In any case, when Cohn does get drunk, he behaves like a lap dog who is trapped in insecurity and loneliness; and, like so many of his kind, finds euphoric power in illusions of masculinity. Of course, that euphoria can easily collapse in a stream of apologies and tears of self-pity, as in the drunken fight with Romero.

For Jake and his companions, then, liquor can fuel the appetites and rebellious instincts, but it cannot defuse fear. Drinking isolates the characters and fragments their relationships, culminating in rebellion, antisocial behavior, and an addiction to social fakery and make-believe. Even their conversations are maddeningly incongruent. We sense that each character talks to himself through a muddled backwash of trivia and banality. Connections are short, focused on externals, and filled with nonsequiturs. Most of the talk is centered on bullfights, food, the quality of the wine, the festival at Pamplona, affairs, or banalities of an insufferable texture; but we never know how anyone *really* feels or even if any intelligence or sensitivity supports this masquerade of maturity and self-sufficiency. Consider the following scene when Jake sees Brett in Paris:

> A taxi passed, some one [*sic*] in it waved, then banged for the driver to stop. The taxi backed up to the curb. In it was Brett.
>
> "Beautiful lady," said Bill. "Going to kidnap us."
>
> "Hullo!" Brett said. "Hullo!"
>
> "This is Bill Gorton. Lady Ashley."
>
> Brett smiled at Bill. "I say I'm just back. Haven't bathed even, Michael comes in to-night."
>
> "Good. Come on and eat with us, and we'll all go to meet him."
>
> "Must clean myself."

"Oh, rot! Come on."

"Must bathe. He doesn't get in till nine."

"Come and have a drink, then, before you bathe."

"Might do that. Now you're not talking rot."

We got in the taxi. The driver looked around.

"Stop at the nearest bistro," I said.

"We might as well go to the Closerie," Brett said. "I can't drink these rotten brandies." (74)

The confabulation between Jake, Bill, and Brett is simple enough and casual enough—seemingly concerned about bathing, kidnapping, bistros, and rotten brandies; but the connections never seem to progress beyond bromides. When these people meet, they seem preoccupied with making arrangements to meet again sometime; if they talk for any length, conversations are cluttered with superficial evaluations of the quality of the booze, the problems of hygiene, and the complications of meeting and/or not meeting again. In one scene, they go to the Lilas; they order whiskey; they talk about travel and promise to meet "later." During the "later" at the Select, they talk about Brett's hat, Michael's nose, and a few other trivialities. Then they break up, go to a fight, meet again the next day back at the Select and start drinking and palavering all over again.

These people are on dangerous ground; communication is restrained and indeterminate: they talk about talking; they talk about "other" people and "other" circumstances; they talk about liquor, about affairs, and travel—zealously avoiding personal references which might unhinge the charade of emotional stability which they have barely managed to erect. Each expects the other to be a mind-reader and to interpret his own obscurity. Each expects the other to provide some understanding of unasked questions and to affirm his integrity and his self-worth. But words don't match actions; actions don't match claims; and fantasies and hopes are totally out of sync with what is possible.

Because alcoholics like Jake, Brett, and Mike are likely to embellish their feelings of intimacy with crisis-driven emotions, any possibility for true intimacy may trigger illusions of selective dependence. None of these people seems to have any real understanding of the meaning of love or friendship—in the deepest sense of the word. In the case of Jake and Brett, both are inclined either to deny that they have any kind of connection or to define the relationship in fanciful or catastrophic terms. The consequences of such perceptions are disastrous because neither party is capable of fulfilling the fantasies or ideals of the other with the rigorous consistency that seems to be demanded. In describing the problems of intimacy as they relate to the alcoholic, *Twelve Steps and Twelve Traditions* notes:

> The primary fact that we fail to recognize is our total inability to form a true partnership with another human being. Our egomania digs two disastrous pitfalls. Either we insist upon dominating the people we know, or we depend upon them far too much. If we lean too heavily on people, they will sooner or later fail us, for they are human, too, and cannot possibly meet our incessant demands. In this way our insecurity grows and festers. (53)

An aggressive, manipulative, and self-centered impulse is thus a primary aspect of the alcoholic perception and the alcoholic's relationships with others. Perhaps this is why Jake and Brett articulate fantasies and hopes that exceed the sphere of normalcy, and perhaps this explains why they have chosen to draw judgements that are grounded in chemically induced, self-centered perceptions. Admittedly, there is some talk about the "problem," but these people seem incapable of sincerity, except to complain or commiserate with a superficial regard for any workable solution. Jake drones on about the "old grievance"; Brett tells him she's been "so miserable" (24); the two of them discuss "that hell" after a rousing kiss in the taxi; they agree to "shut up" about Jake's wound; Brett complains that she has to "pay" for what she's done; Jake tells her not to be a fool (25–26). It seems that any opportunity for a genuine conversation about the pain, the frustrations, and the limits and possibilities imposed by circumstance is frustrated by denials, evasions, unanswered objections, tentative groping, or simply a refusal to consider the matter any further.

As far as Jake and Brett are concerned, it is assumed that genital affection is the only option in a male-female relationship; and, denied that possibility, there is no other recourse but to whine about unkind fate, refuse compromise, and dismiss the possibility that sexuality may involve a great deal more than coitus and penile fascination—as any paraplegic would be most glad to explain. In any case, it is blatantly obvious that Jake would rather withdraw into his own misperceived loneliness, absolve himself of any opportunity for a solution, and get drunk.

Jake's congenital preoccupation with evading any substantive consideration of his circumstances is vividly illustrated in his relationship with Bill Gorton. When Jake is with Gorton, his closest friend, he appears to be having a good time—indeed, the experiences and conversation seem a long way from the standard, alcoholically dysfunctional context of so much of the rest of the novel. However, a careful analysis of his behavior might suggest that the friendship is severely limited—indeed, badly strained—by his fear of personal exposure.

Certainly, when the two go fishing in the Pyrenees, the descriptions and the scene are appealing enough. Jake and Bill take a long walk, bait their hooks, discuss where to fish, toss out their lines, get a nice catch, pack it, eat lunch, drink wine, and discuss eggs and drumsticks. Later, having gotten "cock-eyed" on wine, they have a brief conversation about Jake's "problem":

> "Say," Bill said, "what about this Brett business?"
>
> "What about it?"
>
> "Were you ever in love with her?"
>
> "Sure."
>
> "For how long?"
>
> "Off and on for a hell of a long time."
>
> "Oh, hell!" Bill said. " I'm sorry, fella."
>
> "It's all right," I said. "I don't give a damn any more."
>
> "Really?"
>
> "Really. Only I'd a hell of a lot rather not talk about it." (123–24)

And that's the end of it. Bill says he's going to sleep—and he does.

Jake has apparently decided that intimacy must necessarily be predicated on genital voyaging. As a consequence, his prospects for any kind of connectedness to Brett—or anybody else for that matter—fluctuate with maddening irregularity. "I've had plenty to worry about one time or other. I'm through worrying," he says early in the novel (11). Even so, it seems that he has a remarkable penchant for continuing to worry, deny, and rationalize throughout the remainder of the story; indeed, his drunken escapades are an epic study in self-destruction, complaint, and evasion. He tells us at one point that he's gotten a "little drunk," not in any "positive sense," as he calls it, but "enough to be careless" (21). When he's with Brett in a taxi in Paris, they kiss and discuss how his wound is "funny." "I never think about it," he lies. He burbles on to insist that he's "pretty well through with the subject," having considered it from various "angles" (26–27). Of course, he feels like "hell" every time he stops being through; and, indeed, the entire novel is full of liberally sprinkled affirmations that he has quit thinking about his problem.

In trying to deal with circumstances and frustrations, then, Jake and his circle only seem to know how to run from their problems. In this sense, they are typically alcoholic. Indeed, an escapist impulse and an addiction to evasion and denial are hallmarks of the alcoholic perspective. They dash from Paris to the Pyrenees, from the Pyrenees to Pamplona, from Pamplona to Madrid. They dare not stay in any one place too long, and they certainly dare not find any substantive connection with each other. Instead, they are continually setting up the next drama, the next argument or barroom brawl, or the next shattered romance or fouled relationship.

Jake is a seasoned runner who feels powerless, and he hates it. He sets up a party, a trip, an evening; he scurries off to a bar, a hotel, or a sporting event of some sort; his friends congregate, dish out the dirt, cry, joke, confess. And Jake listens—and he says almost nothing. He has found a hook: silence invites talk; talk invites him in. And he doesn't have to do a thing in return. He is the father confessor who has something on everybody and whose own life is a ludicrous mystery. Except for Bill Gorton—whose own status and understanding of Jake are somewhat questionable—no one really seems to know very much about what Jake is really thinking or what he really feels; and this very quality is his attraction: he represents the possibility of a connection without a commitment, a friendship without the gift of intimacy.

Brett too is an accomplished runner. She runs from a defunct marriage; she runs from Jake when he starts getting too close; she runs to Romero; and, having seduced him, she runs away and returns to poor Jake—and always with a drink, or two, or more for support. For Brett, change as a means of resolving fear is not an inside job; change is something imposed on others for the sake of her own insatiable appetite; and, when she fails, as she invariably must, she founders in self-pity, gets drunk, and crashes Jake's apartment to mourn the cruelty of circumstance and to cry on his shoulder. And then she promptly punishes him because she allowed him to penetrate her shell. Early in the novel, when she drags the Count over to Jake's apartment, she comforts the poor sot, tells him she's leaving, takes him out and dances with him, and concludes the evening with a full measure of bittersweet adieus and farewells. "Good night, Jake. Goodnight darling," she purrs. "I won't see you again" (65). The crescendo ascends a pitch higher. They kiss, she pushes him away, they kiss again, and finally she stumbles away to her hotel.

Brett's oscillations are superficial and insubstantial; half the time, she refuses to consider her options. "Isn't there anything we can do about it?" she wonders (26). Then, having asked the question, she denies the possibility of an answer and chooses to suffer in silence. In one scene, typical of many, she complains, "Let's not talk, Talking's all bilge" (55). Back in Paris at the end of the story, she shows up at Jake's apartment, admits that she's broken up with Romero, and concludes, "Oh, hell!" . . . "Let's not talk about it. Let's never talk about it" (242).

Mike is a runner and escapist of a somewhat more decadent complexion. He runs from his infantile preoccupation with being helpless; he runs from his friends and from "friends" who are not friends. He runs from his anger at being "used"; he runs from his dismal failure as a prospective husband; and he runs from his fears that he may be, after all, little more than a drunk. When we meet this jolly English tippler, he's tight; his nose is bloody; and he wants to get laid by Lady Brett who is "a lovely piece" (80). In Pamplona, he gets drunk, fights with Cohn, and seeks refuge in Brett's room. He's pathetic and decent in a weird sort of way, but there really isn't much to redeem this bankrupt, overindulgent patrician—except in his role as a victim of circumstance and the peripheral benefits of codependence.

Like most practicing alcoholics, Jake and his friends are rebels. They don't seem to recognize boundaries; they are hell-bent on testing and bending the rules; and they are obsessed with denying their connectedness with the normal order of things. While Jake spends some of his time writing, preparing for his vacation, ordering his tickets, and undertaking a few other mundane, everyday affairs; we can hardly regard such behavior as substantive evidence of normalcy—indeed, he is in truth generally removed from the mainstream of life. We know very little about his family back in the States, his relationship with Brett is a disaster, and his work doesn't seem to amount to much. At the "office," he reads the papers, smokes, and sits at the typewriter (writing, I assume). Later, he goes out to watch a politico, has lunch, goes back to the "office later"—to do what, God knows (36–40). Mainly, we are told that he stumbles off to his hotel, to the Rotonde, to his flat; he has some drinks, he hails his friends, he goes to the races, has a scene, or in quiet moments he feels just plain crummy.

This is a world of eating and visiting, of race tracks or of "turning up" some place after a four-day blackout—Bill rubs his forehead to describe his loss of memory during a binge in Vienna (70). It is a world of boxing matches, horse cabs, stuffed animals, and bars where no one is especially interested in returning to the States (or to England) and where the idea of a family—in some cases, even marriage—seems to be out of the question. Playing, drinking, and seducing are far more important than work; and risk-taking and "running" command a high priority. What is more to the point, however, is the fact that we, as readers, have hopefully seen enough insanity, enough emptiness, enough self-destruction and self-reproach to discredit the friendships, the values, the drinking, and the lives of these characters. Those who regard the bullfights, the fishing, and the festival at Pamplona as the central focus of the novel could be missing the point. *The Sun Also Rises* is not simply a novel about sterility or the "code" or about re-bellion or running in meaningless circles. Critical as these themes may be, they skirt some important questions about the integrity of the kind of courage, or should we say lack of courage, that Hemingway has tried to portray. While the ring may indeed be a dramatic proving ground for Romero, its values can have little real or workable impact on Jake or any of his friends, except in their role as spectators—and spectatorship automati-cally excludes involvement. For Romero, the ring may demand grace, self-mastery, and control; his actions may be a pretty thing to watch. However, Jake and his friends need none of this. They have already attempted far too much control of appearances, and they give those appearances far too much power as a means leading to an affirmation of self. As spectators, they have learned too well how to pretend grace and mastery of circum-stances which do not involve them and over which they, in truth, really have no control at all.

When Jake and his companions make judgments and translate them-selves to the morality of the bullring, they are transferring the wreckage of their lives to a harmless, irrelevant arena—insofar as they don't have much prospect of being employed as bullfighters or demonstrating grace under pressure to a few thousand fans and aficionados. Because they have degraded themselves as spectators without insisting on the kind of courage they need to confront their own problems, they serve as little more than sterile witnesses to a fabricated tragedy.

Brett, Cohn, Mike, and Jake appear unaware that the true battle-ground of the self, the personal "bullring" of their fears and their wounds and their addictions, lies in how they perceive themselves and how they deal directly with their misfortunes and circumstances. Whatever enjoy-ments or pleasures or health they find, whatever balancing of life's risks and rewards they realize, will only be possible with an honest and fearless inventory of their own conduct, not a superficial fabrication of a code of courage and sensuality that has little to do with the business of living. However, for these alcoholics, such an inventory would be devastating. It would require a great deal more honesty than they are capable of demon-strating, and it would require too heady a dose of the very courage they claim to admire.

On the surface, then, the Hemingway "code" appears to provide a strict set of rules and values defining how the experiences of life, how courage it-self, can be maximized. In this particular case, however, that "code" is degraded by the behavior of Jake, Mike, Brett, and Cohn. It promises order and meaning and resolution, but it can't deliver. The fishing scenes, the mountain idyll, and the friendships are also red herrings. Jake seeks some kind of serenity and some inner balance and wholeness when he goes fishing with Bill Gorton. But the search doesn't work—it can't work. Again, what Jake seeks has to come first from himself; it cannot be generated from a material setting or escapist impulses. In running from himself—in running to a trout stream or the mountains—he is doomed, for he can only find peace in learning to understand and accept himself for what he is. Fish, drink, and run as he does, Jake has yet to learn to accept the fact that there is a great deal that he cannot change; and he has yet to find the courage to change what he can. So the trip is a bust. His nerves are shattered by the arrival of Cohn, by the drinking, by his loneliness and resentment, and by the pain of his wound.

The Sun Also Rises is a portrait of degeneration without solutions. It is a portrait of estrangement and emotional adolescence and "running"; and it is a portrait of a bankrupt value system that depends far too much on appearances and dramatics. It is a novel about spiritual bankruptcy, codependence, and people who enable each other to withdraw and become emotionally impotent because they support each other in erecting a meaningless façade of self-sufficiency and bathos. In the final analysis, it is a novel about people who feel compelled to fabricate a code of conduct that has very little to do with living and even less to do with their own integrity. As such, it is a portrait of what can begin to happen when emotionally damaged people seek refuge from themselves in the desensitizing and addictive effects of liquor where ignorance, insanity, escape, and waste are manifested in abundance.

Notes

1. The inventory of behavioral characteristics which identifies an alcoholic is quite similar, regardless of who is setting up the description. For example, the Christopher D. Smith Foundation asks, in part, whether the lack of a drink leads to tension and whether drinking is used to relieve tension, to escape worries, to escape guilt, to resolve feelings of inferiority or shyness. It further asks if drinking makes the subject irritable, unambitious, detached, self-centered, and resentful (see Smith Foundation, 212–13). The definitions forwarded by such institutions most certainly can provide us with an excellent profile for use in any analysis of the behaviors and perspectives of Jake, Mike, and Brett.

My own observations, experiences, and studies have led me to believe that:

a. The practicing alcoholic suffers from low self-esteem that will very likely be disguised in a mask of grandiosity. That is, most alcoholics have a massive, all-absorbing ego accompanied by an inferiority complex which threatens to undermine the core of their self-esteem.

b. The practicing alcoholic is likely to feel powerless over events, over the behavior of others, and over the conduct of his own life.

c. This feeling of powerlessness can lead him to try to erect a fantasy of control over people, places, and things.

d. It can lead him to rebel against any symbol of authority, whether perceived or real.

e. It can lead him to the illusion that, because he has his external life seemingly under control, he himself is under control.

f. Thus, he will try to manipulate people and circumstances, and he will try to "use" others in the expectation that they will somehow make his world congruent with his needs.

g. It also seems to me that the practicing alcoholic suffers from a great deal of repressed anger. This anger is a mask disguising his fear about his value as a human being and his inability to control events external to himself; it is a defense, a response to the belief that his most intimate needs cannot or will not be satisfied. Of course, the anger is likely to be directed against those held responsible for withholding gratification.

h. Such anger can become depression—anger turned inward—or sullenness and emotional rigidity. It can also erupt violently when the inability to control exterior events becomes obvious and he becomes frustrated.

i. The practicing alcoholic also has difficulty in understanding and sharing his feelings. As a consequence, he feels lonely; and, indeed, he is often a loner and has difficulty making any kind of stable or long-term commitment to others.

j. Finally, it is not at all unusual for the practicing alcoholic to see life in black and white terms. He cannot compromise: small problems and momentary setbacks may frustrate him and appear catastrophic. He may then become childish and self-pitying, and, ultimately, seek release from his feelings in the euphoric and desensitizing effects of liquor.

2. Among recovery groups such as Alcoholics Anonymous, there is considerable discussion and attention given to the problems of individuals who have chosen not to drink any more, but who insist on behaving much the same as a drunk. That is, they manifest feelings of loneliness, anger, resentment, perfectionism, control, denial, and intolerance in much the same manner as if they were drunk. Such people are commonly referred to as "dry drunks."

Works Consulted

Alcoholics Anonymous: The Story of How Many Thousands of Men and Women Have Recovered From Alcoholism, 3d ed. New York: Alcoholics Anonymous World Services, 1976.

Baker, Carlos. *Ernest Hemingway: A Life Story.* New York: Scribner's, 1969, 160–73.

Barnes, Gordon E. "The Alcoholic Personality." *Alcoholism: Introduction to Theory and Treatment.* Ed. David A. Ward, Rev. 2d ed. Dubuque: Kendall/Hunt, 1980, 148–92.

Bier, Jesse, "Liquor and Caffeine in *The Sun Also Rises.*" *American Notes and Queries* 18 (n.d.), 143–44.

Christopher D. Smith Foundation, Inc. *Understanding Alcohol: For the Patient, the Family, and the Employer.* New York: Scribner's, 1969, 212–13.

Dardis, Tom. "Hemingway: I'm No Rummy." *The Thirsty Muse: Alcohol and the American Writer.* New York: Tichnor & Fields, 1989, 155–209.

Forseth, Roger. "Alcohol and the Writer: Some Biographical and Critical Issues (Hemingway)." *Contemporary Drug Problems* 13 (1986), 361–86.

Gelderman, Carol. "Hemingway's Drinking Fixation." *Lost Generation Journal* 6 (1979), 12–14.

Goodwin, Donald W. "Hemingway: Scenes from New York and Havana." *Alcohol and the Writer.* Kansas City: Andrews and McNeel, 1988, 50–72.

Hemingway, Ernest. *The Sun Also Rises.* New York: Scribner's, 1926.

Knauf, Andrew Louis. "Alcohol as Symbolic Buttress in Hemingway's Long Fiction." *Dissertation Abstracts International* 40:4039A–40A.

Lynn, Kenneth. *Hemingway.* New York: Simon & Schuster, 1987.

Twelve Steps and Twelve Traditions. New York: Alcoholics Anonymous World Services, 1986.

Weston, Drake. *Guidebook for Alcoholics: How to Succeed without Drinking.* New York: Exposition Press, 1964, 39–40.

Contradictory Bodies in
The Sun Also Rises

DEBRA A. MODDELMOG

◆　◆　◆

WITH ITS ATTENTION to male bonding and rituals such as fishing, drinking, and bullfighting, *The Sun Also Rises* has become known as "classic Hemingway." Co-existing with these rituals is a thwarted heterosexual relationship—Jake and Brett's—a romantic situation that is also characteristic of Hemingway's fiction. The repetition of this pattern throughout Hemingway's work (e.g., *A Farewell to Arms, For Whom the Bell Tolls, Across the River and Into the Trees, Islands in the Stream*) suggests that Hemingway felt that the intense homosociality of his fiction demanded equally intense heterosexuality to deflect suspicions that either his male characters or he had homosexual tendencies.[1] Yet a closer look at *The Sun Also Rises* reveals that Hemingway's depiction of gender and sexuality is more complex than this description allows. Ironically, in mapping out this territory of interrogation, I will draw upon the very concepts that I claim Hemingway's work problematizes (masculinity/feminity, homosexuality/heterosexuality). As Gayatri Spivak observes, "There is no way that a deconstructive philosopher can say 'something is not something' when the word is being used as a concept to enable his discourse."[2] Despite this paradox, by tracing how Hemingway's texts bring traditional significations of gender and sexuality into conflict, I hope to illustrate that Hemingway's first novel (like one of his last, *The Garden of Eden*) exposes the intellectual limitations that result when "gender" and "sexuality" are read as innocent acts of nature and as fixed binaries.

Early in *The Sun Also Rises,* a scene occurs that seems to establish the gender and sexual ideologies upon which the story will turn: Jake Barnes and Brett Ashley's meeting at a dance club in which Jake is accompanied by a prostitute, Georgette Hobin, and Brett is accompanied by a group of homosexual men. In a poststructuralist reading that provides the starting point for mine, Cathy and Arnold Davidson observe that by switching dancing partners, these characters arrange themselves in different pairings: Jake and Georgette, Jake and Brett, the young men and Brett, the young men and Georgette. These partner exchanges initially suggest "the fundamental equivalence" of the women as well as of the men. Georgette and Brett are conjoined under the pairing of prostitution/promiscuity, just as Jake and the young men are linked under the pairing of sexually maimed/homosexual. Consequently, this episode reveals the contradictions in Jake's own life. Jake relies upon the homosexuality of the young men to define his manhood (at least his desire is the right kind), but that definition is tested by the joint presence of Georgette and Brett, neither of whom Jake has sex with.[3] As the Davidsons conclude, "The terrifying ambiguity of [Jake's] own sexual limitations and gender preferences may well be one source of his anger (it usually is) with Brett's companions, and another reason why he articulates his anger and hatred for them before he reveals his love for her" (92).

But this perceptive reading illuminates only one of the "fundamental equivalences" set up in this scene; further, it fails to recognize that as these equivalences multiply, the glue connecting the descriptive pair loses its adhesive power. Through a series of interchanges, Jake and Brett are equated differently; established relations dissolve and are rearranged into new relations. What began as an inseparable unit (sexually maimed–homosexual) ends up as free-floating terms (sexually maimed, homosexual), and the characters, particularly Jake and Brett, are revealed as bodies of contradictions. Ultimately these pairings challenge the validity of defining gender and sexuality in terms of binarisms—masculine/feminine, heterosexual/homosexual.

For instance, the pairing of Brett and Georgette, like the pairing of Jake and the homosexual men, is complex and multifaceted. The resemblance between the two women is underscored when Jake, half-asleep, thinks that Brett, who has come to visit him, is Georgette (32). Obviously such a correspondence reveals that both women sleep around, one because she believes it's the way she is made (55), the other because it's the way she makes a living. Yet this explanation of motives reminds us that women's outlets for their desires were closely intertwined with economic necessity in the years following World War I, even in the liberated Left Bank of Paris. As a white, heterosexually identified, upper-class woman, Brett still must depend, both financially and socially, on hooking up with one man or another. As Wendy Martin observes, "If Brett has gained a measure of freedom in leaving the traditional household, she is still very much dependent on men, who provide an arena in which she can be attractive and socially active as well as financially secure."[4]

Brett's self-destructive drinking and her attempts to distance herself from sexual role stereotyping—for example, her short hair is "brushed back like a boy's" (22) and she wears a "man's felt hat" (28)—indicate her resentment of this prescribed arrangement. Susan Gubar reminds us that many women artists of the modernist period escaped the strictures of socially defined femininity by appropriating male clothing, which they identified with freedom.[5] For such women, cross-dressing became "a way of addressing and re-dressing the inequities of culturally-defined categories of masculinity and femininity" (Gubar, 479). Like Catherine Bourne of *The Garden of Eden,* Brett Ashley fits this category of women who were crossing gender lines by cross-dressing and behaving in "masculine ways." Although Brett's wool jersey sweater reveals her to be a woman, the exposure is not enough to counter the effect of her masculine apparel and appearance on the men around her. Pedro Romero's urge to both make her look more "womanly" (242) and marry her might be explained as the response of a man raised to demand clear distinctions between the gender roles of men and women. But the attempt of the more carefree Mike Campbell to convince Brett to buy a new hat (79) and to marry him suggests that Brett is dangerously close to overturning the categories upon which male and female identity, and patriarchal power, depend. The "new woman" must not venture too far outside the old boundaries.

Brett's cross-dressing conveys more than just a social statement about gender. It also evokes suggestions of the transvestism practiced by and associated with lesbians of the time (and since). Sexologists such as Havelock Ellis recognized the so-called mannish woman as only one kind of lesbian; nonetheless, the wearing of men's clothing by women was often viewed as sexual coding. Certainly many lesbians chose to cross-dress in order to announce their sexual preference.[6] One hint that we might read Brett's cross-dressing within this context comes in the parallel set up between her and Georgette. When Jake introduces Georgette to a group seated in the restaurant, he identifies her as his fiancée, Georgette Leblanc. As several scholars have pointed out, Georgette Leblanc was a contemporary singer and actress in Paris—and an acknowledged lesbian.[7] This association consequently deepens the symbolic relationship of Brett to Georgette, linking them in a new equation: independent/lesbian. Brett's transvestism crosses over from gender inversion to sexual sign: not only does Brett desire the lesbian's economic and social autonomy but she also possesses same-sex desire.

In fact, Brett's alcoholism and inability to sustain a relationship might be indications not of nymphomania, with which the critics have often charged her, but of a dissatisfaction with the strictures of the male–female relationship. Brett's announcement, for example, that she can drink safely among homosexual men (22) can be taken to mean that she cannot control her own heterosexual desire, though it could also reveal underlying anxiety toward the heterosexual desire of men. Such an anxiety might be related to her abusive marriage, but that experience need not be its only source. As Brett tells Jake after the break-up with Pedro Romero, "I can't even marry Mike" (242). Of course, soon after this, she declares, "I'm going back to Mike. . . . He's so damned nice and he's so awful. He's my sort of thing" (243). Yet even in giving her reasons for returning to Mike, Brett reveals her inner turmoil and ambivalence. Like Mike, she is both "nice" and "awful," and the novel ends before this promised reunion occurs.

We should be careful not to equate Brett's anxiety about male heterosexual desire with lesbian desire nor to presume that unhappy heterosexual relations are a necessary condition for lesbian desire. In fact, Brett's same-sex desire is hinted at in other ways than her cross-dressing and her frustrations with heterosexual men, namely, through her association with her homosexual companions. As Jake states three times, she is "with them," she is "very much with them" (20). This homosexual identification helps to explain Brett's attraction to Jake who, according to Hemingway in a letter written in 1951, has lost his penis but not his testicles and spermatic cord (*Ernest Hemingway: Selected Letters*, 745).[8] If we accept this explanation, Jake lacks the physical feature that has traditionally been the most important in distinguishing sex as well as male sexual desire.[9] He is a sexual invalid and, as a consequence, sexually in-valid.[10] Jake's maleness, masculinity, and heterosexuality, lined up and linked under the law of compulsory heterosexuality, are separated and problematized. Like a woman, Jake has no penis with which to make love with Brett. Instead, Brett ministers to him, "strok[ing] his head" as he lies on the bed (56), and recognizes that the absent male sex organ makes Jake different from other suitors.[11] In this context, Jake's notion that Brett "only wanted what she couldn't have" (31) takes on added meaning. Besides nonpenile sex, she wants to find some way to accommodate the fluidity of sexual desire and gender identification that characterizes her condition.

Brett's affiliation with homosexual men and her transgendering complicate, in turn, Jake's relationship with her. Jake calls Brett "damned good-looking" and describes her hair as being "brushed back like a boy's" (22), two attributions that dissolve into one in Jake's later identification of Pedro Romero as "a damned good-looking boy" (167). Jake's attraction to Brett can be partially attributed to his homosexual desire, a desire that seems about to break through the surface of Jake's narrative at any time.[12] As the Davidsons observe and as I mentioned earlier, this desire can be seen in Jake's conflicted response to Brett's homosexual companions. It can also be seen in Jake's possession of *afición*, which must be confirmed by the touch of other men (132). To quote the Davidsons, there is something "suspect" in the aficionados vesting so much of their manhood in a boylike matador who woos a bull to death through "girlish flirtation and enticement." As a consequence, "the whole ethos of *afición* resembles a sublimation of sexual desire, and the aficionados—serving, guiding, surrounding the matador out of the ring and applauding him in it—seems all, in a sense, steers" (95).

Jake's descriptions of the meeting of the bull and bullfighter imply more than flirtation; the encounter evokes images of sexual foreplay and consummation. He states, "The bull wanted it again, and Romero's cape filled again, this time on the other side. Each time he let the bull pass so close that the man and the bull and the cape that filled and pivoted ahead of the bull were all one sharply etched mass" (217). Later Jake expresses the climax of the bullfight, the bull's death, in terms reminiscent of sexual climax:

[F]or just an instant [Romero] and the bull were one, Romero way out over the bull, the right arm extended high up to where the hilt of the sword had gone in between the bull's shoulders. Then the figure was broken. There was a little jolt as Romero came clear, and then he was standing, one hand up, facing the bull, his shirt ripped out from under his sleeve, the white blowing in the wind, and the bull, the red sword hilt tight between his shoulders, his head going down and his legs settling. (218–19)

Jake's relationships with Bill Gorton and Pedro Romero constitute two of the more important sources of sublimated homosexual desire. During their fishing trip to the Irati River, Bill tells Jake, "Listen. You're a hell of a good guy, and I'm fonder of you than anybody on earth. I couldn't tell you that in New York. It'd mean I was a faggot" (116). In expressing his fondness for Jake, Bill realizes the risk he takes in declaring strong feelings for an-other man. His words might be construed, by himself as well as by others, as an admission of homosexual love. To avoid being interpreted in that way, Bill must declare homosexual desire an impossibility. However, Bill's phrasing in this passage and his subsequent focus on homosexuality sug-gest that such desire is a very real possibility. For one, his statement "I'm fonder of you than anybody on earth" can be read as "I'm fonder of you than I am of anybody else on earth" or as "I'm fonder of you than anybody else is." Either reading elevates Bill and Jake's relationship to a primary po-sition. It is a connection more binding and important than any other rela-tionship Bill has formed.

In addition, Bill's worry that disclosing his affection for Jake would, in New York, mean that he is "a faggot" indicates Bill's awareness of the insta-bility of the line separating homosocial and homosexual behavior and de-sire. Outside the geographic and psychological boundaries of New York and its taxonomy of deviance, Bill's feelings are platonic; inside those bound-aries, they are homosexual.[13] Bill's concern about the boundaries for same-sex relationships indicates that he cannot be sure about the "purity" of his feelings for Jake or of Jake's for him. In an early draft of the novel, Bill's ob-session and concern are even more apparent. Bill tells Jake that New York circles have marked him (Bill) as "crazy." "Also I'm supposed to be crazy to get married. Would marry anybody at any time. . . . Since Charley Gor-don and I had an apartment together last winter, I suppose I'm a fairy. That probably explains everything." Bill also reinforces his awareness, and fear, of the instability of sexual identity when he attacks the literary world of New York by claiming that "every literary bastard" there "never goes to bed at night not knowing but that he'll wake up in the morning and find himself a fairy. There are plenty of real ones too" (quoted in Mellow, 312–13).

Even though Hemingway eventually cut this passage about fairies and the unstable sexual identities of "literary bastards," the anxieties it ex-presses remain in the published text. Having stated his fondness for Jake, Bill moves the discussion away from their relationship, but he cannot drop the subject of homosexuality: "That [homosexual love] was what the Civil War was about. Abraham Lincoln was a faggot. He was in love with General Grant. So was Jefferson Davis. . . . Sex explains it all. The Colonel's Lady and Judy O'Grady are Lesbians under their skin" (116). By identifying ho-mosexual desire as the cause of all private and public action, a supposedly absurd exaggeration, Bill defuses the tension that expressing his affection for Jake creates. Yet homosexuality is still very much in the air—and "under their skin."

This homosexual current flowing through the text reaches its crisis at the same time that the heterosexuality of the text is also at its highest tension: during the liaison that Jake arranges between Brett and Pedro. As we have seen, Jake describes Pedro in terms that repeat his descriptions of Brett. Further, his first impression of the bullfighter is a physical one—"He was the best-looking boy I have ever seen" (163)—and his later observations continue this focus on Pedro's body. Jake tells Brett that Pedro is "nice to look at" (184), notices his clear, smooth, and very brown skin (185), and describes Pedro's hand as being "very fine" and his wrist as being small (185). Considering the way Jake gazes upon Pedro's body (a body that, like Brett's, blends male and female, masculine and feminine), the moment when Jake brings together Pedro and Brett is also the moment when the text reveals its inability to separate heterosexual from homosexual desire within the desiring body.

This scene has typically been read as the tragic fulfillment of a traditional love triangle in which two men want the same women and desire moves heterosexually: Jake wants Brett who wants Pedro who wants Brett. Yet given the similarity in the way Jake describes Brett and Pedro, given Jake's homoerotic depictions of the bullfighter's meeting with the bull, and given the sexual ambiguities embodied by Brett and Jake, it seems more accurate to view this relationship not as a triangle but as a web in which desire flows in many directions. When Brett and Pedro consummate their desire for each other, Pedro also becomes Jake's surrogate, fulfilling his desire for Brett and hers for him, while Brett becomes Jake's "extension" for satisfying his infatuation with Pedro. Although Jake is physically and phallically absent from Pedro and Brett's "honeymoon" (190), his desire is multiply and symbolically present. Of course, the inadequacy of a figurative presence is disclosed when Brett persists in telling Jake the details of her relationship with Pedro, a verbal reenactment that drives him to overeat and overdrink.

The final scene of the novel situates Jake between the raised baton of the policeman, an obvious phallic symbol and representative of the Law, and the pressure of Brett's body. Such a situation suggests that the novel does not stop trying to bridge the multiple desires of its characters. However, Brett's wishful statement—"we could have had such a damned good time together"—and Jake's ironic question—"Isn't it pretty to think so?" (247)—reveal that at least part of the failure, part of the "lostness," conveyed in the novel is that such a bridge cannot be built. The prescriptions for masculinity and femininity and for heterosexuality and homosexuality are too strong to be destroyed or evaded, even in a time and place of sexual and gender experimentation.

As my analysis suggests, to explore the fundamental equivalences implied in the dancing club scene and their reverberations throughout *The Sun Also Rises* leads to constructing a network of ambiguities and contradictions pertaining to sexuality and gender. As I admitted earlier, in creating such a construction, I have had to draw upon the very concepts that I claim Hemingway's novel calls into question (masculinity/femininity, homosexuality/heterosexuality). But by refusing to qualify or resolve the contradictions surrounding these categories and by focusing attention upon the points at which they conflict, we see that Hemingway's novel puts gender and sexuality into constant motion. Although modern society attempts to stabilize conduct and appearance as masculine or feminine, and desire as homosexual, heterosexual, or bisexual, it is still not easy to contain and categorize desire and behavior. Actions, appearance, and desire in *The Sun Also Rises* spill over the "normal" boundaries of identity and identification so that categories become destabilized and merge with one another.

This is not to say that Brett and Jake have discarded society's scripts for femininity and masculinity, or for heterosexuality and homosexuality, in favor of more contemporary concepts such as transgendered or queer. Their actions, particularly Brett's flirtations and Jake's homophobia, show that they know these scripts well. Nevertheless, as we see by following the several parallels suggested in the club scene, both Jake and Brett continually stray from the lines the scripts demand. The text asks us to suspect, and finally to critique, those systems of representation that are insufficient and hence disabling to efforts to comprehend the human body and its desires.

Notes

1. Peter F. Cohen has recently presented an argument regarding the intense male bonds in *A Farewell to Arms* that coincides with the one I make in this chapter regarding *The Sun Also Rises*. Drawing upon Eve Sedgwick's contention that male homosocial behavior lies on the same continuum as male homosexual desire, Cohen proposes that "Rinaldi 'trafficks' Catherine between himself and Frederic as a means of eroticizing his relationship with his roommate," " 'I Won't Kiss You . . . I'll Send Your English Girl': Homoerotic Desire in *A Farewell to Arms*," *Heming-*

way Review 15, no. 1 (1995), 45. Although my argument posits a more comprehensive circulation of desire among the characters, Cohen has recognized that a Hemingway heroine might serve as an erotic go-between for two Hemingway heroes.

2. Gayatri Spivak, "A Response to 'The Difference Within': Feminism and Critical Theory," in *The Difference Within: Feminism and Critical Theory,* ed. Elizabeth Meese and Alice Parker (Philadelphia: John Benjamin, 1989), 213.

3. Arnold Davidson and Cathy Davidson, "Decoding the Hemingway Hero in *The Sun Also Rises,"* in *New Essays on* The Sun Also Rises, ed. Linda Wagner-Martin (Cambridge: Cambridge University Press, 1987), 89–92.

4. Wendy Martin, "Brett Ashley as New Woman in *The Sun Also Rises,"* in *New Essays on* The Sun Also Rises, ed. Linda Wagner-Martin (Cambridge: Cambridge University Press, 1987), 71.

5. Susan Gubar, "Blessings in Disguise: Cross-Dress as Re-Dressing for Female Modernists," *Massachusetts Review* 22 (1981), 478.

6. George Chauncey observes that Havelock Ellis, like other contemporary sexologists, attempted to differentiate sexual object choice from sexual roles and gender characteristics, an attempt reflected in the distinguishing of the sexual invert from the homosexual. Chauncey also notes, however, that the sexologists were less willing to apply this distinction to women. Hence, whereas Ellis could claim that male homosexuals were not necessarily effeminate or transvestites, he was less capable of separating a woman's behavior in sexual relations from other aspects of her gender role. See Chauncey, "Sexual Inversion," 124–25. For example, although he maintained that transvestism was unrelated to homosexuality, in Ellis's own "Sexual Inversion," he still provided numerous examples of lesbian transvestites and insisted that even lesbians who dressed in "female" attire usually showed some "masculine" traits in their clothing. Ellis also believed that a keen observer could detect "psychic abnormality" in a woman by watching her behavior. "The brusque energetic movements, the attitude of the arms, the direct speech, the inflexions of the voice, the masculine straight-forwardness and sense of honor, and especially the attitude towards men, free from any suggestion either of shyness or audacity will often suggest the underlying psychic abnormality," "Sexual Inversion in Women," *Alienist and Neurologist* 16 (1895), 153.

Ellis's observations reflect his entrenchment in a heterosexual norm, assuming, as Shari Benstock remarks of many critics, that "all lesbian behavior has in common its *reaction* to the norm of compulsory heterosexuality and that all lesbians act out their sexual orientation in the same way—here, through cross-dressing." Benstock points out that different behavior patterns existed among members of the Parisian lesbian community of the 1920s (as they do among lesbian communities today) and suggests that many lesbians of the Left Bank based their choices on the sexuality of their audience. *Women of the Left Bank: Paris, 1900–1940* (Austin: University of Texas Press, 1986), 179–80.

7. Apparently, Hemingway did not feel kindly toward Georgette Leblanc. In a letter to Ezra Pound (c. 2 May 1924), Hemingway noted that Margaret Anderson was in Paris with "Georgette Mangeuse [man-eater] le Blanc," *Ernest Hemingway: Selected Letters, 1917–1961,* ed. Carlos Baker (New York: Scribner's, 1981), 115. But whether he knew her personally is uncertain. According to Bertram Sarason, Margaret Anderson claimed that Leblanc had never met Hemingway and did not know her name had been mentioned in the novel. *Hemingway and The Sun Set* (Washington, D.C.: Microcard Editions, 1972), 81. Interestingly, Jake's identification of Georgette Hobin as Georgette Leblanc suggests a special kind of knowledge about prostitutes that circulated at the time. In "Sexual Inversion," Havelock Ellis remarks that the frequency of homosexuality among prostitutes is very high, especially in Paris, 210. He quotes a friend who states, "From my experience of the Parisian prostitute, I gather that Lesbianism in Paris is extremely prevalent; indeed, one might almost say normal. In particular, most of the chahut-dancers of the Moulin-Rouge, Casino de Paris, and the other public balls are notorious for going in couples, and, for the most part, they prefer not to be separated, even in their most professional moments with the other sex," 211.

8. Also compare Hemingway's description several years later during his interview with George Plimpton in which he states that Jake's testicles "were intact and not damaged. Thus he was capable of all normal feelings as a *man* but incapable of consummating them. The important distinction is that his wound was physical and not psychological and that he was not emasculated," Interview, in *Writers at Work: The Paris Review Interviews,* 2d ser., ed. George Plimpton (New York: Penguin, 1977), 230; original emphasis. [Reprinted in this volume.]

9. Although this kind of statement does not need verifying, given the phallo-centrism of our society, a quote from Havelock Ellis will contextualize Jake's wound in its historical time: "It is easy to understand why the penis should occupy this special place in man's thoughts as the supreme sexual organ. It is the one conspicuous and prominent portion of the sexual apparatus, while its aptitude for swelling and erecting itself involuntarily, under the influence of sexual emotion, gives it a peculiar and almost unique position in the body. At the same time it is the point at which, in the male body, all voluptuous sensation is concentrated, the only normal masculine center of sex," "Erotic Symbolism," vol. 3, *Studies in the Psychology of Sex* (New York: Random House, 1936), 123.

10. Peter Messent's essay on *The Sun Also Rises,* in *New Readings of the American Novel* (London: Macmillan Education, 1990), 92, suggested this play on words. Although he does not state the matter as I have, he also seems to have borrowed this idea

from Sandra M. Gilbert, "Costumes of the Mind: Transvestism as Metaphor in Modern Literature," *Critical Inquiry* 7 (1980), 409.

11. Peter Messent has also recently explored gender fluidity in *The Sun Also Rises,* and his reading lends support to many of the suppositions I set forth here. Messent states, "In *The Sun Also Rises,* gender roles have lost all stability," 112. Among other things, he points to Georgette's sexual forwardness with Jake, Brett's pre-dawn visit to Jake's room after he retired there with a "headache," the count's bringing of roses to Jake, and Jake's crying, 114.

12. As support for this argument, consider Susan Gubar's suggestion that seductive cross-dressers "can function as sex symbols for men, reflecting masculine attitudes that range from an attempt to eroticize (and thereby possess) the independent woman to only slightly submerged homosexual fantasies," 483. While I do not discount the first possibility (eroticism in the service of possession), here I am tracing the latter function.

13. In *Gay New York* (New York: Basic Books, 1994), George Chauncey argues that only in the 1930s, 1940s, and 1950s "did the now-conventional division of men into 'homosexuals' and 'heterosexuals,' based on the sex of their sexual partners, replace the division of men into 'fairies' and 'normal men' on the basis of their imaginary gender status as the hegemonic way of understanding sexuality," 13. But Chauncey also notes that "exclusive heterosexuality became a precondition for a man's identification as 'normal' in middle-class culture at least two generations before it did so in much of Euro-American and African-American working class culture," 14. To outside observers of the homosexual subculture, "faggot," in the 1930s, would have been the equivalent of "queer" and "fairy." However, to insiders, "queer" was reserved for men who had a homosexual interest, whereas "fairy" and "faggot" referred only to those men "who dressed or behaved in what they considered to be a flamboyantly effeminate manner," *Gay New York,* 15–16. Bill's comment about how his words and feelings might be interpreted in New York seem to indicate an awareness that he would be seen as inverting norms of both gender and sexuality.

Whiteness and the Rejected Other in *The Sun Also Rises*

DANIEL S. TRABER

◆　◆　◆

WORK IN THE FIELD of whiteness studies commonly treats white racial identity in terms of its constructed quality and the privileges unfairly rewarded to white people. The prevalent critical standpoint is thus that whites work to protect whiteness. In contrast, this essay will focus on a white literary character—authored, perhaps surprisingly, by Ernest Hemingway—who rejects particular dominant versions of whiteness. In *The Sun Also Rises,* Jake Barnes has often, and rightly, been treated as a conflicted protagonist attempting to strike a balance between pre- and postwar narratives to endure a meaningless world. In this light, he can be read as a figure of hybridity who mixes identities to avoid claiming allegiance to any one totalizing narrative. Ultimately, it is the Basque peasants, situated sufficiently outside and within the center, to whom Hemingway has Jake turn as a viable Other to give his world meaning. But rather than concentrate on how this Spanish Other is represented in the novel, I wish to interrogate those forms of marginality Jake withdraws from, specifically Jews and homosexuals.

Jake is easily read as anti-Semitic and homophobic, but by examining how "whiteness" is used to denote a privileged economic and social class we can move closer to a more nuanced understanding of Hemingway's intentions as subversive, though hardly without paradox. What follows is not necessarily to be taken as an apologia intent on clearing Hemingway, or Jake, of charges of homophobia or racism; however, I do intend to complicate the way Hemingway is today so easily written off in American literary studies—put on exhibit as a fossilized exemplar of all that is wrong with the canon. Hemingway's evaluation and fictional treatment of forms of otherness according to a rejected notion of centered whiteness reveals a complicated critical politics existing simultaneously with prejudice. Jake's convoluted identity quest allows us to see how marginality is deployed by Hemingway, and Jake's refusal of particular othered identities exposes something other than a facile bigotry.

Michael Harper argues that Hemingway has a "preoccupation with characters who exist on the fringes of society . . . [and] it is among the outcast and the despised, the incompletely or unsuccessfully 'socialized,' that an alternative has the best chance of flourishing."[1] In the relationship Hemingway has with various marginal identities and the center this idea is both true and untrue. As a character in transition and exploring options of subjectivity, Jake's beliefs and practices are underpinned by politics. The anti-Semitism voiced in the novel has always been problematic for readers, and recent critical interest in Jake's homophobia has reopened the issue of how forms of otherness—women, Jews, gays, and blacks—are approached by Hemingway. But Robert Stephens's rationale for the plot's exclusion of certain characters calls attention to the fact that white, Christian, heterosexual men and women are equally guilty of breaking the Hemingway code:

> The outsiders are those like Robert Cohn, Mrs. Braddocks, Robert Prentiss, the artist Zizi, the bal musette homosexuals, and the Paris and Pamplona tourists who are unhaunted by *nada,* have no real cause for rebellion against their societies, and are messy and undisciplined as they imitate without comprehension the actions of the insiders.[2]

Of course, these are specific characters with specific narrative functions— to express ideas through word and action—but it is a mistake to disregard how some social types are given more degrading duties than others. The narrative snipes directed at those occupying certain socially marginal subject positions exhibit a bias more attuned to a mindset of the past than any supposed freedom of progressive modern thought. To understand the criterion Jake uses to determine the forms of marginality worth appropriating it is necessary to analyze the groups chosen to portray the negative side of the Lost Generation. And Cohn and the *bal musette* homosexuals are the figures who best delineate where such boundaries get drawn.

Hemingway's ability to offer social commentary and facilitate characterization through a self-conscious manipulation of derogatory racial and ethnic slurs—a deft maneuvering that absolutely proves he is capable of recognizing racism—is already found in the story collection *In Our Time,* published prior to *The Sun Also Rises.* An unequivocal example of this is found in the chapter 8 vignette featuring the word "wops." This piece depicts American nativism at its worst, resulting in the death of two foreigners by a policeman named Boyle who fires without warning. While his partner is worried about the possible repercussions of the act, the murderer fully understands the racial climate of the times: "They're wops, ain't they? Who the hell is going to make any trouble?"[3] It is with the heaviest of critical irony that an Irish American cop claims he "can tell wops a mile off," since the victims are actually Hungarians. Hemingway is critiquing the kind of assimilation a "Boyle" makes once he adopts the hatred toward the Other—defined as anyone different from himself—that constitutes "white" America's racial policy.

A more complex application of racial slurs occurs in "The Battler," where the African American character Bugs is referred to through a careful shuttling between the terms "negro" and "nigger." One might accuse Hemingway of essentialist racism in having Nick "know" Bugs is black by his voice and walk before he can more clearly see the man, but the significance of Nick's perceptions becomes clearer once Bugs's submissive demeanor around Ad Francis and Nick is established. "The negro" is the term most frequently used in reference to Bugs, but it is those "nigger legs" and the deferential "Mister" that Bugs uses when addressing the white men that tell us more about Bugs's oppressed condition as a black man and Hemingway's possible racial politics.[4] While "negro" lacks the intentional racism of "nigger" (putting aside the issue of how scientific discourses created this racial nomenclature and conferred legitimacy upon institutionalized racism), it nonetheless remains problematic, since Hemingway has named Bugs yet continually chooses to identify him by a racial category, in effect reducing him to that category. However, race may be exactly what Hemingway hopes to emphasize, for by constantly reminding the reader of Bugs's blackness he offers a foil to Ad's psychotic behavior and the train brakeman's own violent treatment of Nick. Of course, this plot tactic opens the question of a black character once again being placed in the stereotypical dutiful and benevolent role; however, such a degree of ambiguity in Hemingway's management of otherness should forestall a too easy condemnation or apology for the way he presents such figures.[5]

In *The Sun Also Rises,* any overly generalized conclusion about Hemingway's opinion of Jews as a group proves equally difficult. In Hemingway's letters we find anti-Semitic slurs used casually, yet the correspondence also exhibits close friendships with Jews, particularly Harold Loeb (the source for Robert Cohn) and Gertrude Stein.[6] It is unwise to draw too close a connection between Hemingway's work and his life without recognizing how he manipulates the "facts," as critics like Frederic Svoboda and Michael S. Reynolds remind us.[7] Nonetheless, it is significant that Hemingway openly expresses feelings of friendship for Harold Loeb in his letters. Prior to their falling out one is struck by how insistent Hemingway is that Loeb come to visit him; he is "sad as hell," he tells Loeb, "that you're not coming [to Austria]. We'd have had such a hell of a good time."[8] In his apology to Loeb, written the night of their infamous argument in Pamplona, Hemingway is effusive in his repentance and highly self-critical: "I'm thoroly ashamed of the way I acted and the stinking, unjust uncalled for things I said."[9] Even this limited evidence suggests that Hemingway is more guilty, at least in *The Sun Also Rises,* of being angry with a particular Jew and permitting himself to take the low road of racist stereotyping to "fight" Loeb in his writing than of wielding an uncritical anti-Semitism. Yet such a biographical explanation does not fully account for how Hemingway uses the Jewish Other in his first novel.

Criticism of Robert Cohn's negative depiction as a Jewish character is hardly the result of any recent awakening in ethical consciousness, for it followed close on the heels of the novel's publication. In a December 1926 letter to Maxwell Perkins, in which Hemingway dismisses the reaction of critics to the immoral and "unattractive" characters, he is prompted to defend his portrayal of Cohn: "And why not make a Jew a bounder in literature as well as in life? Do Jews always have to be so splendid in writing?"[10] This rhetorical appeal to common sense and the logic of realism has failed to convince many readers there is no ulterior motive behind a Jew being selected to play the author's primary whipping boy. And rightly so, for our ability to make sense of Cohn, as well as how otherness as a whole is articulated by Hemingway, depends on answering the question of this character's function in the novel.

Linda Wagner-Martin reads the stereotyping as Hemingway keeping to his pattern of splitting off from a mentor, in this case Gertrude Stein—a Jew whose lesbianism was hardly kept in the closet. This explanation carries weight when one recalls how Jake feminizes Cohn by accusing him of being "moulded by the two women who had trained him," suggesting that the author feared being considered solely the product of Stein's influence.[11] Wagner-Martin's idea becomes doubly significant in view of the history of Harold Loeb and Hemingway's relationship. In *The Way It Was* (1959), Loeb's memoirs of the period, he claims to have helped get *In Our Time* published by Liveright. Both Hemingway's letters and Loeb's narrative tell a story of two close friends who genuinely care for, enjoy, and respect each other until their falling out over a woman. In fact, he and Hemingway shared the same opinion of the Lost Generation. Loeb criticizes Duff Twysden's fiancé, Pat Guthrie, as "typical, I suspected, of that fraction of the British upper class which chooses parasitism for a vocation."[12] This similarity of opinion, in conjunction with Loeb's assistance with the publishers, may be why Hemingway wanted to cut himself off from his one-time friend. Loeb's recollections of the time also reveal, if we are willing to take him at his word thirty years after the events, the extent to which Hemingway manipulates his characterization of Robert Cohn. There is a good deal that corresponds to Loeb's life, but the details informing Jake's rejection of Cohn do not; namely, the elite social background of the upper class that Hemingway/Jake associates Cohn with, but that Loeb presents himself as having rejected.

This authorial control over character adds credence to Josephine Knopf's reading, which locates Cohn in Jewish literary traditions as the stock type "shlemiel," a bumbling trickster who consistently fails, yet serves as a device for social criticism.[13] Knopf convincingly argues that Cohn's infractions of the expatriate code offer Hemingway an opportunity to present this Jewish character as "somewhat beyond the pale of the peculiar society in which he functioned, and somewhat superior to it," thus having the chance "either to make meaningful social commentary or to develop insights concerning the condition of man."[14] But Hemingway does not take that opening; instead, he uses Cohn as the foil to Jake (despite their being doubles as writers who have certain romantic impulses) and relies on a characterization easily read as suggesting that "the traits of meanness, corruption, and weakness are somehow closely bound up with Jewishness."[15]

Michael Reynolds appeals for a degree of clemency being granted to Hemingway on the grounds of historical context and accuracy: anti-Semitism, as well as anti-Catholicism and racism, were rampant during this period, so Hemingway is to be treated as a man shaped by his time: "To fault Hemingway for his prejudice is to read the novel anachronistically. . . . The novel's anti-Semitism tells us little about its author but a good deal about America in 1926. To forget how we were in the twenties is to read the novel out of context."[16] This evasion strikes me as too easy, as though Hemingway were incapable of changing his opinions, especially when we recall that Jake mentions how Robert became "race-conscious" at Princeton (4). The phrase implies that Hemingway, as well as his narrator, understands what it means to treat someone differently because of race or ethnicity—and, consequently, that some will consider anti-Semitic utterances in the novel to be immoral. Hence, Hemingway depicts Jake as *choosing* to express certain "racist" opinions about Robert, based on his Jewishness, that cannot simply be traced to Hemingway's socialization in a specific historical moment.[17] This is a conscious act of labeling; therefore, it behooves us to analyze why that choice is made.

To Reynolds's credit (as well as John Rouch's) he does observe the control Hemingway has over representing *Jake's* representation of Robert Cohn.[18] But what of the authorial and narratorial control Jake is granted by Hemingway? To overlook the centrality of Jake Barnes as the narrator diminishes our understanding of the novel's purpose: Hemingway's possible message of hope and durability for a society so mired in meaninglessness. Jake is as guilty as anyone of making prejudiced comments (most memorably about noses, stubbornness, and money), but much of the overtly malicious anti-Semitism in the novel is put in the mouths of the people whom Jake is gradually growing tired of—those he deliberately depicts himself casting aside. Mike's cruel treatment of Cohn during the festival, by continually targeting his Jewishness, is hardly intended to win the approbation of readers. Indeed, the other members of the group are shocked by the level of hatred Mike spews forth. It is even explicitly condemned by Bill Gorton—"I don't like Cohn . . . but nobody has any business to talk like Mike"—who has proven himself bigoted toward Jews and blacks (145). Yet a character like Bill proves useful for noting how Hemingway complicates matters, since he often plays the role of comic relief. Bill's frequent use of irony, added on top of Jake's own, causes some of his racist comments to fall into a gray area. A prime example is when he speaks of an African-American boxer being cheated in Vienna. Bill begins his story by saying there is "injustice everywhere" but then uses the term "nigger" throughout; Hemingway/Jake even has Bill toss in a touch of supposed black dialect with "musta" (71). Is this to be read as a racist blindspot or an example of facetious (even cynical) dark humor? It is hard to tell, for although there are several unequivocal moments when Bill speaks the language of racism with reference to Cohn, his instances of anticonservative irony, such as the several times he openly ridicules organized religion, work to confuse the political identity one can attach to him; thus Hemingway/Jake disrupts the reader's ability to make meaning or achieve sure closure.[19]

The same ambiguity can be applied to Jake's varied responses to the Other. At the club Zelli's, after dinner with Brett and Count Mippipopolous, Jake nonchalantly refers to the jazz musician as a "nigger drummer" who is "all teeth and lips" (62). There are neither details nor commentary offered to suggest a sense of irony. Nor does Jake interpret (and thus license the reader to interpret) the drummer's behavior—including his spoken "Hahre you?" and "Thaats good"—as the mask an African American must don to appease the white folks who pay his salary. This representation of a black Other (the only one Jake "himself" makes in the novel) seems an irrefutable example of racism on Hemingway/Jake's part. Yet consider the significance of the preceding chapter, in which Jake calls attention to his authorial position by confessing complicity in negatively representing Cohn: "somehow I feel I have not shown Robert Cohn clearly" and "I probably have not brought it [Robert's cheerfulness] out" (45). Here he suggests the impossibility of objective writing and that his statements should not be taken as unquestionable truths. No matter how stripped down the language or submerged the iceberg, authorial bias will enter the (re)presentation of characters and events. As with the treatment of Bugs in "The Battler," it would seem Hemingway is subtly undermining the very racism he has his characters display.

Hemingway ensures that any analysis of Jake is slippery because so many of his statements about Cohn are contradictory as articulations of either inclusion or exclusion. Jake says he likes Cohn (he even includes him in his prayers at the cathedral in Pamplona [97]), but he will later claim to dislike him; he feels sorry for Cohn and then deliberately withholds sympathy; he feminizes Cohn as highly emotional and childish, yet has this unmasculine man physically conquer the novel's two code heroes by knocking Jake out and pummeling Pedro Romero into a bloody mess. Additionally, given Jake's Catholicism, a fact he often mentions, Jake and Cohn are both members of religious groups suffering prejudice against immigrants during the nineteenth and twentieth centuries.[20] Karen Brodkin notes that nineteenth-century "anti-Catholicism and anti-Semitism overlapped and fused with racial stigmatization of southern and eastern Europeans;" add to this the Ku Klux Klan's powerful and popular nativist voice in the 1920s against these religious Others and we have Hemingway deploying a strategically placed ambivalence which forces one to find a reason, beyond simply charging the author and/or narrator with anti-Semitism and racism, to understand why Cohn is anathema to Jake.[21]

Some reasons for Cohn being depicted so negatively are obvious: he has sex with Brett (a pleasure Jake will never be able to experience), he does not follow the code (especially the rule about emotional control in public), and as Jake's double figure he is an ever-present reminder of Jake's own proclivity for sentimental yearning. Jake has the same impossible romantic feelings for Brett, but he learns how to deal with them and continue existing without experiencing a full-fledged breakdown like Robert. Jake has achieved the kind of identity Cohn never will; he can be read as a hybrid made from equal parts of the old and new narratives who makes the leap a person like Cohn is incapable of making. Of all his offenses, the major one is still Cohn's inability to live according to the code, but this should be linked to what proves an equally important facet of Cohn's characterization: his social background.[22]

Robert is the product of one of the wealthiest and oldest Jewish families in New York. (Harold Loeb was born in 1891, related to the Guggenheims on his mother's side.) Hemingway may have come from an upper middle-class environment but that facet of Hemingway's life is never clearly ascribed to Jake. Thus it is notable that in a text so concerned with details and using words sparingly that the reader is given scenes and signifiers that emphasize Cohn's privileged upbringing. I will point to three key moments. First, during an argument over Brett, Robert angrily stands up and demands that Jake "take back" a disparaging but true remark he made about Brett. Jake responds with, "Oh, cut out the prep-school stuff" (39). Second, after the fight in Pamplona (once again over Brett) in which Robert knocks Jake out, in the midst of describing Cohn's bawling apology Jake mentions that he is wearing "a white polo shirt [a button-down oxford], the kind he'd worn at Princeton" (194). Third, Cohn offers a social climber's reason for being impressed by Brett: her "breeding" and title (38).

These instances mark Robert as a well-born, well-bred and well-financed person; he is the antithesis of the marginality found in the Basque peasants, and that is why Jake turns away from Cohn as a source of otherness. Robert's consciousness is shaped by his connection to the Ivy League set and connotes a deeply held world view rooted in the status quo that Jake finds retrograde. Cohn's mentality and behavior—prepared to fight to protect the good name of his "lady love" (178)—are indicative of values he has been taught in prestigious schools and read in romantic novels. Jake too refers to the past to understand his place in the world, but the ideals Cohn supports are useless to him. Hence, the rejection of Robert Cohn supersedes merely his "race"; it is the combination of social origin and code-breaking that invalidates him.[23]

Jean-Paul Sartre's philosophy of otherness posits that forms of marginality can be used to break the binds of society, allowing one to become more "authentic" by rejecting a society's normative values.[24] In *Anti-Semite and Jew,* he theorizes Jewish otherness (admittedly in a romantic and often essentialist manner) as a subversive threat to white Western society's self-conception as "civilized" and superior. Therefore, according to Sartre, non-Jews should try to emulate the Jewish Other by placing themselves outside the center; Jews themselves should resist the desire to assimilate into bourgeois society or to "pass" for non-Semite. Sartre's perspective cannot be wholly attributed to Jake; nevertheless, it does offer a perspective for understanding Jake's reaction to Cohn that allows us to go deeper than noting a callous anti-Semitism. Like Sartre's "inauthentic Jew," Cohn has spent his life trying to shape himself according to the mainstream standards of "civility;" thus, he fails to be a transgressive source at the level of social marginality.[25] This character offers a way to think about whiteness as the dominant identity of the center, one constituting a specific economic and social class based on the assumed superiority of a certain race.

The signifiers of the American upper class—boarding school, Princeton, polo shirts—attributed to Cohn can also be read as marking a virulent form of privileged white identity. Indeed, the details Jake gives the reader suggest that Cohn's wealthy family—which, being one of the oldest, arrived before the massive wave of Jewish immigration in the late nineteenth and early twentieth centuries—has trained him to desire assimilation in order to carry on the family's mission of achieving acceptance. Cohn occupies a privileged place at the center of marginalized peoples, all the while trying to gain access to that more central culture of affluent whites. Jake uses a biblical allusion to describe Cohn's reaction to Brett as akin to the Hebrews' upon entering the "promised land," and this reference can be extended as a comment on the Americanized version of the promised land as wealth and higher social status—the dream Brett represents in Cohn's imagination (22). Thus Robert is depicted by Hemingway/Jake as accepting legitimized hierarchical notions of racial superiority and discarding the subversive potential of his own otherness.

Ron Berman comments on this situation: "Cohn too wants to be transformed, but the issue resolves itself into one of social identity: he wants not only to escape Paris and the civilized condition but to escape himself as he is seen by others. Cohn is a rootless Jew . . . who imitates exhausted Protestantism."[26] Yet, while noting that "Cohn becomes or tries to become what Hemingway refused to become," Berman misses a particular ramification of this move by focusing solely on the non-Semites' reactions to Cohn as a "false gentleman" in a defensive response to his attempted assimilation (45, 44).[27] This is surely applicable to the characters other than

Jake who speak of Brett needing to stay with her own "kind," but the novel's narrator expresses no concern about the matter (102, 203). It is rather the problem of Cohn's willingness to adopt that identity itself that bothers Jake. What is revealed is not the source for his occasional expressions of anti-Semitism, but instead Jake's repudiation of Cohn's maneuvering to affiliate himself with an elitist Anglo-Saxonism through the likes of Brett and Mike (the holders of "true" Anglo-Saxon "blood") that will give him further access to all the privileges and abuses the upper class enjoy with their closed version of whiteness. This is the identity Cohn desires; therefore, Jake chooses to dissociate himself from Cohn in the same way he eventually dismisses Brett and Mike.

The novel's negative treatment of otherness may seem more obvious with homosexuality, but it too has deeper ramifications as a comment on the code and, at a further level, on race. At the Parisian *bal musette,* a group of young gay men arrives with Brett, at which point Jake commences to objectify them according to their appearance and behavior, all the while scornfully referring to the group as "them" or "they." In their article deconstructing the novel's code hero, Arnold and Cathy Davidson theorize Jake's negative reaction as an act of othering: "Jake may be ill-equipped to deal with Brett's sexuality, but not from lack of desire. Lacking such desire, the gay men who accompany Brett are thus defined as Other—not men, not Jake."[28] Jake's dislike for this group stems from their having the ability to sexually "act like men" but choosing to conduct themselves otherwise when Jake lacks that choice. Several critics have called attention to the fact that Jake finds himself in the role of a feminized male due to his war wound; therefore, he too is a sexual Other, yet one aiming to reassure himself of his own masculinity in conventional terms.[29]

In Paris, Hemingway presents a world of inverted gender roles: boys who like boys; girls who dress like boys; boys who weep like girls and plead with their lovers; boys who must perform sex like girls because they lack a penis (which is not the sole means of truly distinguishing one from the other). I agree with Peter Messent and David Blackmore that Hemingway views these changes more as a threat than signs of a new world open to diverse, multiple forms of being.[30] Queerness threatens Jake's discourse of masculinity, reminding him how the loss of the phallus undermines that narrative, and he is not interested in adopting such a subject position. He may like Brett's short haircut, but as concerns his own sense of gender he would prefer to maintain the old values, where men are assumed to be "men." That Jake essentializes homosexuals—"They are like that"—so as to configure them as another negative example supporting his social philosophy is obvious; otherwise the reader would get a more "positive" gay character. But such an alternative never makes an entrance, and the Burguete fishing trip episode with Bill and Harris works hard to posit an idealized homosocial relationship as a counterbalance to homosexuality: men being friends with men, no strings attached.[31]

Significantly, however, Jake once again admits to breaking with postwar values of accepting difference in his refusal to condone queerness. His statement, "I know they are supposed to be amusing, and you should be tolerant" (20), carries the same implications of mentioning Cohn becoming "race-conscious" at college. Jake evaluates his own reaction as negative and unjust; he acknowledges his own failure to live up to a "modern," progressive standard (one based on the stereotype of homosexuals as "amusing"). During the fishing trip, Bill addresses the more sophisticated, lenient attitude toward diversity found in Europe and points to a growing anxiety in America. He says to Jake, "Listen. You're a hell of a guy, and I'm fonder of you than anybody on earth. I couldn't tell you that in New York. It'd mean I was a faggot" (116). In Europe, homosocial relationships are not as suspect as back home. Nevertheless, back in Paris Jake wants "to swing on one, any one, anything to shatter that superior, simpering composure" (20). He uses stereotypical signs the reader is meant to associate with queerness so as to separate these men from heterosexuals like himself. The encoded smile he shares with the policeman when Brett's crowd enters connotes his attempt to salvage a sense of stability. Jake's feelings here, on the edge of violence, can be read as symptomatic of the continued problem of prejudice in America, but additionally as an outgrowth of the challenges to provincialism made by emerging subjectivities coming out of the closet. Beyond Jake's homophobia, what else is Hemingway trying to expose through this character's voice and story? Jake's refusal to blend queer men's marginal subjectivity into his own identity is surely founded in prejudice, a closed notion of what constitutes proper masculinity, but, as with Cohn's Jewishness, it is subtly offered to the reader as something extra—a dislike for jerks.

This othering further expresses Jake's conception of the code in the novel. He overhears one of the effeminate men speak of dancing with the prostitute Georgette for a laugh: "I do declare. There is an actual harlot. I'm going to dance with her, Lett. You watch me" (20). Eventually they all take part in the joke by dancing with her, objectifying Georgette as a toy for their amusement, and this infuriates Jake. He may use Georgette to keep up masculine appearances, as the Davidsons suggest, but Jake does not treat her with outright disrespect or intentionally hire her so as to humiliate her in front of his friends (admittedly, this semblance of respect is dulled by Jake's joking about her "wonderful smile" which objectifies Georgette for the benefit of the reader [8]).[32] As a *poule,* Georgette is also a marginal social figure, an Other, but she understands the code and Jake *does* respect her for that. Certainly Jake does not want to be gay, but it is the personality of this group that is used to mark the kind of people in general he wants to separate himself from.[33] This is where Wolfgang Rudat should look to answer his question about what Jake thinks "he has that makes him superior to gays."[34] It is a matter of how he chooses to treat people that distinguishes him from the way the homosexuals are represented as acting. For even when Jake dislikes someone, and the novel is littered with people he dislikes, he is rarely shown ridiculing them publicly in the manner of Lett and his friends. Still, Hemingway/Jake's irony cuts through this moment. The smile passed between Jake and the policeman is a nonverbal example of his ability to ridicule, and on another level Jake and the homosexuals actually do behave similarly: Jake uses a version of the Other (the gay men) to make himself feel superior *morally* in the public constituted by the reader, while Lett and the boys use a different version of the Other (Georgette) to make themselves feel superior *socially* in the public realm of the club.

But what is truly curious in this scene is the way Hemingway has Jake cunningly connect the homosexuals' pompous behavior to a form of racial centeredness. Jake's description of the men when they enter the club includes a very particular detail: he calls attention to their "white hands" and "white faces" (20). The Davidsons offer an explication: "The suggestion is that the faces are pale, like the powdered faces of women; that the hands are white in contradistinction to the tanned hands of real men—the dark, leathery hands of a Basque shepherd."[35] This is compelling, but to insist that Jake's singling out of "whiteness does not mark race" is problematic because he forces the reader to "see" the whiteness of the homosexuals rather than pass over it as an invisible, assumed norm. None of Jake's friends have workers' hands, those who are not writers are ne'er-do-wells like Mike and Brett, and she is hardly a woman of the "powdered face" type. So what is the motivation for racially naming these men as white when the assumption of whiteness is adequate for the other characters?

The suggestion is that the homosexuals represent not only the kind of Other Jake repudiates, they are also the kind of white people he wishes to dissociate himself from. To name the homosexuals' race implicitly creates a hierarchy of whiteness which is composed of varying shades, so to speak, each carrying a different sense of values in Jake's mind. The homosexuals' whiteness represents that of privileged nonworkers who exploit those different from themselves (here on a class level) for enjoyment. In a sense, they are not "Other" enough in that they maintain the condescending attitude of slumming tourists. They enter the environment of the *bal musette* as foreigners exploiting the exotic; indeed, this accusation is fairly applicable to all the expatriates at the club, which is usually a gathering place for the working class. "Five nights a week the working people of the Pantheon quarter danced there. One night a week it was the dancing-club" (19). The expatriates take over the club for one night rather than using it the way the workers do during the rest of the week; they impose a different meaning on it as a social space, one that cuts it off from the local culture. This symbolizes a refusal to acclimate by expatriates and tourists alike, thus conflating the two. It is symptomatic of a colonialist mentality that perpetuates a negative view of marginality to establish one group's sense of superiority over those posited as Other.

The difference between Jake and the expatriates who behave this way infuses a sense of class consciousness into his system of judging people, which can then be read back onto Jake's friends without the narrator having to directly state it. Jake's friends rise above neither their class elitism nor, by extension, their race. The *bal musette* scene quietly works to prepare the reader for judging their actions and attitudes during the Pamplona festival. They are all associated with this kind of whiteness as they exhibit the elements of "bad form" they attribute to the busloads of American and British tourists. Rather than showing respect for the culture they are in, they abuse it for their own pleasure. In one scene, a drunken Bill buys shoe-shines for Mike, having several boys working at once, because he finds it entertaining to throw money at the subaltern for a form of song and dance. Brett's own pleasure is fulfilled by "corrupting" Pedro Romero, which breaks the local cultural code of the aficionados by imposing her own values on someone who is for Brett the local Other. And, of course, Jake is eventually complicit with this process by bringing Brett and Pedro together. This colonialist type of whiteness unintentionally gets the better of Jake, and that is part of Hemingway's point. He is also commenting on the expatriates' failure to cut themselves completely off from past narratives by showing how easily one falls back into the old practices. To remedy this, one must find a way to combine the old and new in a precarious balance.

The great paradox in the novel's critique of elitism as a form of racial identity is that Hemingway accomplishes it by targeting figures from marginalized groups. The treatment of Cohn and the homosexuals points to a conscious system of exclusion, albeit one that Jake thinks is based on a higher sense of values, so his transgression is seemingly compromised. For Earl Rovit, it is Hemingway's own upper middle-class background in Oak Park that results in the author's

> casual racist, anti-immigrant, anti-Semitic, antiurban sex chauvinism . . . [and] nostalgia for preindustrialized America that was, in reality, merely a fantasy of childhood. These "new" alien Americans—immigrant, working-class, or bourgeoisie—were patently "not one of us."[36]

I have shown that Hemingway does not include Jake in that supposed "us." It should also be noted that Cohn's family would not consider itself part of those "'new' alien Americans," so Cohn's denigrated Jewishness in the novel cannot be positioned so easily as expressing anti-immigrant sentiment. Nonetheless, Rovit does offer a productive means for thinking about otherness in the novel by relating Hemingway's social training to Jake's own "way of accenting individualism [that] characteristically asserts selfhood by excluding . . . [other people] rather than by absorbing creatively from others to strengthen that self."[37] This speaks to the situation with Cohn and the homosexuals; they are indeed the repugnant Other that threatens Jake's own sense of self. The problem here is that Rovit does not acknowledge how Jake is still in the process of creating that self, and that one always works from a narrative of exclusion when constituting an identity. Whether that subjectivity is based on outsider or mainstream sources, choices are made about what and how much enters the mix. He also disregards how Jake uses his experience in Spain where he does turn to a form of marginality "creatively" in order to construct his individuality.

It is the Spain chapters that offer a version of difference Jake deems worthy of integration. Cohn and the homosexuals show us people classified as Others who adopt the exclusionary practices of the center, be it respect for title and family or the arrogant mistreatment of "inferiors." This in turn emphasizes the way Jake, a figure who moves with and is accepted by the center, chooses a marginal group in Spain to develop his subjectivity, albeit a group that satisfies his desire for a modicum of traditionalism—found in a sense of order and a conventional model of masculinity. It is the conflict between staid morality and modern alienation that leads to Spain's eventual significance in the novel. Jake's need for a personal center to give him the ground from which to make moral decisions and structure his life demarcates Spanish culture as posing a better standard. The romanticized Spanish subaltern is marked as a useful source for hybridity: a form of fixity and communitarian sensibility resorting neither to the constrictive morality of the American middle class nor to the highly individualistic and hollow practices of the expatriate as romantic poseur or "authentic" libertine. Instead, Jake turns to a space he hopes will allow him to effectively interpret existence and find a way to just "live in it" (148). Ultimately, that space also fails to fulfill Jake's desires, but that remains beyond the borders of my investigation here.

Notes

1. Michael Harper, "Men without Politics: Hemingway's Social Consciousness," *New Orleans Review* 12, no. 1 (1985), 19.

2. Robert O. Stephens, "Ernest Hemingway and the Rhetoric of Escape," in *Ernest Hemingway's* The Sun Also Rises, ed. Harold Bloom (New York: Chelsea, 1987), 53.

3. Ernest Hemingway, *In Our Time* (1925; New York: Scribner's, 1996), 79.

4. Hemingway, *In Our Time*, 57.

5. Michael Reynolds narrates how Hemingway submitted "The Battler" as a substitute story at the request of Liveright before they would publish *In Our Time*. Hemingway used "nigger"—"the word most in use by the society that raised him" and which was "true to his ear, to the sounds of the time," according to Reynolds—but the publisher changed it to "negro." See *Hemingway: The Paris Years* (New York: Norton, 1989), 279. However, that both words appear suggests that Hemingway had some final control over usage. For another discussion of Hemingway's use of African-American characters see Toni Morrison's *Playing in the Dark: Whiteness and the Literary Imagination* (Cambridge: Harvard University Press, 1992), which analyzes this problem in *To Have and Have Not*.

6. For the sake of honesty, I have cataloged Hemingway's less than egalitarian moments toward groups other to his own sense of self. In his 1923–1927 correspondence in *Selected Letters: 1917–1961*, ed. Carlos Baker (New York: Scribner's , 1981) one finds five explicit references to Jews, the first three of which can be read as directly anti-Semitic (May 2, 1924; July 19, 1924; May 21, 1926; Dec. 21, 1926); one use of "coon" (Apr. 22, 1925); and three references to "fairies," the first of which seems to carry a hint of irony (Sept. 15, 1927; Oct. 8, 1927; Dec. 13, 1927).

7. Frederick Joseph Svoboda, *Hemingway &* The Sun Also Rises: *The Crafting of a Style* (Lawrence: University Press of Kansas, 1983), and Michael S. Reynolds, The Sun Also Rises: *A Novel of the Twenties* (Boston: Twayne, 1988). The first-person structure of the novel, along with the autobiographical roots of the events described, presents all the usual problems about where to draw the line between author and narrator. Hemingway creates Jake as both narrator and author of the text, and while

that does not entirely relieve him of authorial responsibility for any racist content it certainly complicates matters. Despite Hemingway's self-promotion as a writer who does not hide behind language, he is a cagey author who consciously presents ideas in a way to forestall the reader from arriving at any "one true" interpretation. Thus I will use "Hemingway/Jake" or note the "dual" authorship in other ways when I think it necessary to mark the importance of considering both the real author and the constructed one as responsible for manipulating the novel's formal elements with a specific intention.

8. *Selected Letters,* 142.

9. *Selected Letters,* 66.

10. *Selected Letters,* 240.

11. Ernest Hemingway, *The Sun Also Rises* (New York: Scribner's, 1986), 45. Hereafter cited parenthetically.

12. Harold Loeb, *The Way It Was* (New York: Criterion, 1959), 250.

13. Josephine Z. Knopf, "Meyer Wolfsheim and Robert Cohn: A Study of a Jewish Type and Stereotype," in *Ernest Hemingway's* The Sun Also Rises, ed. Harold Bloom (New York: Chelsea, 1987), 67.

14. Knopf, "Wolfsheim and Cohn," 68.

15. Knopf, "Wolfsheim and Cohn," 70.

16. Michael S. Reynolds, "The *Sun* in Its Time: Recovering the Historical Context," in *New Essays on* The Sun Also Rises, ed. Linda Wagner-Martin (Cambridge: Cambridge University Press, 1987), 54.

17. I apply scare quotes to the term racist because placing Jews within racialist categories is by no means the consensus. For some, like Janet Helms in *Black and White Racial Identity: Theory, Research, and Practice* (Westport: Greenwood, 1996), ethnicity is defined as a group identity based on shared cultural behavior, values, and beliefs, so the distinction between Semite and Jew is one between race and ethnicity. But there are those like Karen Brodkin who continue to refer to Jews as a race, although she complicates this with the term "ethnoracial" identity in *How Jews Became White Folks, and What That Says about Race in America* (New Brunswick: Rutgers University Press, 1998). The trajectory of racial thinking concerning Jews has its own history. Matthew Frye Jacobson informs us that in the late nineteenth century, American political discourse often relied on a notion of whiteness but the word "did not carry the same meaning that it does in the late twentieth century: both in nineteenth-century science and in popular understanding the white community itself comprised many sharply distinguishable races. The categories 'Celt,' 'Slav,' 'Hebrew' and 'Anglo-Saxon' represented an order of difference deeper than any current notions of 'ethnicity.'" See *Special Sorrows: The Diasporic Imagination of Irish, Polish, and Jewish Immigrants in the United States* (Cambridge: Harvard University Press, 1995), 185. Within this hierarchy of the shades of pale, Jews, like so many other

immigrant groups, were typically held racially as not-quite-white and thus less American. It is during the early twentieth century, with the rise of nativist attacks against "dark" immigrants integrating themselves into American life, that scientific narratives about race hold sway over more cultural-influenced arguments by attributing social and behavioral characteristics to biological and geographical/ national determinants. Sander Gilman's *The Jew's Body* (London: Routledge, 1991) discusses at length scientific theories about the superiority of the Anglo-Saxon blood of northwest Europe that differentiated between true Americans and immigrants, between the inheritors of a pure race and those "mongrelized" inferior Others weakening it. Thus Jews were not considered purely "white" during the period that Hemingway wrote *The Sun Also Rises*. According to Karen Brodkin, Jews did not "become" white in American popular consciousness until after World War II, when larger numbers moved from ethnically distinct urban neighborhoods to suburbs where they were able to assimilate and share in the economic and social privileges accorded to "whites."

18. Michael S. Reynolds, The Sun Also Rises: *A Novel of the Twenties* (Boston: Twayne, 1988), and John S. Rouch, "Jake Barnes as Narrator," *Modern Fiction Studies* 11 (1965–1966), 361–70.

19. See James Hinkle, "What's Funny in *The Sun Also Rises,*" *Hemingway Review* 4, no. 2 (1985), 31–41 [reprinted in this volume], for a closer study of the context and narrative function of humor in the novel.

20. The choice to make Jake a Catholic becomes all the more weighted with meaning when we recall that Hemingway had not himself converted at this time. The rituals of Catholicism, a system of order so lacking in the modern world, and the conflict arising from Jake's failure to believe in them devoutly are used symbolically in the novel. However, to overlook the equivalent prejudice expressed toward Catholics and Jews during this period will miss the subtle manner in which Hemingway complicates a reader's possible reactions to both Barnes and Cohn.

21. Brodkin, *How Jews Became White Folks,* 55. Also see Walter Benn Michaels's *Our America: Nativism, Modernism, and Pluralism* (Durham: Duke University Press, 1995) for an extended study of nativism and modernist American literature. Michael's few remarks on *The Sun Also Rises* (26–29, 72–74) are concerned with the treatment of Cohn as a Jew, and I hope to problematize Michaels's reading that Cohn is a character used solely to evoke a negative, parochial response to immigrants.

22. Wolfgang E. H. Rudat, "Anti-Semitism in *The Sun Also Rises*: Traumas, Jealousies, and the Genesis of Cohn," *American Imago* 49 (1992), 263–75, mentions the economic difference between Loeb and Hemingway as a factor in Cohn's negative characterization but more as a matter of envy. Rudat focuses on how Cohn can be used to understand the issue of Jake's sexuality in the novel.

23. It may be countered that Brett and Mike are equally dependent on titles

and origins in "good" families but that they do not come under the same kind of censure as Robert. This is valid to a point, for while they are lively, witty, and more adept at heavy drinking, their social credentials influence their behavior as negatively as Cohn's, indeed, more so. These characters use their names to insulate them from responsibility and repercussions; however, their class status hardly protects them from criticism in the novel. It is not Hemingway's intention that readers "like" Brett and Mike or wish to emulate their parasitic and elitist practices. Marc Baldwin states it well: "The social hierarchy, based on 'breeding' and money, does not necessarily correspond to the natural *class* exhibited by those simple people who work for a living and assume no pretentious airs of superiority." "Class Consciousness and the Ideology of Dominance in *The Sun Also Rises,*" *McNeese Review* 32 (1994), 16.

24. Jean-Paul Sartre, *Anti-Semite and Jew* (New York: Schocken, 1965). Also see Stuart Zane Charmé's *Vulgarity and Authenticity: Dimensions of Otherness in the World of Jean-Paul Sartre* (Amherst: University of Massachusetts Press, 1991) for a study of this issue.

25. Sander Gilman's *The Jew's Body* documents how many Jews desired to be accepted as phenotypically and culturally white in the 1920s (179, 238).

26. Ron Berman, "Protestant, Catholic, Jew: *The Sun Also Rises,*" *Hemingway Review* 18, no. 1 (1998), 43.

27. Berman, "Protestant, Catholic, Jew," 45 and 44.

28. Arnold E. Davidson and Cathy N. Davidson. "Decoding the Hemingway Hero in *The Sun Also Rises,*" in *New Essays on* The Sun Also Rises, ed. Linda Wagner-Martin (Cambridge: Cambridge University Press, 1987), 90.

29. See the Davidsons' article; Nancy R. Comley and Robert Scholes's *Hemingway's Genders: Rereading the Hemingway Text* (New Haven: Yale University Press, 1994); Wolfgang Rudat's "Hemingway on Sexual Otherness: What's Really Funny in *The Sun Also Rises,*" in *Hemingway Repossessed,* ed. Kenneth Rosen (Westport, CT: Greenwood, 1994), 169–79; and Peter Messent's *Ernest Hemingway* (New York: St. Martin's, 1992). All these critics also point to how Hemingway problematizes sexual pairing at the club through three groups: the heterosexual Brett enters with her gay friends; the wounded Jake arrives with the prostitute Georgette (whose very profession is the act Jake cannot perform); and the scene closes with Georgette dancing with the homosexuals as Brett and Jake leave.

30. Messent, *Ernest Hemingway,* 102, and David Blackmore, " 'In New York It'd Mean I Was a . . .': Masculine Anxiety and Period Discourses of Sexuality in *The Sun Also Rises,*" *Hemingway Review* 18, no. 1 (1998), 65.

31. See Blackmore for an application of Freudian theories on latent homosexuality contemporary with the novel's publication. Blackmore offers intriguing analyses of a homoerotic subtext in the bullfighting and Burguete fishing trip

episodes, but their validity depends on how much credence one is willing to grant Freud, as well as assuming Hemingway uses them *sans* parody.

32. Davidson and Davidson, "Decoding the Hemingway Hero," 91.

33. In an earlier draft of the novel, Hemingway has Jake ruminate negatively on the Parisian Left Bank homosexuals as a group, as an undifferentiated "they":

> This Paris is a very sad and dull place and it has few permanent in-habitants. It seems as though the Fairies lived there permanently but this is a mistake because they take flight like the birds and go off to Brussels or London or the Basque coast to return again even more like the birds. . . . It is interesting that they go away and quite pleasant but the pleasure is diminished by the fact that one can not count on it and many times they are gone for several days and one does not notice it and so can not enjoy it. Once I remember they were all gone to Brussels for a week and were back before I noticed they were gone away and a week's enjoyment of their absence was lost. (Quoted in Reynolds, *Hemingway: The Paris Years,* 33–34)

This is unquestionably an expression of Hemingway's (and consequently Jake's) ho-mophobia, yet it is significant that he cut this passage out of the final draft. For whatever reason, it does not appear in the text; so we are left with the characters from the *bal musette* scene as a point of comparison to later "masculine" moments in trying to make sense of Hemingway's reasons for depicting homosexuals negatively and deciding to cast "them" as a negative form of whiteness.

34. Rudat, "Hemingway on Sexual Otherness," 74.

35. Davidson and Davidson, "Decoding the Hemingway Hero," 90.

36. Earl Rovit, "On Psychic Retrenchment in Hemingway," in *Hemingway: Essays of Reassessment,* ed. Frank Scafella (New York: Oxford University Press, 1991), 187.

37. Rovit, "On Psychic Retrenchment in Hemingway," 184.

Suggested Reading

◆ ◆ ◆

Baker, Carlos. *Ernest Hemingway: A Life Story.* New York: Scribner's, 1969.

————, ed. *Ernest Hemingway: Selected Letters, 1917–1961.* New York: Scribner's, 1981.

Baskett, Sam S. "'An Image to Dance Around': Brett and Her Lovers in *The Sun Also Rises,*" *Centennial Review* 22 (1978), 45–69.

Capellan, Angel. *Hemingway and the Hispanic World.* Ann Arbor: UMI Research Press, 1985.

Comley, Nancy, and Robert Scholes. *Hemingway's Genders: Rereading the Hemingway Text.* New Haven: Yale University Press, 1994.

Crowley, John. *"The White Logic": Alcoholism and Gender in American Modernist Fiction.* Amherst: University of Massachusetts Press, 1994.

Diliberto, Gioia. *Hadley.* New York: Ticknor & Fields, 1992.

Donaldson, Scott, ed. *The Cambridge Companion to Hemingway.* Cambridge: Cambridge University Press, 1996.

————. "Fitzgerald's Blue Pencil," *French Connections, Hemingway and Fitzgerald Abroad,* ed. J. Gerald Kennedy and Jackson R. Bryer. New York: St. Martin's, 1998, 15–29.

Eby, Carl. *Hemingway's Fetishism: Psychoanalysis and the Mirror of Manhood.* Albany: SUNY Press, 1999.

Ganzel, Dewey. "*Cabestro* and *Vaquilla*: The Symbolic Structure of *The Sun Also Rises,*" *Sewanee Review* 76 (1968), 26–48.

Hemingway, Mary Walsh. *How It Was*. New York: Knopf, 1976.

Hemingway Review 6, no. 1 (1986), commemorative issue for *The Sun Also Rises*.

Lansky, Ellen. "The Barnes Complex: Ernest Hemingway, Djuna Barnes, *The Sun Also Rises*, and *Nightwood*," *The Languages of Addiction*, ed. Jane Lilienfeld and Jeffrey Oxford. New York: St. Martin's, 1999.

Loeb, Harold. *The Way It Was*. New York: Criterion, 1959.

Kennedy, J. Gerald. *Imagining Paris*. New Haven: Yale University Press, 1993.

Kert, Bernice. *The Hemingway Women*. New York: Norton, 1983.

Reynolds, Michael S. "False Dawn: *The Sun Also Rises* Manuscript," *A Fair Day in the Affections: Literary Essays in Honor of Robert B. White, Jr.,* ed. Jack D. Durant and M. Thomas Hester. Raleigh, N.C.: Winston Press, 1981.

————. *Hemingway: The American Homecoming*. Oxford: Blackwell, 1992.

————. *Hemingway: The Paris Years.* Oxford: Blackwell, 1989.

————. *Hemingway's Reading 1910–1940: An Inventory*. Princeton, N.J.: Princeton University Press, 1976.

Rovit, Earl. *Ernest Hemingway*. Boston: Twayne, 1963.

Sanford, Marcelline Hemingway. *At the Hemingways* (*with 50 Years of Correspondence between Ernest and Marcelline Hemingway*). Moscow: University of Idaho Press, 1999.

Sarason, Bertram D. *Hemingway and the Sun Set*. Washington, D.C.: Microcard, 1972.

Schwartz, Nina. "Lovers' Discourse in *The Sun Also Rises*: A Cock and Bull Story," *Criticism* 26, no. 1 (1984), 49–69.

Spilka, Mark. *Hemingway's Quarrel with Androgyny*. Lincoln: University of Nebraska Press, 1990.

Svoboda, Frederic Joseph. *Hemingway and* The Sun Also Rises: *The Crafting of a Style*. Lawrence: University Press of Kansas, 1983.

Wagner, Linda W., ed. *Ernest Hemingway: Five Decades of Criticism*. East Lansing: Michigan State University Press, 1974.

————, ed. *Ernest Hemingway: Six Decades of Criticism*. East Lansing: Michigan State University Press, 1987.

Wagner-Martin, Linda, ed. *Hemingway: Seven Decades of Criticism*. East Lansing: Michigan State University Press, 1998.

————, ed. *A Historical Guide to Ernest Hemingway*. New York: Oxford University Press, 2000.

————, ed. *New Essays on The Sun Also Rises*. New York: Cambridge University Press, 1987.

————. "Racial and Sexual Coding in *The Sun Also Rises*," *Hemingway Review*, 10, no. 2 (Spring 1991), 39–41.

White, William, ed. *Byline: Ernest Hemingway.* New York: Scribner's, 1967.
————. *The Merrill Studies in "The Sun Also Rises."* Columbus: Charles E. Merrill, 1969.
Wilentz, Gay. "(Re)Teaching Hemingway: Anti-Semitism as a Thematic Device in *The Sun Also Rises,*" *College English* 52, no. 2 (1990), 186–93.